Where the Bugs wear Boots

The Story of a Liverpool Survivor

George Russell

This 2nd edition published by the author George Russell
ISBN 978-1-897771-01-3

Printed by Flexipress, Ormskirk, Lancashire. L39 4QB

Dedication

This book is dedicated to my wife Viv who typed the manuscripts and removed some of the political incorrectness and to my children, Maddy and Lisa: this trio of fabulous ladies have kept me on track and away from the Edge to the best of their abilities through many happy and sad times.

Thanks

Thanks for the foreword by the illustrious Peter Howard-Browne of Cape Town, whose holy-cow-butchery and presentations never fail to challenge and delight me; his interest and encouragement kept me working to complete this book.

Thanks for the cover artwork by the fabulous Rodney Matthews, whose artistic skills never cease to amaze me and whose friendship has encouraged me. The dude is a genius! To view or purchase samples of Rodney's amazing work, visit his website and prepare to be dazzled! www.rodneymatthews.com

Thanks to all the people who encouraged and helped us practically particularly in the hard times but most of all to Jesus without whom this book would never have been written.

Additional copies of this book, the Structured Learning memory and study skills course and other products may be ordered by e-mail, writing or accessing my website.

george3russell@yahoo.co.uk

G Russell, Russell Associates,
PO Box 136, LIVERPOOL, L9 0LZ.

www.georgerussell.biz

Contents

Foreword

The title may seem odd enough. But then again, this is an unusual book. And the author is unusual too. His daughter Maddy feels I am equally unusual so it's appropriate that I write this foreword. Touché. What makes George unusual is that he looks like a large and imposing Hell's Angel bruiser, (and has obviously done some bruising in his colourful life) yet he is a learned man with a university degree in Chemistry who loves his God, his wife and his family.

George's life-story reminds me of a comment by Emile Zola: 'If you ask what I am here to do in this world, I will say I am here to live my life out loud.' Which, really, is the only way to live! This is clearly not a book for the faint hearted nor the beige civil servant types who are too afraid to really live.

If in life you judge a book by its cover, you could end up denying yourself the exquisite pleasure of something well worth reading. When I met George in Liverpool I liked him in an instant and I knew that I had met one of God's rough diamonds - the kind of guy every church needs - colourful, mysterious, engaging and very interesting.

George's book is part history (and very interesting as history books go), part (very honest) autobiography, part (engagingly funny) comedy, part (interesting) philosophy and (practical and earthed) theology. His style is large and dramatic - so is he - and flows with the ease of a well told story. Some of it will disturb you - he's not the kind of guy to apologise for it either. All these ingredients make his book unusual and yet very accessible at the same time. I know you will enjoy the read. I did. But then again I am unusual.

Peter Howard-Browne
Cape Town, South Africa

Introduction

Many have asked me about the title of this book. When I was a lad, people used to say it was so rough in Bootle that even the bugs wore boots from whence came the title 'Where the bugs wear boots'. In fact, Bootle is no rougher than many other areas of Liverpool but has an undeserved bad reputation. I was born on the 25th of March 1941 in Bootle, a suburb of the great city of Liverpool. Bootle was later absorbed into the Sefton area, much to the dismay of the residents of rather more salubrious areas like Crosby, Birkdale and Southport. Not only was I born in Bootle, but I went to Bootle Grammar School, then Liverpool University and have lived and worked in the Liverpool area all my life. I have travelled widely, visited many pleasant places in England and beyond, but I choose to live in Liverpool. I'm not about to give a free advert for the city and its many attractions, but for readers who don't know the city let me paint a picture.

The City of Liverpool is one of the most well known cities in the world; with its legendary musicians, entertainers, colourful citizens and beautiful architecture, Liverpool is truly unique. Inhabitants of Liverpool are referred to as Liverpudlians but are also known as 'Scousers', in reference to a local meal known as 'scouse, a form of stew. During hard times when meat was unavailable and the family pets were beginning to look worried, the vegetarian version was called 'blind' scouse. So now you know! The word scouse has also become synonymous with the Liverpool accent and dialect. In 2007, the city celebrated its 800th anniversary, and in 2008 it held the European Capital of Culture title.

The main shopping centre of Liverpool is one of the largest shopping districts in Great Britain. It starts on the Mersey at the Albert Dock and heads inland for a couple of miles, covering the original seven streets of Liverpool and much more. Liverpool also has several buildings that are famous city landmarks. Dominating the waterfront is the Royal Liver Building with its twin towers topped by sculptures of the liver bird, a mythical creature after which the city is said to have been named. Other famous buildings include the Town Hall, built in 1749, and St. George's Hall, which dates from 1842 and served as both a court building and public hall. The inner city surrounds town and has many older houses. This area also includes Liverpool University and the Anglican and Roman Catholic Cathedrals.

There are a wide variety of cultural activities and sports events. The Walker Art Gallery has one of the best collections outside London, as does the Tate of the North at the Albert Dock. Liverpool also has an orchestra, several theatres, many live music venues and several radio stations. The Grand National, one of the greatest steeplechase events in the world takes place each spring at Aintree. Liverpool is also home to two of the best football teams around; not Liverpool and Liverpool Reserves as Bill Shankly used to joke, but Everton and Liverpool.

There are some cities that people seem to love, Paris and New York being good examples. For some reason Liverpool is a place you either love or hate; many hating the city without cause. The following example reveals the attitude of some. The writer chose to remain anonymous, so we were unable to send a patriotic mob round to show him forgiveness and understanding.

A list of things <u>never</u> said by Scousers:
- *My specialist subject is Shakespeare.*
- *Duct tape **won't** fix that.*
- *Come to think of it, I'll have a dry white wine.*
- *You can't feed **that** to the dog.*
- *Lets not fight over this **now**.*
- *We're vegetarians.*
- *Too many empty beer bottles detract from the décor.*
- *Spitting is such a nasty habit.*
- *I've got two cases of PG Tips for the Cup Final.*
- *Checkmate!*
- *Hey, here's a Channel 5 movie that we haven't seen.*
- *I **don't** have a favourite football team.*

So, knock back a couple of double espressos and read on. If you are unimpressed, depressed or freaked out after reading it, pass the book on to someone you know who is searching for the meaning of life!

If you come across words or phrases you are unfamiliar with, check them in the Glossary on page 257.

Chapter 1

Right place, wrong time

It was eight o'clock on the 3rd of May, 1941. My parents sat down for their evening meal with their ten 'guests'. The 'guests' of course were relatives whose homes had been blown up or had unexploded bombs wedged in the roof, in the garden or in one case, in the toilet. A large pot of stew with very little meat but plenty of home grown vegetables was steaming in the centre of the table. The sound of a loud shouting in the street broke the silence just as my dad was about to say grace. My mother drew back the thick curtains to look: just blackness and silence again. A loud rapping on the window almost made her take off vertically. 'Put that light out!' a loud voice shouted. It was feared that the bright lights of the city would provide an easy target for enemy bombers, so from 1 September 1939 major cities like Liverpool were ordered to black out any light that could be seen from the sky. Air raid precaution wardens, most of whom were part time volunteers with full time day jobs, supervised the blackout. They patrolled the streets watching for the slightest chink of light and supervised people getting into air raid shelters. People were required to cover their house windows with anything that would prevent light escaping - paper, curtains, blinds and even paint. These items quickly became dear and hard to find. Fortunately we had thick curtains to retain some heat in winter: mother closed them over rapidly.

Just as the meal finished an undulating wailing sound broke the flow of conversation. It wasn't the Martian fighting machines; it was not the War of the Worlds but the War of the Nations; the Second World War. White faced, everyone began to collect their few belongings and move out of the back door. I was asleep in the kitchen; someone carried me outside into the Andersen Shelter with the others. Why they bothered I don't know - the shelter had a concrete base but only a thin piece of corrugated iron and half a metre of topsoil to 'protect' from the bombs. I woke to the drone of aircraft and the thumping of the anti-aircraft guns. Then the bombs began to fall. There were butterfly

1

bombs with wing-like tails, which enabled them to flutter slowly to the ground long after the bomber had disappeared, oil bombs, which exploded and spread burning oil in all directions, incendiary bombs clipped in containers of 12 or so which spread all over the place as they whistled down onto the City. Then there was the dreaded delayed action time-bomb; there was no way to tell when these would explode after they landed in the streets. Inside the flimsy air raid shelter everyone flinched and braced themselves for the impact. There was a succession of bone-shaking thuds as the bombs fell nearby; some cracks appeared in the walls and dust trickled down, then the lights went out. Some screamed, some prayed; others just sat shaking with fear. They all knew that the shelter would not survive a direct hit and neither would they. Torches were hastily switched on, and candles or night-lights were lit. The ordeal went on for hours. It gradually went quiet then the welcome one-note sound of the 'All-Clear' siren was heard: as usual I slept through it all, but then I was only six weeks old.

Some thirty years later we were staying in a caravan on a working farm in North Wales. My youngest daughter Lisa, around three years old, expressed the wish to watch the cows being milked and the necessary arrangements were made with Mr Jones, the farmer. At the appointed time we arrived. The cows were all in pens, carefully linked to the suction apparatus and at the flick of a switch the white fluid began to squirt into the containers. Lisa stood at the rear end of a cow called Daisy, marvelling at the wonders of science. I was personally tired of the healthy outdoor smells and returned to the caravan to read a comic book while my wife cooked dinner. Cows, as you may know, do not urinate like other animals, with a leg in the air and a controlled stream directed away from themselves. They dump several litres within a few seconds, with no prior warning and in an omni-directional way. Lisa arrived back at the caravan, totally marinated, blinking like a toad in a sand heap. After a quick shower and a change of clothing she requested a return to the milking sheds, not wanting to miss any more of the performance. She returned to her original position, this time wearing her wellies. Daisy was her favourite cow but she must have had a bad pint, a vicious bog-roll in-the-freezer Vindaloo or too much All Bran. Lisa returned less than 10 minutes later, this time coated in liquid excrement, a classic case of being in the right place at the wrong time. This certainly describes my birth in Bootle, Liverpool, in the March of 1941.

Where the Bugs wear Boots

Bootle is mentioned in William the Conqueror's Domesday Book. Most historians suggest, or guess, that Bootle was originally settled by wild Anglian raiders after Ethelfrith's victory over the Britons at Chester in 613 AD. Linacre, next door to Bootle, was settled by Vikings around 900 AD when a new phrase was invented, 'There goes the neighbourhood!' Local historians describe the Bootle of old as pasture and ploughed land skirted by marshes on the Mersey estuary side. Apparently a golden shore curved around Bootle Bay with salmon and otter among the varied fauna. In the early 19th century Bootle was a delectable spot; the Strand Promenade was one of the many pleasant approaches to the beach. Successful businessmen had mansions built for themselves in the vicinity. This turned out to be a poor investment as the threat of global war created the need for larger and deeper docks than the existing Port of Liverpool system; Bootle Bay was the obvious choice and the leisure activities for the Bootle rich were over. Over three and a half thousand Irish navvies descended on the beach engaged in dock and railway construction. As the dock system reached the town boundary, the already considerable social division became even greater. Rich people lived behind high hedges and exotic curtains: grand style living for the families of the wealthy with live-in maids, croquet on the lawn and elegant garden parties. In the dockland area, bad housing, primitive sanitation, and disease epidemics characterised the ghettos of the under-privileged. Vermin ruled OK. On special occasions called 'Rat Days' you could get a shilling for every rat carcass brought in. Houses of ill-repute flourished; the police were totally understaffed and drunkenness, prostitution and violent crime characterised the dockland area. A 1888 Watch Committee rated Bootle against other townships in the area. Chester; quiet. Southport; quiet. Birkenhead; rough. Bootle; exceptionally rough, hence, 'Bootle, where the bugs wear boots'

The docks brought more wealth to the wealthy and elevated Bootle to a place of importance but by 1941 it also became a prime target for German bombing missions, mainly because of the warships in the deep-water docks. The first bombs fell on August 29th at 10.22 p.m.; at first incendiaries, then High Explosive bombs and finally parachute mines. Between the 2nd and 8th of May 1941, when I was 6 weeks old, the bombing increased to saturation level; known as the May Blitz. The seven nights of bombing damaged over 75% of the built-up area of Bootle with 191 major bomb blasts. 20,000 people were rendered homeless and those whose houses were intact had no mains water, gas or electricity. Sewage seeped into the streets and there was no public transport because of the bomb craters in the streets. Over a third of the shops were destroyed and many made their way nightly to school halls, churches or the fields in outlying areas like Maghull. As I mentioned earlier, many of our relatives were bombed out or had unexploded bombs in their back yards, so our three bedroom semi with windows intact became a night-time hotel with eight family members plus children and pets squashed in with my parents and I. During the day they would scuttle back to what was left of their homes to salvage items they considered valuable and discourage looters.

On December 7th, the American fleet at Pearl Harbour was attacked by the Japanese. Interestingly, the day before, the OK was given for the Manhattan Project to commence. This was a project researching the feasibility of an atomic bomb. Most items were rationed at this time; bacon, butter, sugar, bread and then clothing. The in-films released or escaped that year were 'Citizen Kane' and 'How green was my valley', but cinema-going was not on my family's agenda; their priority was survival.

Chapter 2

Meet the family

My Dad's family originally lived in Olivia Street, Bootle, and then moved to Crosby. Dad was a fireman; at the onset of war he and virtually all of the Fire Brigade and HM Police volunteered for active service and were turned down as they were needed at home. Unfortunately, no-one thought to pass this information to the rectal-scrapings-for-brains who accused them of cowardice, sometimes even as they were being carried out of burning buildings by the firemen. On one occasion my Dad carried a woman and child from a burning house having sustained a broken arm when a wall collapsed on him as he was reaching them. His reward? A white feather and a heap of abuse because he was not shooting Germans. I am still amazed when old folks talk like wartime was the 'good old days'.

My Dad had a strong sense of humour which was genetically transferred to me. I recall several examples. They had an articulated skeleton at the fire station which could be set in any position: this was used for teaching First Aid. My Dad once placed Horace (the skeleton) in the ladies toilet as if he was reading the Liverpool Echo: it seemed a good idea at the time. Several of the more querulous types had minor accidents as a result of Horace's presence in the bogs. Horace was fully articulated and various bits could be removed for demonstration purposes. On another occasion my Dad removed the hand and surreptitiously dropped it in the gravy in the canteen. He hovered near the servery waiting for the reaction as each person helped him or herself to gravy. The second officer entered the canteen, selected a pie and, of course, up came the skeletal hand on the ladle, dripping with greasy congealing gravy. He was surprised and amused simultaneously; amid the chaos of war most Scousers retained their ability to see the funny side of many situations.

Once during the blackout my Dad was sent with another officer to pick up a corpse from a bombed building. Negotiating the bomb craters in the road they arrived at their destination, no mean feat in pitch blackness, and loaded the body into the back of the van which had no back doors; a bomb blast had wrecked them. His companion went to find a place in the bombsite to relieve himself and my Dad had a brainwave. He switched on the interior light then hid under the back of the van with a long piece of wood he had found in the road. With this stick he was able to switch on the lamp in the rear of the van without being seen. His companion returned, assumed my Dad had also gone to the universal toilet and switched off the light illuminating the body. As he went to sit in the front he heard the switch click on. He called out but no answer. After three repeats of the exercise he was in a state of shock and shouted at the corpse, 'I know you're dead you bastard!' He was not amused when my Dad revealed the trick.

My Dad got all the good jobs; he was frequently sent to remove dead bodies from the docks. Almost a year after the War a businessman was sitting on the dockside to eat his lunch when he looked into the dock and saw a ghastly face looking up at him. The body had been in the water for a long time and as they pulled the corpse out of the dock, the arm came off and the body splashed back into the water. The flesh was pulpy and even worse, covered with shrimps which were tucking into the luckless individual. This tale was shared at tea-time, of course. That evening we had tripe and onion, why I don't know. I can't think of anything more repulsive than tripe (apart from shrimps).

I have no recollection of my Dad's dad at all, apart from the story passed down which I will now relate. Billy Russell and his mate were on their way home on foot. They'd been on a drinking spree and began an argument in the Baltic Fleet public house. As they got to the Albert Dock the argument turned into a fight. Grandad Russell punched his friend who flew backwards into the dock. They were both full of the spirit, but Grandad realised his mate was drowning. Kicking off his boots and removing his jacket, he dived into the murky waters of the dock and dragged his spluttering friend to safety. As they emerged a policeman stood on the dockside demanding names and addresses. A few weeks later he was notified that he had been awarded a Humane Society medal for his rescue effort; the policeman hadn't seen him knock his friend in the water, just the rescue!

Billy Russell's wife, whom we called Granny Russell, was a large lady. She ate all the things that we are now told are bad and ate very few healthy things, but she was fit as a fiddle until she died at 80 odd. One of her favourite meals was bacon and eggs. She used to pour the fat remaining after the fry up onto her plate, add a dollop of brown sauce then mop up the unsaturated animal fat with a piece of bread. My main memories of her are her hobbit-like physique (including the beard), the enormous wart on her shiny moon face and her biceps which delivered the knock-out punch at Chester Zoo about which I will comment later.

My Dad had an older brother, Alf, a 6 foot 6 gorilla who was a Regimental Sergeant-Major in the Army. He had a pet spaniel with huge droopy ears which he called Gunner; at meal-times it was fitted with a nylon stocking on its head to keep its ears out of the dog food. Uncle Alf once smuggled a monkey from India into the UK, not difficult in the turmoil of global war. This beast, within minutes of arriving at our house, had frightened the cat, shredded the curtains and peed all over the window. The dude had to go. I never found out what happened to him but meat was scarce and people were desperate.

My Auntie Lil inherited the build and ability to deliver a fair forearm smash from my grandma. Most summers we spent in her huge house in Waterloo where she lived with Uncle Sam. She was in charge of a care home and spent most of her time cleaning up incontinent geriatrics. Not the greatest job in the world, but someone had to do it; it certainly cured her of persistent nail-biting. Her henpecked husband, Uncle Sam was a joiner. The attic of the house was a well fitted joiner's shop, with roof windows allowing light to enter the room. Connected to this was an unlit room where the water tank resided, a place of doom, gloom and the perpetual sound of running water. They called this the Mother Attic and we were forbidden to enter - like the shuttered room, we were afraid but also had to know what was in there. We often stood in the doorway then chickened out. One day my brother bought a blue plastic gun, which was a novelty torch. We crept upstairs to look in the Mother Attic. The torch was not that powerful, the battery almost flat from all the puffer fish experiments: this consisted of placing the mouth on the end of the torch and inflating the cheeks, but what we did see was hideous and had us racing downstairs in panic. There behind the huge tank was what I first thought was a monkey, slowly swinging. As we approached the face was visible, grotesque and with demonic little eyes that glowed as the torch swept across them: a horrible almost-human face. The frightening homunculus was, in fact, an Indian curio, carved from a branch of a tree: a monkey with a human face, glass eyes and a weird painted waistcoat. Many years later I inherited it - and it swayed to and fro in my office until eventually it disappeared. It was ugly, spooky and I was slightly afraid of it. Ultimately my wife, Viv, admitted she had never liked it and had sent it to the refuse dump in the sky. Secretly, I was glad. The twittering noise it made after midnight spooked everyone that visited us.

Uncle Sam died when I was quite young, well I hope he did - they buried him anyway. I remember his visits in his later days. He had part of one of his fingers missing from an accident in the joiners shop - but no-one would tell me how the amputation occurred. He had the quaint habit of pointing with the stump to emphasise what he was saying. He was a just-about-living example of upper respiratory tract infections. He smoked heavily and had a number of problems which sounded exotic: pleurisy, dropsy, angina and chronic bronchitis; he summed it all up as 'trouble with the bronicals'. He carried around a shiny flip-top sputum cup, in which he kept his collection of phlegm. When in our home, which had a coal fire, he would hawk horribly, his face red, with an increasing sound like an underground train as the tasty phlegm rattled around the air passages until he voided it. I guess he intended the fire to be their destination but it frequently hit the front of the grate because of his weak lungs and gozzy eyes. The sputum hissed and crackled as it flowed under gravity down the hot surface. In the morning, the grate looked like a snail family's big-day-out had occurred overnight. My mother, like Queen Victoria before her, was not amused. My efforts to emulate my good uncle went unrewarded but not unpunished.

Our whole area became smokeless and not before time. Some of the fogs or smogs we experienced were almost 'end of the worldy'. The air was yellowish, often for days and it made you choke and burned your eyes. We were made to wear linen handkerchiefs across our mouths and noses: coming home from school we looked like a cattle rustlers' convention, with huge black spots at the nostrils where at least some of the carbon crud had been filtered from the air. The alternatives to proper coal, which bubbled, roared and entertained as well as keeping us warm, were gas fires, electric fires or smokeless fuel, which was totally over-priced. We picked up a second-hand three bar electric fire, though we only ever used two at a time to save money.

Where the Bugs wear Boots

One day Uncle Sam arrived, complete with his portable spittoon. He was no chicken, his eyes were failing like the majority of his bodily systems and so when he deemed it time to expectorate, he began a succession of coughing and grozzling, then directed the phlegm at the hazy source of heat - namely our electric fire. I would like to report an amazing flash-back, a two metre-long spark that singed his eyebrows but, in reality, a short circuit occurred and our three-bar fire became a two-bar. I was still quite young when he died and on being informed of his sad demise, so I am told, I was more concerned at the whereabouts of his sputum cup than his extinction. This was probably because I thought it was a beer tankard, an interesting Holy Grailish object - shiny and mysterious - (and I had magpie tendencies). I never really understood the function of the shiny cup and lid. Any attempt to investigate had always led to disgusted looks and vicious condemnation; only when I was older did I realise what I had been spared by not flipping the lid.

I don't know anything about Uncle Charlie other than he was torpedoed in the North Sea, or the ship he was serving on was, and that I was named after him.

Cousin Bill was in the Merchant Navy, his ship was also torpedoed during the War and he spent several days in sub-zero water. He survived by keeping his greatcoat on, treading water and reciting all the psalms and hymns he knew; watching his companions dip beneath the waves one-by-one. He was a brilliant pianist with a performers' licence; I recall that he abandoned a career as a concert pianist to run the choir in a local mission church. I stayed with them now and again and learned about the old days at sea or I would shout out the name of a classical composition and he would play it from memory. He and his wife Margery were keen Christians and encouraged me to go to their church, called Bankhall Mission on Stanley Road. The building was precariously poised on the edge of the railway embankment and the seats were coated with varnish that never completely gelled: this had the effect of leaving an accurate bum print of the last person to sit on them and a wild sound when bum and seat parted - a bit like a zip unfastening. The pews also had wire hat racks that were just the right height for my feet and produced a deep 'Jaws Harp' sound when touched. They gave me a shilling every time I attended church, which was not for very long: the stress was worth at least half a crown!

Where the Bugs wear Boots

Bill's love for the sea was such that he bought a house overlooking the River Mersey and they had season tickets for the Isle of Man ferry. Every time I have sailed to the Isle of Man I have provided ground bait for the fishes, apart from one occasion when I wished I could vomit and hopefully then feel better, but was unable to. On this occasion Viv and I travelled with Marge and Bill who kindly treated us to a meal in the on-board restaurant: we'd never dined there before as a bank loan was usually required to pay the bill. After dinner we found a nice place to lie in the sun and relax. The Irish Sea can be fairly choppy on occasions; on this occasion it was extremely so. We were sailing on the Lady of Man, a steamship fitted with stabilisers which reduced the amount of pitching from side to side. Unfortunately the major movement on this occasion was a sickening rocking from stem to stern. Marge and Bill travelled regularly to the Isle of Man and not only had season tickets: they also had seasoned stomachs. Viv and I lay on our deck chairs as sick as parrots, greener than a chlorophyll sandwich. An obese lady next to Viv was sprawled on her deck chair like a beached whale. As each wave hit the ship, a corresponding wave of anti-peristalsis caused her to roll on one side and spew horribly onto a steaming heap of something she had prepared earlier, smack in the centre of her copy of the Daily Mirror. The sea was so rough that even some of the crew joined in the spewfest.

I got up and staggered some distance from our honking neighbour when another fat lady pushed past me, hand across mouth towards the rail. She never made it to the rail before the inevitable happened. All the way up to the rail and the rail itself was coated in white greb; I suspected she had overdosed on apple crumble earlier. After voiding her dinner she returned to obscurity just as a dapper chappie carrying a stick-seat and expensive binoculars arrived on deck. Obviously a seasoned traveller he showed no sign of sea-sickness as he strode purposefully across to the space that the big woman had marked out. He showed no sense of smell either as he plonked his elbows down in the regurgitated apple crumble and scanned the horizon with his binoculars. The woman attempting to recreate the Devils Tower in fresh vomit retched again. Viv had seen enough, she raced to the toilet which was awash with puke and full of professional honkers: there was her expensive lunch gone in three seconds. The next three hours was a nightmare; I lay on a coil of rope, wanting to vomit but unable to do so.

Where the Bugs wear Boots

I had an Auntie Edith whom I saw infrequently. She was a frail lady with chronic arthritis in her hands. She used to go for hot wax treatment - I don't think it did much good. Her husband, Alf, was almost completely deaf, which he attributed to German mortar bombs in the poppy fields. Other relatives reckon he was never there, so make your own minds up! He had a weird sense of humour; when I was young I thought he was just mad. At a family wedding he explained to me how during the War the Gurkhas crept silently around, testing the way boots were laced (crossed for British, straight for German) If the laces were tied German style, the throats were slit - as he told the tale he would throw his head back, move his thumb across his throat and make a horrific death rattle. He was scary, but there was more to come. Later on he took a kitchen knife, gripped it in his teeth and began to wriggle under the huge table where the guests were sitting, checking out the boot-lace style. To my relief he did no more than cut any laces which were incorrectly tied. As the party proceeded, with his inhibitions totally gone, he vanished for five minutes or so. When he returned, he was 'dressed' in nothing but a bath towel and two saucepan lids strategically held with string against his scrawny upper body - a pre-Madonna metal bra. He leaped onto the table but after a painfully short parody of a hula-dance, he slipped on a plate of sandwiches, destroyed a trifle, and then fell off onto the floor and into obscurity. I recall the ignominy of the war hero being removed, a pimply buttock peeking out from the towel which was unwinding dangerously as they dragged him into the kitchen and obscurity. I decided to look for a more positive role model.

My Mother was adopted by the Horton family; her mother died when she was born; quite a common occurrence in the early days of not-too-antiseptic surgery and her Dad died not long afterwards. The Hortons originally lived in Aigburth but eventually moved out to Croxteth. My mother was an amazing person with a beautiful, gentle spirit sustained by her faith. She was a real Christian and demanded honesty and truthfulness from her children; as I grew older this became a major problem for me. She was also a great cook and most hospitable: she could produce meals for many almost out of thin air. She worked as a secretary for a firm of solicitors in the city centre. Quite a number of her relatives died when I was young and the thought of this happening to my parents worried me. I frequently tried to make Mum promise to take pills that would give her everlasting life; unfortunately such medication

11

didn't exist.

Everyone wore hats or things on their heads in those days and when a funeral procession went past we had to take our hats off and keep still. I never understood why the ladies didn't remove their hats or head-scarves, but it wasn't a big deal, I was too busy observing the exotic limousines dedicated to corpse transport. Mum used to sing to us when we were very small, but virtually every song made me cry. 'I'm forever blowing bubbles', a song of yesteryear about the short life of bubbles compared to the brevity of life and relationships had me howling over the fate of the poor bubbles. A few years later and I would parody the same song but feature the fate of the geek who passed wind excessively in a bath with too much soap in it. Another weepie around the same time was 'Rudolph the red nosed reindeer'. It wasn't his red nose that upset me but the way his so-called friends excluded him from their games. I knew what he felt like, as they say, 'Been there, done that, got the T-shirt'.

I only saw Grandma Horton, the lady who adopted my Mum, once when I was older. I took the Overhead Railway from Seaforth to Aigburth, an amazing trip along the dockside, with all manner of cranes and ships from all over the world. Grandma Horton lived in a huge terraced house which was dark and gloomy; I recall the dado rail and the muddy maroon coated anaglypta paper underneath. Grandma Horton was dying and according to some quirky Victorian ritual, we were all expected to see her on her way out and to look forward to seeing her corpse glammed up with make-up after she died. The only lighting in the house was gaslight, flickering eerily as if it knew she was on her last legs. I was led to a downstairs room; the stench was unbearable. The black edged bedcover was horribly stained, the occupant was unmoving apart from shallow breathing. A bucket full of black clotted blood greeted me as I was pushed to the bedside and her hand was placed on mine - it was icy cold. I stood there, not knowing what I was supposed to do or say. I don't think she was aware of anything on the morphine with which she was overdosed. As I turned to get out of the room she let out a bloodcurdling shriek and began to vomit blood. My Aunt Emmy picked up the bucket, realised it had not been emptied and had to watch helplessly as the stream of part clotted gunge flowed across the bedcover. I ran from the room; how I didn't puke I will never know. I couldn't wait to get out into the fresh air, blinking in the daylight and feeling the cleansing rain on my face. She died four days later. I rode my bicycle at full speed into a brick wall so I was unable to attend the corpse viewing, the wake or the burial. I never saw her in her younger and better days: the ruler of the house with a wooden pastry rolling pin for a sceptre.

Her husband, Grandpa Horton, had one major claim to fame; his barbershop was close to Goodison Park, the home of Everton Football Club. Dixie Dean, the celebrated centre-forward, was one of his esteemed customers among many other Everton players. Grandpa Horton liked his ale and frequently came home in a more than happy state. His children didn't mind. He would hand out his small change with a lop-sided grin, then walk into the kitchen where he was often disciplined by his wife: a thwack across the head with the rolling pin kept for the purpose. One Friday night he failed to return from the pub at closing time. A search party was sent out and he was eventually found on his knees under a street lamp on Walton Road, trying to pick up what he thought was a silver shilling. A closer inspection by the less inebriated revealed a golly, a circular gobbet of sputum which someone had kindly left for his entertainment. A few blows about the head with the rolling pin helped him to sober up and once again he promised to give up the ale, or at least reduce his consumption of the amber nectar. He did manage a few days without a drop of the 'hard stuff' but then an incident occurred which placed him right back on the ale wagon, never to escape until 'death did him part'.

Times were hard and any job on the side was a welcome addition to the household finances. A customer in the barber-shop, a male nurse at Newsham General Hospital, suggested there was money to be had shaving corpses. Apparently facial hair continues to grow after death and requires shaving to make the cadaver look more handsome. Grandpa Horton was not happy with the idea but Grandma's 'look' and the bumps on his head convinced him to give it a go. It was a cold winter's night, pitch black as he arrived clutching his shaving mug, shaving soap and collection of cut-throat razors. These razors used to fascinate me. I was told they were sharp and to keep away, yet he seemed unable to cut the old leather strap he carried around with him. I needed to solve the puzzle. One evening while he was out I found the bag of barber-shop tools, removed a razor and cut through the leather strap and the end of my finger with ease.

Where the Bugs wear Boots

Back at the hospital, the old bloke he had to shave had died in a chair and to straighten him out for burial they had weighed down his knees with several planks of wood and some house bricks. His jaw was bandaged shut and there were two pennies keeping his eyelids shut until they stayed that way by themselves. Far from happy, Grandpa Horton lathered up and shaved the near side of the corpse without incident. The trolley was against the wall and his shaky hands were unable to release the corroded wheel locks: he also needed the toilet but there was no-one around and he had no idea where it was. Anxious to get the job done as soon as possible he leaned across the body to lather the other side. As he did so a brick slid off one of the planks and landed on his toe. The same plank now see-sawed into his crotch and the corpse's knees came up and thumped into his chest, but worse than any of this was the horrific moan as the corpse reverted to a seated position and air was dragged across the vocal cords. With the pennies dropping off with the movement, the eyelids slowly opened. Shocked beyond measure and no longer needing the toilet, he ran home, leaving his gear for one of the kids to pick up the next day. After a change of under and outer-wear he returned to the pub until closing time. Some friends delivered him to the door, so bladdered that he felt no pain from the rolling pin.

Auntie Gertie was a dressmaker; she and Auntie Ivy worked in an attic in a spooky old shop on Brownlow Hill, pulled down years ago. I often called in to see them on the way to or from Liverpool University where I was studying for a Chemistry degree. The buildings either side had been demolished many years before: the shop was very narrow and high with a steep staircase at the back which went up three storeys and down into a cellar. The shop had a permanent smell of stale urine from the rack of clothes awaiting alterations, I could cope with that by holding my breath 'till I got to the top of the stairs; coping with the little dwarf that lived and worked in the cellar was a different story. I'll tell you more about that later. Auntie Ivy had eyes like an owl, but a beak like a falcon. I never really got to know her and her family, but her son was famous because he had a 16 inch collar when he was only 12 years old. This fact was waved before me to discourage me as I only had a scrawny 15inch neck. Anyway, John-Boy had a large collar size because he was a fat git, not because he was a genius or hung like a donkey.

Uncle Harry was a foreman in an engineering business on Aintree

Road. He lived in a small hotel in Orrell Park, had exotic foreign holidays and rode fast motorcycles. He was fun to talk to and helped me select my first motorcycle from a shop in Manchester. His main claim to fame was that he worked for the company that installed the Liver Birds on the top of the Royal Liver Building at the Pier Head. There is an old brown photo somewhere of Uncle Harry doing a handstand on top of one of the birds. The photo was taken just before they raised the bird from the flat roof to its present position, but you can't tell that from the photo. Another interesting habit he had was to test electrical wires or sockets by licking a finger then touching the live contact: not a lead I was prepared to follow.

Auntie Clara was the nearest thing to a real sister that my Mum had. She looked after us when Mum visited the hospital after Dad had the first stroke: she always brought edible goodies for brother Dave and me. On other occasions she bought encyclopaedias for us which we read avidly. Books like The Wonder Book of Science, The Wonder Book of How it's Done etc. After absorbing the information, we cut them up and stuck bits on the wall. They'd probably be worth a few bob now but then we never thought about the future, life in the present was hard enough.

Auntie Emmie was only five foot one in height and width, a true hobbit clone. When younger she was a cinema cleaner and usherette at the Astoria and Victory cinemas. When they could find no one else they let her sell the ice creams in the wax tubs with the splintery wooden spoons. She would stand in the spotlight, a beatific grin from ear to ear, sixteen stone of flobster; I'm surprised anyone bought ice creams with such an object lesson. Her aim in life was to eat everything edible in the universe. She had her own reinforced armchair with a built-in footstool which was placed exactly perpendicular to the gas fire. Looking back now, she was the perfect illustration of a human black hole for any cosmology seminar. She would lie there like a beached whale with food in various containers on the floor beside her. She often had sweets lined up along the arm of the chair, half of them with the wrappers removed. I asked her once why she did this. She explained it was so that she could chain-eat and waste no time removing the wrappings. She was a very happy person but slow moving. One Christmas she brought in a bowl of custard to go on the pudding and dropped it in the hall. Some 'unspoilt' custard remained in the largest fragment of the bowl and she

15

decided to eat it. She lacerated her tongue on some glass fragments lurking beneath the custard and needed seven stitches in it. Yecchh! Her son Tom taught me to play chess, to ride a bicycle and approximate to as decent a human being as a 15 year old boy can be. Unfortunately, he emigrated to Australia with his family and with his influence gone, my development was again in chaos.

Chapter 3

Early days

One of my children once asked me what I did during The War. My reply was 'most of the time I lay on my back and peed myself!' Before they wrote me off as the wimp of the century, I explained that I was only a baby at the time. I don't recall the end of the war or the house full of relations who were bombed out. I don't recall being force-fed omelettes made from dried egg but I can well imagine it. My Dad said my uncle Alf used to use dried egg omelettes to sole and heel his army boots, and why not? My earliest recollections of life are grasshoppers. I recall sitting on top of a huge mound of earth, observing grasshoppers and catching some in an almost clean jam jar. I knew that the 'mountain' in the garden was called an air-raid shelter; when they came and took away the corrugated-iron part of it a huge rectangular concrete-lined hole in the ground was left. My suggestion to make a crocodile enclosure was ignored: the hole was filled in and I had to make do with snakes, lizards and tree frogs as companions. After the War these Andersen shelters were offered for sale to those that had the money; few of our neighbours really wanted a dark concrete based shed full of spiders and permanent dampness. All the cats in the neighbourhood used ours as a combination toilet and brothel and my folks were glad to see the back of it.

We lived in Park Lane, Bootle, with the cemetery at the bottom of the street and the railway station at the top end. Almost opposite the station, further up the hill was Dolly's sweet shop; we called the hill Dolly's Brew. Dolly was a Gagool figure, extremely old and wrinkly with minimal hygiene standards. I suspected she might be a witch. The shop window was always full of iced buns, cream cakes and flies. She ritually licked her twisted fingers as she opened the conical paper sweet bags then dropped the chosen delicacies in one-by-one as she totted up the price. Walking back down the hill, peeling back the lolly ice wrapper or dipping into the spittle fingered sweets, you could see the bowling green and the wooded area that screened off the railway. At different times of day this patch of land was inhabited by bowlers, snoggers, perverts and

17

kids sorting out arguments by means of a fist-fight.

As I mentioned earlier, many of our relatives lived with us when I was really young as their houses had been bombed or were unsafe. I got a lot of attention as a baby which helped program me for later life. As things got back to normal, the temporarily homeless relatives returned to their own homes; I think my Mum was glad! I was born in Bootle Maternity Hospital in Balliol Road but my brother Dave, destined for greater things, first saw daylight in Blundellsands Nursing home for the upwardly mobile. When Mum and Dad arrived home with him in May 1944 just a few days old, I was, to say the least, disappointed. He couldn't speak, he just lay there and gurgled and worst of all, he couldn't play football. I'd built up this mental picture of a slightly smaller version of me that would be happy to play in goal. Part of this pseudo-prophesy would be shown to be false in the future when he captained the school team and was a prolific goal scorer and rock-solid defender, but never played in goal. The war was still progressing, if that's the right word for it, and we were too young to be evacuated out into the country somewhere. Dave had a full-body baby gas mask with a bellows and filter, but was not aware of it. I was issued with a horrible red Mickey Mouse face gas mask with a strong rubbery smell. It had to fit tightly and consequently bit into my chin and pulled my hair when putting it on or taking it off. I'm glad to say we never had to use them in a real gas attack but we had to practise wearing them now and again.

It was wartime and most luxury items were scarce. The toys I had as a child were not very well made and didn't last long; the one exception was a teddy bear with the ingenious name of Teddy for whom I knitted an Everton FC scarf. It was 3 cm wide, almost 30 cm long and took me several weeks to produce. Another favourite was Bun, a fluffy rabbit on which I had occasion to vomit; no amount of washing and cleaning could remove the aroma of stale puke so he went on the fire along with anything else that was burnable. Someone bought me a dog on wheels which my parents christened 'Peter'. When I sat on him he collapsed and a wicked rusty metal spike protruded from each leg. Peter followed Bun to the front room inferno. My favourite toy was a small white dog called Spot who had no spots and wobbly eyes; he also consisted of a wire frame stuffed with horsehair. I bit one of his eyes out and Mum managed to fish the tasty morsel out of my toothless slobbering mouth. It was made of glass with a twisted metal spike to hold it in place. Spot was so precious that he wasn't even put on the fire, he just vanished: I guess the aliens abducted him. Not only were toys badly made, virtually everything was expensive and ingenuity ruled. The coal we were getting was rubbish with a lot of useless little bits and a lot of coal dust, we called it 'slack'. When shoes were no longer serviceable, we filled them with slack and put them on the fire. We recycled old bits of soap into one 'new' block and made 'spills' to convey fire from the coal fire to the cooker, cigarettes or the upstairs gas fire. Every home had rocking cardboard parrots impregnated with DDT insecticide swinging on the mantelpiece. Beneath them were heaps of dead flies, a pleasant alternative to the horrible brown sticky fly papers hanging from the ceiling covered with rotting fly corpses; my uncle Harry said they were used to make Eccles Cakes or 'fly pies' as we called them.

Some of the things we ate still stick in my memory now as they stuck in my craw then: dripping butties - rancid animal fat spread on bread with added salt; sugar butties where the salt was replaced with granulated sugar; conny-onny butties employing condensed milk as the filling. Tripe, raw in vinegar or boiled in milk, was still like chewing rubber or a synthetic golly, almost worse than drinking the contents of a spittoon although I never got to experience that. Then there was Spam, a slimy meat product of dubious origin which could be incorporated into any meal including porridge and trifle. Virol was a sweet, gooey substance used to make babies' dummies more tasty. It caused the teeth to rot and is probably responsible for the popular song, 'All I want for Christmas is my two front teeth'.

If the parentals got hold of any margarine they would soften it in front of the fire and add a bit of milk to make it 'buttery'. The neighbours once gave me a taste of their pseudo-strawberries; they sliced some tomatoes, added sugar and milk and left the concoction in the coal cellar to cool down. They were old and I suspect their taste buds were due for replacement; it certainly didn't taste like strawberries to me. Finally, the ultimate pleasure, toast made on the coal fire with a toasting fork; it was easy to burn the fingers, even easier to burn the toast, but the resultant charcoal reduced the family flatulence.

DIY healthcare also flourished: a spoonful of castor oil was administered once a week to keep the bowels ticking over whether you needed it or not. Cod-liver oil and malt was administered regularly to prevent colds and flu. The fish oil and 'malt' separated on standing. If I heard the sound as my Mum shook up the filthy concoction I used to hide, but was ultimately captured and dosed with the muck. The malt was supposed to make it taste better, but didn't work. The fish-breath produced if you burped could cost you friendships. Goose grease was another popular cure-all if you could get hold of it: an old sock soaked in goose grease placed round the neck for a sore throat, or solid grease spread on the chest then covered with brown paper was indicated for chesty coughs or the 'bronicals. 'Spitting is forbidden' notices on public transport reminded us that absolutely nothing was to be wasted. Every home had the statutory three plaster ducks on a wall somewhere and a collection of Toby jugs in the kitchen. Toby jugs are, not as one might think, a women's complaint, but evil looking containers moulded in the shape of an inebriate Victorian tosser in a three-cornered hat. Ugly, almost hateful but probably worth a few bob nowadays.

Money being scarce, days out were selected with 'free' or 'cheap' as the criterion. The riverside gardens at Waterloo, near my Auntie Lil's house, were well kept and were a good place to take butties for a picnic: you could see the different ships entering and leaving the port of Liverpool. Sometimes I timed them as they passed the measured-mile buoys in the river and worked out their speed. Other times I just watched the grass growing and wondered if aliens really did exist. Another cheap trip was to Otterspool before the construction of the new promenade and Riverside Walk. Like the vampire haunts in the movies, it was safe enough during daylight hours but some weird characters hung about after dark. On a visit to Mum's family in Aigburth I went to the 'Cazzie' near the old iron foundry where a dead horse had been washed up by the tide. It must have been in the water a long time and was rotten; I could smell it well before I saw it. The flesh was so sloppy that it squidged when the horrible little kids stood on it and dropped bricks on it. I began to realise that I wasn't the lowest form of life that my teachers had told me I was.

Speke Hall, adjacent to Liverpool Airport, was cheap if you took your own food and didn't go in the old mansion itself. Exploring the woods at the back you could walk along an elevated path and see the aeroplanes taking off from the airport. Nowadays you have to pay to get in the grounds but it's still worth it. A similar cheap day out was a visit to Croxteth Hall, again provided you didn't want to go round the Hall itself. We took butties and crisps, a bottle of juice and four plastic cups and found a place to sit down in the spacious grounds amid hundreds of fellow paupers with the same idea. After 'dinner' most of the kids wanted ice creams from a scrofulous vendor on a tricycle. My dad's warnings that he probably made the ice cream in a dirty cellar with unwashed hands (possibly true) did not put us off so he had to pay up. After the ice cream we now needed amusement so we went to look at the lake which had several huge willow trees hanging over the water. Many years later I took my own children to Croxteth Park. The largest of the willow trees did not have a 'climb me' sign but I knew it would have done in an alternate universe. To a chorus of approval from the kids, and disapproval from my wife, I began my ascent. I got quite a way up and shouted to the kids but there was no answer, other than 'Get down! Get out of the park!' in a deep officious voice. I descended to find my wife trying to explain my behaviour to a park security policeman on a huge horse. When the parkie saw I was not a young scally (but an older one) he scratched his head, reset his cap and galloped off to find some other miscreants somewhere else in the park.

Returning to my childhood cheap days out, probably the best outing by far was the tour of Scott's Bakery on Dunnings Bridge Road. The tour round the factory was boring when you'd done it once a week for a month but at the end it led into a large marquee on the grass at the front of the factory where you got a free cup of tea and one of the cakes that they made in the factory. The last time the family visited I noticed a cigarette-end in a vat of jam, no doubt put there by a public spirited visitor; it did make the tea and cakes seem less appealing though.

Considering the risks my dad took, and some of the injuries he sustained in rescuing idiots who smoked in bed, the pay was not that good in the Fire Brigade. For this reason my mum used to shop at Sturlas on Linacre Road. The shop had a system of hire-purchase and stamps you could save to buy school clothing; I don't recall much more other than two things which were utterly memorable. The first was the way that money was transferred to the office; assistants put the cash in a tube and popped it into a system of hissing vacuum pipes that ran across the high ceiling. Highly impressed I was! The second was memorable because it was horrible: to get to Sturlas we had to cross a bridge that spanned the Leeds-Liverpool canal. I was convinced a troll lived under it but that did not deter my crossing. The bridge was adjacent to the local tannery and the permanent stench was sickening; I don't know how the local residents tolerated it. Many years later they had a sale of Afghan coats in the students union at the university. Entering the hall the smell hit me; the coats were improperly cured and the stench of the tannery filled the place. I thought to check a coat in case the smell was from the many students in the place and dry-retched as I sniffed. I left the building and purchased a donkey jacket; the type not made from donkeys!

Where the Bugs wear Boots

A final slice of nostalgia features memories of some of the sounds of the 40s that you don't hear very much today, like the one 'o clock gun; a cannon that was fired at 1300 hours around the docks somewhere. To be in the area when it went off was to risk dropping your lunch, whether you'd eaten it or not. When there was fog on the river a very loud siren sounded, they called it the Bootle Bull, it used to scare the knickers off me as a child; if I was playing in the garden, I'd go indoors until it stopped. A more welcome sound was the clip-clop and rattle of the rag and bone man's horse and cart and the strangled, 'Any old iron?' which sounded more like, 'A-O-I-O'. He'd take anything, if you were lucky you might get a goldfish for £40 worth of scrap metal. Towards the end of the day he sometimes gave away the goldfish, which were in a bit of a state by then. Had he possessed one brain cell more he could have given them a bit of fresh air and shade, and kept them for the next day, but we didn't mind. Some nights we'd be listening to the radio or reading when there would be a frenzied knocking on the door. My Mum would open the door, with me peering from behind her to greet a scrofulous neighbour requesting a loan. 'Gorra shillun for de lecky?' which meant their electricity meter needed feeding and they had no shillings. We looked forward to the 'Lecky man' coming to read the meter because when he'd counted all the coins you got some 'divvy' back and we could have a chippy tea or some other treat. Another nostalgic sound was the twitter of my friend Bagsey's dad's chickens when we went to feed them with mashed up stale bread on the plot near Ford station. The tiny yellow balls of fluff were only fed once a day and they freaked out at feeding time.

Fire engines were fitted with bells in those days, as they went to extinguish fires and rescue people, they cleared the traffic by means of a beefy fireman who rang the bell like he had something against the clapper. We were visiting my Dad at the fire station once when the alarm bell sounded. I think my feet left the ground for an instant, then I was pulled out of the way as hordes of men jumped onto the shiny pole that led down to the place where the fire engines were kept, some still fastening their uniforms, then off down Strand Road with the bells clanging loudly. They called it the 'greasy pole', but it wasn't greasy to the touch. I couldn't resist the temptation to leap onto the pole and, being unaware that you have to grip the thing with your legs to control the rate of descent; I dropped like a stone and twisted my ankle. It was not as easy as it looked; many years later I saw someone on a trampoline just bouncing up and down like a frog in a bucket. When they stopped I leaped onto the thing, bounced on my head and spent six weeks in a neck brace. As Clint Eastwood puts it, 'A man ought to know his limitations!'

Going to the pictures wasn't too expensive; we usually went to the Regal cinema which eventually became Allinsons Club, now demolished to make room new buildings. The cinema was opposite to the White House pub in Litherland, now a fast-food emporium. We visited the Regal whatever the weather and by the same route, which included a back alley that resonated when you ran down it. The alley led onto Hawthorne Road and there glowing in the distance were the mercury and sodium lamps of the Lancashire Tar distillery, a visual feast for any young Sci-Fi freak. There was a permanent creosote atmosphere which could clear one's sinuses in seconds; little did I suspect that I would work there as a chemist many years later. My parents had to drag me past the distillery and into the cinema. A miserable, fat lady used to show us to the seats we had to sit in but when she had gone we usually moved somewhere better, away from the seedy old perverts with raincoats on their knees and irritating people who talked during the movie.

The screen was at first hidden by a weird pleated curtain with coloured lights shining from above and below making an interesting pattern. When the show was about to begin the lights dimmed and the curtain automatically rose up to reveal the screen. There would be a few low-budget adverts and maybe a trailer for the film being shown later in the week. If we were lucky there might be a short cartoon but we always had to suffer the Pathé News with the same boring voice accompanying the black and white newsreel footage. At last the U Certificate; the film was about to begin. I liked the MGM pictures because of the roaring lion at the beginning. Some films I recall are 'Annie Get your Gun', 'Across the Wide Missouri', and 'The Greatest Show on Earth'. In most performances there would be an ice-cream break where the big woman, who scowled with the effort of showing everyone to their seats, now stood with a forced smile in the spotlight bearing a tray of ice creams.

In central Liverpool was the Punch and Judy show located on the edge of St George's Plateau. There I learned the amazing tale of the infamous, psychotic Mr Punch, his regularly battered wife, his murdered baby and the futile attempts of the Law and a hungry crocodile to give him his just deserts. I never found out where 'Professor' Codman obtained his degree but the whole thing gob-smacked me. I had to be regularly dragged away, particularly when the hat came around to take up a collection. I practised some of the classic rhetoric; 'That's the way to do it!' usually after Mr Punch had bludgeoned someone to death, 'Judy, Judy, Judy!', 'You hold the baby!' and 'Where's the sausages?' I even bought a so-called 'double throat' that was supposed to aid ventriloquists to squeak like Mr Punch. I nearly swallowed mine and never really succeeded in getting the voice right.

We lived next door to Tom and Nellie Boulton, an elderly couple. Tom drove an old motorcycle and sidecar; if they passed you on the road, Nellie would do a reasonable Queen Elizabeth II impression as she waved through the yellowed plastic sidecar window. I think they were fairly well-off; they were certainly the first in the street to get a television. The TV was like a huge packing case with a tiny nine-inch screen on one side and an equally small loudspeaker on the other. This engineering marvel had a picture which twitched and rotated but Tom and Nellie belonged to a cult which forbade the touching of Line Hold or Frame Hold controls. They did purchase a 'magnifier' for the TV, a huge perspex contraption full of glycerine which made the picture slightly bigger but totally distorted everything. Many years later my in-laws had the same 'never adjust' belief about the colour control on their colour TV; the skin tone was permanently set on purple.

Nellie, a very kind lady, let all the kids in to see Muffin the Mule once a week. Muffin was boring but not as boring as Annette Mills, the human who patronised it. This television pioneer spoke to Muffin as if she suspected he was only a puppet and addressed the audience as if they were brain-dead. Nevertheless we all sat totally enthralled. To be honest, Muffin was just a stupid puppet, no attempt to hide the strings. The character I really liked was Peregrine the Penguin. He was mildly offensive with a clicking beak and was constantly nagged by the almost human Annette Mills. He had attitude and was a forerunner for future Puppets-with-attitude like Zippy and Spud. As the programme ended with the haunting strains of 'We love Muffin the Mule', the Boulton's flatulent black dog was admitted to the room and we began to file out. I guess too much excitement could have jeopardised the soft furnishings. Over half the young viewers were incontinent; all of them were with my pen-knife pushed up their noses.

The Boulton's dog was a spaniel called Mac, black and smelly, with a tongue that dangled onto its paws. Never did I encounter a dog with such flatulence, noisy but deadly. It was years later that I discovered the secret. During the summer months Mac was force fed with great lumps of sulphur which Nellie claimed 'cooled the blood'. It also explains how the dog could disperse a street full of people in seven seconds without any obvious effort. In some grotty joke shops at the seaside you can still get 'fart powder'; powdered sulphur to sprinkle on your friend's curry and enhance his or her biochemical warfare potential. The Boultons were good neighbours in other ways; once when my Mum was ill, Nellie brought a huge bowl of soup made with bacon bones. I remember how salty it was, but it soon had Mum back on her feet. We had a rabbit called Judy who strayed through the hedge into the Boulton's garden and never came back. My theory was that Mrs B had probably poisoned her, but I had no proof. I suspected the bacon rib soup may have been 'Judy soup' and when the next consignment arrived I poured mine away while no one was looking and filled up later with jam butties.

Opposite our house lived the Pierce family, Charlie and Maggie and their only daughter, Ivy. Ivy's claim to fame was her 'ability' to sleep with her eyes open. She was rather pale when young and could easily have been accidentally buried alive if she had fallen asleep in the cemetery. Charlie was a Cockney, a wizened little gnome of a man with a brown, leathery monkey-face. He worked down at the docks as a labourer, his main occupation was steam-cleaning the fish oil tanks. He smelled unbelievably badly all the time. He would take a bath, drain off the water and repeat the procedure but despite this he was permanently fishy. As he walked up Park Lane on his way home it was not uncommon to see two or three cats following his slipstream, or sniffing round their front door after he had entered.

Maggie was another good neighbour, quite a bit older than Mum and with many health problems. She made the mistake once of confiding her incontinence problem to Mum while Uncle Harry was within earshot. He promptly renamed her 'Piddle-Pants-Percy' which, because of its innovative use of alliteration, stuck fast in my mind. I had to be reprogrammed regularly with a wooden spoon until I no longer referred to her by her new name. Ivy married Köra, a Norwegian translator who could read and speak some six languages. He was a brain-on-legs and their first and only child was the same. Carl was playing the violin at an early age and irritating us normal kids with his genius. One year Köra won the title of 'Mr Handsome Man of Bootle', an oxymoron if ever I heard one. The award didn't mean too much in those days and means even less now. We looked after their goldfish, Cleo, when they went on holiday to Norway and it went and died on us. Mum and I toured the pet shops and rag and bone men with the corpse in a paper bag trying to get a reasonable match. When they returned they claimed we had been too liberal with the ant's eggs as 'Cleo' had put on weight. Ivy claimed the fish had missed them and had a change of personality. We didn't have the heart to put them wise.

Our back garden faced that of Mr and Mrs Corrin. I probably got to know them the best because I was always asking for my football back; they had amazing patience. Any day in summer if the weather was good, they set up a large snooker table in their garden and the games would commence. One of the family; their son-in-law I think, had lost a hand in the War and had a gadget with an X-shaped snooker rest fitted to the stump. It looked like a branding iron or an alien implant to me, as I had problems distinguishing science fiction from science reality at that time. The War had been over for two or three years and there were many young men with bits missing, complete with medals but with limited job prospects: as the song goes, 'Heroes, just for one day.'

Each year on November 5th most streets had a bonfire party to celebrate Guy Fawkes' attempt to blow up the Houses of Parliament in 1605. Any loose timber was in danger of being stolen and used, gates, fences, even trees. Some people took the opportunity of Bonfire Night to get rid of unwanted chairs, settees and such like. Everyone came out to share fireworks, cups of tea and sausages or potatoes on dirty bamboo garden canes. When I moaned about the grubby state of the canes I was told, 'You'll eat more than a peck of muck before you die'. Nevertheless I was still made to wash my hands after going to the toilet and forbidden to eat sweets I found in the street. With so much to burn the fire usually went out of control, the tarmac ignited and the Fire Brigade arrived, once or twice with my Dad driving the fire engine, and all the children grizzled as the flames were extinguished.

Uncle Harry had contacts with a fireworks wholesaler and usually brought cases of them to the party. I used to stash a box of rockets and several boxes of bangers to create mayhem into the New Year. After he died we had to buy our own and started collecting them weekly as we could afford them. The family cat was always sniffing at the cardboard box that we kept them in, what appealed to him I don't know, but we put the box in the sideboard out of his way. It was two days to Bonfire Night and I came home from school to find the sideboard doors open; as I rushed to check the fireworks I was met by a horrific stench. The cat had opened the doors, got into the sideboard and relieved himself on our precious fireworks collection. Mum was in the garden as I went to moan, then realising that the oven, our main source of heat, was on, I ran back to the sideboard, grabbed the dripping box of fireworks and shoved them into the oven. Several minutes later I heard Mum shouting, 'What's that awful smell?' My automatic reply was, 'Nothing' but if you've ever put coal that has been sprayed with TCP (tom cat pee) on a fire you will know that it isn't 'nothing'. She pulled the steaming box out of the oven, all the back part was charred. The cat was jumping around and I was shrieking as Mum took the box outside. Fortunately the cat had done a thorough job of soaking the fireworks and none of them ignited. My Dad examined them; some were deemed useable, the others were thrown in the bin.

Very few people owned cars in 1945 in the area I lived in. As I mentioned earlier, our next door neighbour had a motorcycle combination, and over the road lived the Malins who owned the sausage factory in Seaforth. They had several cars down their drive. As the years went by more people got cars. First the privets would be uprooted, part of the wall would disappear then wooden or metal gates would arrive. Ultimately the council would come and drop the kerb and create a ramp leading to the new drive. Dad drove various types of fire engine but we didn't have a car, firstly because they were too expensive, but also because the sub-station he was based at was at the bottom of our street about seven minutes walk away. We generally got about on foot or got the bus; one of my favourite outings was to the laundry with Dad's shirts, we took the bus to the Rotunda on Scotland Road. This was once a theatre; then after a bomb took it out, an emergency water supply for the Fire Service during the War. From the Rotunda a tram ran all the way to the laundry in Fazakerley. I know it came from the Dingle tram sheds, where it went after Fazakerley I never knew. I was intrigued by the way trams were steered, not with a steering wheel like a bus, but with handles. Sometimes the tram would be turned round by the driver pulling the electrical contact round then steering from the other end of the vehicle; then all the seats could be flipped to face the new direction. I used to take it upon myself to flip all the seats until the other passengers or Mum indicated that their patience was exhausted. After the trams disappeared the tram lines remained for a long time: I frequently got my bicycle tyres caught in them and bit the dust.

There was no television, the playing fields were infested with big kids (bullies) and the perverts hung round the toilets, which were so gross you'd have to be real desperate to use them anyway. Most of the time, therefore, we played in the street: there was not a lot to do; grass grows too slowly to have any future as a spectator sport, so we often got into trouble. We regularly played chicken with the buses on the 57 and 57A route, hiding behind the huge old elm trees then rushing across the road to see who had the guts to be last across. There were four or five of us and it got a bit hair-raising on occasions. A bus once caught my pullover and ripped it as I raced in front of it, stupid I know, but it seemed exciting at the time. Another equally stupid pastime was throwing things at the pensioners coming from the allotments, their 'sit up and beg' antique bicycles loaded up with leeks and cabbages. We frequently had to out-run these senior citizens who would have scalped us were they able to catch up.

The asphalt road surface was very gooey in hot weather and we used to make tar babies (see the story of Brer Rabbit) out of lolly-ice sticks and launch them at people's front doors or leave them stuck on car bonnets etc. Another craze was marbles. I bought them in huge quantities and claimed to have won them, but I was soon cleaned out as I was useless at the game. I kept some special heavy ones which I incorporated in a knotted handkerchief for thwacking lesser beings on the head. Virtually every street activity was dirty, anti-social or dangerous.

Several rich kids in the street had footballs and cricket gear; we poor kids were sometimes allowed to play and we slowly outgrew the more crazy activities for a while. Metalgob was a very rich kid; his nickname originated from the corrective device for wonky teeth which he wore for years. His parents bought him a genuine cricket bat made of willow with twine bands on the blade, rubber handle and always sticky with linseed oil. On special occasions, when his mother allowed, he appeared in the street with his bat and a game of pseudo-cricket took place. This consisted of Metalgob batting for most of the time and the rest of us mere mortals fielding for him. When he was bowled out or caught he would remind us whose bat it was. If we moaned enough about not getting an opportunity to bat he would mince off down the road for his tea - with his bat. He manipulated us by allowing us all a short spell with the bat, just enough to keep us fielding; then he would whine, 'Ah, let me have the bat'. Eventually his teeth were deemed perfect and the brace removed: the name Metalgob was now no longer accurate. I was interested in Native American culture at this time, particularly their names which reflected their characters or achievements. I duly renamed him 'Ah-let-me-have-the-bat'. I hassled my mother to get me a cricket bat. All she could afford was a cheap one, more like a rounders bat, cut out of one piece of wood that hurt your fingers if you hit a cork ball too hard. In the street we used a tennis ball which wasn't too bad; at least we had independence. 'Ah-let-me-have-the-bat' ruled no more!

Street cricket was a bit dangerous; Park Lane was part of a major bus route and the neighbours didn't like having their windows broken. Games began with 10 or so lads, girls were not allowed to play. The numbers slowly dropped as kids were called in for meals or baths. One day a boy's older sister was sent to summon him in for bed and he told her to 'F**k Off'. I'd never heard the expression before, but every one seemed impressed and it obviously infuriated the sister who chased him down the street. Thinking about it now, it amazes me that a bit of Anglo-Saxon frequently offends the gentile, yet they will come out with 'Omigod!' or 'Christ' without even thinking that they are disrespecting the Being who will one day judge their words and behaviour. Anyway back to the Park Lane street cricket club…

Some twenty minutes later, our numbers down to about six, my Mum appeared at the gate and called me in. It seemed a good idea to tell her to 'F**k Off' also. Within seconds I was over her knee and the bat was compromising my gluteus maximus. Somewhere between the seventh and tenth smack the handle snapped off. We were independent no more. I don't recall ever playing cricket in the street again and it was many years before I used the F-word anywhere near my mother.

To enforce obedience has never been easy because all members of the human race, and I'll give kids the benefit of the doubt; want to do things their own way. My mum never used the Bogeyman, or God, or my Dad, as a threat or lever. I never once heard her threaten, 'Wait until your father gets home!' She believed in instant justice so we knew what we had done wrong and why we were being punished. To this end she carried a secret weapon everywhere she went with us; one of my Dad's old slippers. One day we visited the local shops; I was around 7 and Dave was 4. We behaved reasonably well until boredom set in. The last call was at the butcher's shop; I hated this shop because of the smell of blood; the smell of death. Along two walls were iron rails with half animal corpses hanging from meat-hooks, dripping congealing blood onto the sawdust on the floor. Refrigeration was not as advanced or available as it is now. There was the continuous buzz of flies and sticky stalactites; fly papers covering the ceiling, almost black with the hateful bluebottles. I'm amazed that these shops weren't closed down by the health authorities. There was a long queue and to pass the time I invented a new game: throwing blood-soaked sawdust at my brother.

Dave quickly grasped the rules of the game and devised an almost identical version. My Mum was consistent, we always got one public warning. We were told to stop or else and, like the good children we were, we stopped for several seconds then continued the game. Asking the person behind her to look after her place in the queue, she took out the slipper and gave Dave a good thwack on the bum with the slipper; I got two because I was older, the originator of the stupidity and supposedly the more responsible. In today's Looney Tunes society this method of correction may sound barbaric and possibly illegal, but it worked. It's important for children to learn obedience; I'm not convinced that reasoning with a child is effective when the intellect is as yet undeveloped.

Chapter 4

Starting school

I don't recall my first day in Primary school other than the trauma of being separated from my Mum. I was only four and a half, extremely wimpy and a lever was necessary to remove me from my mother's side. I have no recollection of the teachers other than fear. We learned to count using counters with distinct patterns for the numbers; for example five was always represented as four dots in a square formation with the fifth in the middle. My strongest recollections are the multiplication tables; we used to stand by our desks and chant them like a mantra. One two is two; two twos are four; three twos are six and so on up to twelve. At this time there was no thought of decimalisation, you may remember there were twelve old pence in an old shilling. Looking round at the other children chanting, intense concentration on their faces, amused me greatly. I learned my tables fairly quickly as Mum and Dad rehearsed them with me so I would sometimes just open and shut my mouth with the metre of the chant, like a mad goldfish saying 'Bob'. The hawk-eyed teacher would stop the chant and make me stand on my chair while the others continued. To reinforce the message she would thwack me across the legs several times with a wooden 12 inch ruler.

Mental arithmetic was a pain, in more ways than one. The teacher selected pupils at 'random'; she always seemed to select me several times in a session but I generally got the answer right. Those who did not were encouraged to do better next time with the ubiquitous 12 inch ruler. I once threw it out of the window when she was not looking but she had a stash of them and I went home with an extra perfectly linear bruise on my leg.

I was the tallest in the class which, of course, meant that any anonymous misdemeanour must have been perpetrated by me or someone looking just like me. Sometimes I really was guilty. The teacher decided that we would combine Handicraft and English by performing a glove-puppet version of Charles Dickens' Great Expectations. This was called Pip and the Convict and was not exceptionally close to the original. We were split into groups and two or three kids made a puppet for each character in the play: my group had to make a vicar. I was never that good with papier-maché but I created a thin-faced evil looking vicar complete with dog collar made from a bandage. I wanted mine to be used in the play but the other two were much better so I sabotaged them. Puppet noses are notoriously unstable as the large gob of paper and paste takes a long time to dry. It took a moment to remove the noses from the competition as we were going home and in the morning I was the first to be shocked by the event and thankful that my vicar still had his nose. The teacher, however, was not born the previous day, in fact she was born in the Dark Ages and wrote the vicar out of the play. I was allowed to take my creation home. I used my vicar as you would a football all the way home, by which time the nose came off - a case of poetic justice.

Drama was used frequently to attempt to enlarge our horizons from playing mindless schoolyard games like Lallio or absorbing every word of the Dandy and Beano. The start of my acting career was a part in a Mummers play, a weird version of the story of St George and the Dragon. I secretly wanted to play the part of Saint George, because my name is George, but was given the non-speaking part of Jack Finney the Fool. This involved walking on and off stage, totally embarrassed, in a poorly made crêpe paper jester suit; I now knew what it was like to die on stage at the Glasgow Empire. The play ended with the audience scratching their heads wondering what it was all about. Years later I understood the confusion when I saw '2001, A Space Odyssey' at the movies.

I attained my thespian heights in yet another non-speaking part, this time the executioner in The Red Shoes. A girl in the class was having ballet and tap dancing lessons and had the makings of a severe personality defect at the age of seven. Thanks to her mother's pressure on the teacher she got the part of the ballet dancer who finds these spooky shoes which won't come off once she puts them on. Because I was the tallest in the class I was to be the executioner with my head in a brown paper-bag mask for the whole performance. My Dad made me a realistic headsman's axe from a brush handle and a piece of plywood. In the story the ballerina seems condemned to dance forever and decides on extreme measures to solve the problem: to have her feet amputated by George the executioner. For five seconds I was on stage just about to do the business, when the fattest fairy godmother ever bounced on stage and cried, 'Executioner, stay your hand!' and my moment of glory was over. I often wonder to what extent these rôles influenced my character development over the following years.

Eventually my teachers realised that not every misdemeanour was my doing and I was given some level of responsibility in the class. I had the title Tadpole Monitor and had T-shirts been available at this time I would have pestered my folks for one with a Tadpole Monitor logo. The main part of the job was to change the water, which was always cloudy and evil-smelling because the teacher insisted on using minced offal as tadpole food. The recommended dilution procedure was slow and tedious and had to be done in the staff room. There was no plug in the sink so I put a jam jar over the plughole then carefully emptied the tank full of froglets into the sink. Unfortunately the rotten meaty water caused the jam jar to float then tip over. In seconds easily half the critters had escaped into their new ecosystem; the Bootle sewers. On an infrequent visit to Sunday School I heard about the Plagues and envisioned hordes of mutant frogs infesting the sewers, preying on the rats and growing to Godzilloid proportions; the Army, Navy and Air Force being helpless to stop them. Frog: the movie. Frog 2, Son of Frog and so on. In moments of less crazy imagination I pictured the staff sat around in the lunch break, each with a grinning frog peeking out of the teacup: a world of frogs hopping about; the school closed indefinitely. It would have worked for me!

I have always liked frogs since finding McGregor in our grid at home. He was, in fact, a skinny old toad but I thought he was a frog. I soon fattened him up with a variety of insects and table scraps. He appeared to prefer insects but wasn't fussy on beetles. I could identify with that. Then he vanished; I don't think the aliens abducted him; it was probably Ginger the family cat, a vicious orange predator, totally feral and likely to eat anything that moved.

I kept reptiles as pets for years; they didn't carry tales, they never told lies and best of all they were always happy. All lizards, snakes, tree frogs and terrapins have a permanent grin. When parents were displeased, when neighbours griped about the thud of the football on the wall, when teachers criticised and when my so called friends weren't on speaking terms with me, I could guarantee sympathy from my 'smiling' reptile friends.

My recollections of my primary education are a little hazy but my experiences at Junior school were etched into my subconscious. Some idiot once said that schooldays were the happiest days of their life: not at my school. Even at junior level, most of the staff controlled classes by fear and intimidation. They had their favourites and those they disliked. The psychotic teacher portrayed in Pink Floyd's 'The Wall' would have been offered the headship of my school starting immediately. We were taught what to think, not how to think. I don't recall too much encouragement but plenty of criticism. I can just about remember Miss D'Arcy, old and wrinkled, hair tied back in a bun, with cockatrice eyes and a razor tongue. She was well hard and not to be crossed in any way. Mr Hughes and Mr Downs were a bit more friendly but always reeked of rancid sweat and tobacco.

When entering school we were herded into the classroom with little or no opportunity to visit the toilets if required. Miss D'Arcy reckoned if you were old enough to be in her class, then you were old enough to wait until break before going to the toilet. This is an interesting theory, but practically unworkable. Her attitude towards the kids in the class induced stress-incontinence and if she was in a bad mood, there wouldn't be a dry pair of knickers in the room. On one happy occasion, a boy called Joe put up his hand and asked to be excused. No dice! Five minutes later he came out with the classic one liner, 'Me bum's aching, Miss!' Still no mercy and within the next five minutes the poor lad had pancaked his underpants and had to sit through the rest of the lesson as described. Why his parents did not visit the school and lay a fat lip on the old shrew, I don't know. The classroom certainly was a scary place on occasions but the place of real terror was The Yard.

Between lessons we were pushed out into the schoolyard, a bleak expanse of cracked concrete with all the violence of a Tarantino movie. The toilets were situated as far away from the school buildings as possible, for obvious reasons, with the boys on the left and the girls on the right of the main entrance. The boys' bogs were an atrocity in themselves, with no roof so the elements could cleanse the facility, but it didn't work. As far as I was concerned, the bogs were a definite no-go area. Some weird kids hung around them, the smell could strip paint and rot the plaque off your teeth. At lunch time I always walked home, relieved myself there then walked back to school in time for the bell. This also meant I only had to hang round in the yard in the morning and afternoon breaks.

The schoolyard was an unpleasant ecosystem with an interesting 'food web' comprising four distinct species. The first were the predators, bullies with severe behavioural problems: most of whom should have been strangled at birth. Next, of course, were their victims; any child that was too large, too small or different, scuttling around the yard clutching a white handkerchief, hoping someone else would be picked on. Then there were the footballers, trying to emulate their Evertonian or Liverpudlian heroes with a tennis ball. No prisoners were taken in these games and there were grazed knees to be plastered after every game. The 'Game' was a good way to avoid the bullies as they would never ever cross the invisible boundaries of the pitch.

Finally there were the so-called Cocks of the school, the top dogs, alpha males who had proved their position by right of combat. These kids weren't all bullies, they just swaggered about and relied on past fights for their position. Frequent fights would ensue to sort out the pecking order and identify the Cock of the school. These kids were hard and thick as bricks: just ripe for manipulation. By the use of the occasional boiled sweet, piece of chewing gum and the demonstration of some limited martial art training from Uncle Harry who was a judo Black Belt, I bought an uneasy friendship with these psychos. If I was in a good mood I would wander round the yard, find some bully plying his trade and 'dead-leg' him, or kick him in the groin if I felt he was being too mean. If anyone retaliated I would explain that if I got any grief the Cocks would have him for dinner - a dangerous game indeed.

A number of exotic methods of torture or payback were employed in our school; what amazed me was that the patrolling teachers never seemed to witness any of them. The 'dead-leg' was the application of the kneecap at high speed into the thigh muscle of the victim producing an instant muscle spasm. An interesting but stupid variation was the 'double whammy' where two people would dead-leg someone simultaneously. It was possible to walk normally after twenty minutes or so; I'm glad to say that I never had the pleasure of a double whammy, but gave and received quite a few of the single version.

The 'bumps' was another rather dangerous practice: a group of brain-deads would grab someone by the legs and arms and bump them up and down on the concrete until the participant cheered up. In view of the potential for spinal injury a teacher would occasionally interrupt this ritual. Some kids would hang around the railings that separated our yard from that of the senior girls, a frightening group comprising some 80% trainee slappers. The price for ogling these slags was considerable. The arms would be pushed through the railings then bent back against the joint to partially dislocate the elbow. This stupid ritual was known as 'the bars'. It was usually only practised on kids daft enough to stand by the railings gawping at the slappers.

Sometimes the yard was actually used for school activities! There was no grass nearby so the yard was used for games in all weathers. On a daily basis each child built up a collection of grazes, bruises and plasters. Thinking back I wonder if Elastoplast had a representative on the governing body - who knows? We were only allowed to wear white shorts, white socks and white training shoes. For team games we were identified by thin coloured hoops of red, green, blue and yellow fabric. In late Autumn it was hard to referee games between the blue and green teams because the average skin colour was blue-purple with the cold. The officiating teacher of course would be wearing a tracksuit or overcoat.

These were the days before smokeless fuels. Atmospheric pollution ruled OK and as autumn arrived, we prepared for smog. Smog was a combination of fog, caused by the mixing of warm and cold air fronts with the soot, sulphur and acidic crud in the air around industrial areas. In daylight smog appeared like thick yellow soup that produced itchy running eyes and sore throats. At night you could hardly see anything at all. Everyone wore handkerchiefs over their mouths and noses to filter out at least some of the muck in the air. After a few minutes out in the smog you could see great black spots over the nostrils where some of the carbon had filtered out. The best way to deal with smog was to stay indoors.

When we got home from school it was time for tea. It was usually just Mum, Dave and me because Dad worked some weird shifts with the Fire Brigade. I was made to bathe in a large tin bath in front of the fire then listen to the radio while Mum got Dave to sleep. My favourites were 'Dick Barton, Special Agent' and 'Journey into Space'. Before sleeping I was allowed to read a less exciting text, for example 'Just William'.

At weekends we could stay up a bit later and often went shopping in Liverpool. Auntie Clara would arrive with presents each week and we would all get the bus to Liverpool. We always visited Coopers with its amazing coffee scented atmosphere, frequently shopped at the Co-op because of the 'divvy'; I liked the way money was placed in little containers and launched by means of a piece of elastic along wires to a cashier station in the sky; minutes later the change would come crashing back. Some shops had a posher system where cash was put in tubes and sucked up into outer space with a whooshing noise. Sometimes we entered Blacklers, a veritable time warp of a shop with huge corsets and other cheeky items pinned high in the sky and a basement that can only be likened to Aladdin's cave.

As a treat I was allowed to buy one American comic then we were off to one of the continuous performance cartoon cinemas in the city centre, the Liverpool News Theatre or the Tatler. There would also usually be an episode of one of the many serials made at the time: my favourites were Batman and Flash Gordon. I have been an Evertonian since I was five, in those days I used to stand in my Dad's inside pocket in the Gwladys Street ground. Some Saturdays I went to see Everton FC with my Dad while my brother Dave went shopping in Liverpool with Mum. One special Saturday afternoon we all met up in the city centre and went for a meal out, not something I had experienced before. I recall this occasion quite vividly because of what happened. At the time I thought we were moving into life in the fast lane. My Dad had been promoted again within the Fire Service and had transferred to the Fire Station at Strand Road, Bootle. He was talking about getting season tickets for Everton and life was good. The restaurant seemed very posh, there were lacy cloths on the rectangular tables and all the men wore ties. We found a table with three chairs and a stool and sat down when a large waitress appeared, puffing and panting, my Dad said like a grampus, demanding to know in a surly way what we wanted. She was not happy that we had not yet decided what to order and moved away like it was a major effort. Dad, Mum and I chose sausage and chips; I told you it was posh! Brother Dave could not make his mind up. The waitress took so long to return that Dad decided we would go somewhere else, as we stood up to go she wobbled over so we ordered.

After a ridiculously long wait three meals arrived, three plates of sausage and chips. Dad asked for new knives and forks, as the knives on the table were streaked with grease and two of the forks had bits of antique egg jammed in them. 'Big Bertha' shuffled off muttering to replace the 'eating irons'. The chips were soggy and oozed lukewarm fat; the sausages were small and overcooked, not unlike dog turds; the peas were hard and swimming with water which, with the grease floating on it, made amazing interference patterns. My Dad was all for sending the stuff back, but Mum was afraid of the Gorgon waitress and what she might do, so we began to eat.

Dave had eventually ordered egg and chips but his meal still hadn't arrived. I imagined the cook chasing the hen round the kitchen. Dave had tucked the tablecloth under his chin and was looking around to see the admiring glances of the rest of the customers who hadn't thought to do the same. No one was amused; all lips were curled along with grimaces of disapproval. We were almost half way through the awful meal, still no sign of the egg and chips, when Dave groaned 'I'm faint for lack of nourishment', and slumped back on the stool which he thought was a chair. He had unfortunately pushed the tablecloth a little too securely into his shirt and as he fell to the floor, so did our plates and everything else on the table. Our beloved waitress moved in, smirking like she had predicted it would happen. Dad quickly paid what we owed; the cheeky rats tried to charge for the egg and chips which never arrived, and we left in disgrace and embarrassment. You could have cooked an egg on Mum's red face, Dave was screeching, coated with various food remnants, I was whining because I was still hungry. To bring a suitable end to a perfect day, it was pouring with rain as we squelched through the darkening streets to the Old Haymarket for the bus home, Dad trying not to laugh.

On the only family holiday I can recall we visited the Cheshire Broads at Winsford in Cheshire. Let me explain that the Cheshire Broads are not female reprobates. The Broads consisted of chalets scattered along the banks of the River Weaver in Cheshire. It could possibly be a marina now, when we visited many years ago it was grim. We stayed in a chalet which was utterly gross, a shed with windows with dead flies and crud everywhere; it took Mum three hours or so to clean it up. The river Weaver was a sewer, muddy and full of litter, including barges holed and sunk in the water, but to us it was a jungle to be explored. My brother found a dead fish which he claimed was only asleep and so he put it in a bucket. He 'fed' it with worms, bread and scraps from the table but it wasn't hungry. He frequently stirred the water with a stick and claimed the circular movement of the corpse was a sign it was waking up. By the end of the week the fish had a weird fungal coating and the water smelt like a gorilla's jockstrap. Despite my brother's protests, the fish was launched back into the river from whence it had come; the bucket was just launched.

It rained a great deal of the time so Mum and Dad decided to take us all to the Zoo at Chester. The zoo was full of weird and exotic creatures doing weird and exotic things. Llamas masticating, monkeys masturbating, horses fornicating and gibbons defecating, and hurling the results of their efforts at the human passers by. At each turn I constantly wanted to know what was going on and was told to shut up or taken to get ice cream. The zoo was and still is vast, we seemed to be walking all day and Granny was knackered so we sat down for a bit then went to get a cup of tea.

I've always been fairly observant. On a visit to my Grandma's I observed that her bloomers, flying at half-mast on the washing line were almost as large as the play tent I had at home; I was about 5 or 6 years old at this time. This amazing fact was stored away in my subconscious until we moved off after our tea-break and I noticed her bloomers were just visible as she staggered along. Then I had an idea: none of the people crowded around knew that my Grandma's gargantuan knickers could house a family of dwarves. Eager to share the secret and glean a little attention for myself I lifted up the corner of her skirt from behind and walked along to the amusement of the spectators. My next recollection was waking up outside the Pachyderm House with a crowd around me. My mother later explained that Granny had heard the laughter, felt the cold draught and solved the problem with a swift back-hander on the ear. I moved ahead on the learning curve of life, her secret was now safe with me!

Another outing that was not so enjoyable was the frequent visits to the dentist. For some reason the family patronised the infamous Baker's dental practice on Great Mersey Street. Everyone I knew had horror tales about the practice, like the old lady who was turned inside out as Baker tried to extract her wisdom teeth. Eventually I had tales of my own to tell. I'm sure he had a side business selling necklaces made of human teeth: he never extracted just one tooth at a time but made a habit of removing the teeth adjacent to the aching one as well as the bad one. Visits were so traumatic that I used to hang onto the Gothic columns either side of the door and my Mum often had to enlist the help of a passer-by to release my grip. Even my mum frequently referred to Mr Baker as 'The Butcher'.

I hated the dentist. I hated the weird tasting spring that he rammed in my mouth to hold my jaws open to almost breaking point. I hated the soft rubber, evil-smelling mask that conveyed the anaesthetic mixture: it was like snogging a lukewarm octopus with halitosis. I hated the view up his hairy nostrils as my brain vibrated with the effect of the knockout gas. I frequently felt pain while 'under' as he economised on the nitrous oxide and tried to get into the high speed dental extraction section of the Guinness Book of Records. But what I hated most was the disgusting recovery room. This white tiled excuse for a slaughter house had a waist high channel with continuously flowing water into which all his patients spat blood, bits of teeth or puked up their last meal as the gas mixture made many of his customers vomit like parrots.

Through the years, Mr Baker and friends stole so many of my teeth that my gums shrank and my second teeth grew in a haphazard way. My canines were a little protuberant and I used to draw back my lips over them because I thought I looked hard; a cross between Humphrey Bogart and Bela Lugosi. A more accurate comparison would be somewhere between Larry the Lamb and a constipated fruit bat. Mum and Dad decided I was too ugly to go on as I was so I was taken to an orthodontist in Rodney Street called Joseph Angelman. After a few impressions, my favourite being Quasimodo, and a few weeks' wait, I was sporting a brace on my teeth like one of the rich kids. This marvel of torture technology made my teeth ache and my breath smell like an armadillo's underpants, thanks to the food that stuck beneath the palate and rotted. I kept 'accidentally' breaking the brace and was taken back each time to have it replaced. After what seemed an eternity I was deemed cute enough to need no more tooth straightening. My big nose, which was a problem of much greater magnitude, was left intact.

To end my childhood memories of outings I remember with least affection, I must mention the annual Fire Brigade Party. A few weeks before Christmas my Dad would bring home my invitation to the party at Strand Road Fire Station. I hated this event, always asked to be excused but was always persuaded to go. My first objection was that it meant an extra bath. Secondly, I didn't know any of the other kids and had no wish to remedy the situation. As I sat there with a 'gob on' few people spoke to me, apart from a few patronising adults who were determined that I would enjoy myself at any cost. The games were grim and enforced; wallflowers were not allowed. I visited the toilets each time volunteers were wanted; I wonder whether they thought I had a bladder problem. Oranges and Lemons, Pin the tail on the donkey, Pass the parcel, Musical Chairs; all stupid, pointless games, milked to death until a winner emerged or someone died of boredom. I looked at these bleating, prancing fools and wondered if they had something wrong with them. Had something come adrift in their collective upper-storeys, or was the problem with me? The food was OK and I needed no encouragement to over-eat. The climax of the evening was the arrival of a fat bearded old fart in an ill-fitting red suit. As our names were called out we had to walk to the front of the hall and accept a parcel from this badger-breathed old Santa Claus clone. Then at last I was free to go home to bed.

Our doctor was part of a family practice in Bootle; he was well past retirement age but had no intention of giving up. There was no system for being seen by a doctor; you told a receptionist you had arrived then sat down amid the turbulent mass of human offal. When the previous patient had departed the doctor would come to the door of the waiting room and say in sepulchral tones, 'Next Please'. Because there was no proper appointment system, several people would jump up and argue over who was really next. His surgery was, to be kind, Gothic, dark and dusty, all the surfaces cluttered with old bottles, urinals and books. There was a square porcelain sink where he mixed medicines; he often mixed up a concoction for patients rather than writing a prescription. As you arrived and were asked to sit down he would begin writing a prescription then ask what the problem was. To be honest if I knew what was wrong I would be the doctor, but never mind - you always got something to swallow, rub on or shove where daylight was minimal. Some time during the consultation you would be asked, 'And how are the bowels?' If your bowels were OK it tended to baffle him and he'd send you to a specialist.

My brother Dave came down with a bad fever; he was unable to retain anything he ate and had lost several stone within a few days. Our Victorian gentleman doctor reckoned it was only pneumonia and not to worry. At home we had a copy of a large book called 'Everything Within'. It was heavy enough to stun a horse and full of all kinds of information: old wives recipes, letter writing etiquette, how to address ones betters, etc. It also had a medical section which I read now and again and pestered my parents with embarrassing questions. This old book probably saved Dave's life. The symptoms of pneumonia described in the book really did not fit Dave's symptoms. Dad demanded a second opinion and within a matter of hours we were all sitting in the old Aintree Isolation Hospital. Dave didn't have pneumonia; he had para-typhoid and was dangerously ill for a time. After a series of tests we were allowed home but Dave was kept in for several weeks; we had to talk to him through a glass partition until he was no longer contagious. Dave liked cream cakes and Dolly's kiosk, which he regularly patronised, had no proper covers on the cakes and was a flies' social club. The specialist reckoned some poxy bluebottle carrying the para-typhoid bacteria had used Dave's cream bun as a temporary toilet. Dave made a complete recovery and life continued; we changed our doctor and no longer bought cakes unless they were covered.

It was autumn 1949 and everyone was talking about 'The Third Man', a movie thriller starring Orson Welles. The theme from the film, played on the zither, was selling well. Clothes rationing had ended and the musical play 'South Pacific' was running in New York. One of the songs, 'Some enchanted evening' was in competition with 'Rudolph the red nosed reindeer' both being released in time for Christmas. Everton were having a good season and I hopped about in the kitchen with my home-made blue and white scarf waiting for Dad to come home; he didn't come home. Mrs Pierce from over the road came over with a phone message, Mum went out and Mrs Pierce looked after us, a pattern we got used to over the next six months.

Dad was locking up the stores at Strand Road fire station when he suffered a massive stroke. It was several hours before someone found him: his big overcoat had saved his life in the freezing cold of the stores. He was in a coma for months. When he came out of it he was paralysed down one side of his body and unable to speak properly. With physiotherapy and horrific leather and metal callipers he was eventually able to shuffle around but he was not the same person. Dave and I sent home-made 'Get well soon' cards to Walton hospital each week. As therapy, Mum let Dave and I redecorate the hall with a lick of Brilliant White emulsion over the peeling anaglypta. The job was due to be completed on the day Dad came home. As he was being helped down the front path, I accidentally knocked over a tin of paint; non-drip was non-existent then and the brilliant white waterfall was just reaching the first step as the front door opened and Dad came in. The last time I saw him was as a six foot five giant, the rock solid centre half, the fireman able to shoulder his way through locked doors into burning homes and carry out two people at once. As he entered the house at a snail's pace, both legs in metal callipers, it was a shock to my system. Bent over, face distorted with the effort of walking he was a hemiplegic dwarf, it was the worst day of my life. It wasn't a great day for the whole family but I was a selfish little rat and only appreciated things that benefited myself.

My Mum and dad were members of an evangelical church in Bootle. As the weeks and months dragged by, few of these good people called to visit. The pastor called every week but his sombre clothing and miserable face depressed me. Before he left, he always knelt down on one knee like a medieval suitor and said solemnly, 'Let us pray'. The first time he did this I thought he said, 'Let us play' and jumped on to his back. He was not amused and my Mum and Dad had to try and look like they weren't either.

Dad had been in the Bootle Fire Service for more than 24 years and was coming up to 25 years and a pension that would have made life more pleasant for us. The Fire Service management kindly made the decision to chop him off; give him a cheap clock with his name on and save all that money that we might have lived on. Times became very difficult indeed with very little cash coming in. We could seldom afford coal but kept the gas cooker on with the oven door open to warm the house. We virtually lived in the kitchen in winter; when we had visitors Mum would light the fire in the dining room. Any old shoes or slippers we filled with slack, (the coal dust that represented 30 percent of the sack at that time). I frequently followed the coal man's wagon on my bike and collected any pieces that fell to the ground; sometimes he dropped the odd lump because he felt sorry for me. To stay warm we would burn anything. Once the fire was hot we tied old tree branches or planks to a chair and fed them into the fire as they burned. Then I had a great idea; I would dig a hole and find a coal seam! My mother humoured me; at least it kept me doing something that wasn't bad. After an hour or so I proudly announced my find; there was a quantity of coal and earth in the pit I had dug out. There are no known coal seams in Bootle and my mother became suspicious, particularly as the level of coal never changed. Like a real miracle, as the coal was removed, so there was more to replace it. With minimal pressure on the throat I confessed: my 'coal mine' in fact led to next-door's coal-bunker from which the abundant supply was flowing.

It is a tribute to my parents that in all the years of poverty, (we are talking beans on toast as the only meal of the day on occasions), with virtually no help from the government, the church or family, they never took anything without paying for it. They frequently had to take me back to places from which I had 'borrowed' sundry items when they found out. I got progressively skilled in avoiding being found out. Times were hard, at every knock at the door we all hid under the window in case it was the rent man: we were 6 months behind with the rent at one stage. Two of the local housewives had an 'arrangement' with the rent man: they dropped their knickers and only paid half the required amount. It was years later that I guessed the nature of these 'arrangements'.

At first Dad was totally housebound dragging himself from the front room where his bed was, to the toilet. Throughout his illness he maintained that God knew what He was doing with him; I couldn't see it! Mum had no life at all, most of her time was seeing to Dad with no home helps or anything. I took advantage of the situation; less supervision meant increased freedom to scavenge, steal, vandalise and get into trouble. With weekly physiotherapy Dad became more mobile, the council constructed a driveway and garage and ultimately supplied an electric invalid carriage. They found him a job in the reception at Bootle Town Hall which paid little, but gave him the dignity of working for a living and enabled Mum to return to secretarial work and some financial security.

My Grandad was in the Lodge (Orange, not Yates' Wine) although at times the difference was indistinguishable. My parents were not particularly biased in any way although some relatives attempted to involve us in the Irish problem. Sometimes our street (or five of us anyway) would launch an attack on another street (generally less than five). Now and again civil war broke out. The 'proddy dogs' versus 'red-neck pigs' meant in fact my brother and I against the rest of the kids in our street.

To give Mum a break from looking after Dad on her own, we spent many summer holidays in sunny Waterloo at Auntie Lil's big house. Dave and I were left to amuse ourselves for long periods. On rainy days we explored the many floors of the house, at first just playing Hide-and-

Seek. When the novelty wore off we spiced up the game by filling our water pistols with red ink in a wild precursor of 'paint-ball' before it was invented, and crept round the house hunting each other. We were not too popular as various walls were discovered splashed with ink, not to mention our clothes which, by the end of a game, were ruined. No detergent at that time could cope with the red ink stains.

In our explorations we found a half bottle of gin in a wardrobe. It did not have a label that said 'Drink me!' but we had a compulsion to see what it tasted like: compulsion changed to revulsion; rat urine comes to mind. To avoid discovery, we refilled the bottle with water from the toilet. We never found out to whom it belonged as no one complained about the taste, not surprising as toilet water tastes considerably better than gin.

From one of the windows in the huge landing we could see into a window in part of the house that Auntie Lil sub-let to two antique spinsters. We could see some weird statues which we peppered with rice from our glass tubes: these I produced because we were banned from having catapults, spud guns or pea shooters. The statues were, in fact, standard Roman Catholic Mother and Child effigies, but I'd never seen the like before. To me they were just targets, no disrespect was intended. The ladies however were totally mystified by the amount of rice spread all over the landing. When the ladies shared their Miracle of the Rice with Auntie Lil, she feigned mild interest then beat us up later.

One rainy day we ventured up to the attic. We were afraid to enter the Mother Attic as I mentioned earlier, but there was a huge seafarer's chest with brass hinges just inside the door with a visible-only-to-me label that said, 'Open me!' I had to obey. Inside there was no pirates' treasure but a vast collection of weird body armour. These suits were heavy, reinforced with sheets of bone and had a complex lacing system at the back. With great difficulty my brother and I put on the armour, lacing each other in, then found some broom handles and began to joust, sword fence etc. I 'accidentally' thwacked my brother's knuckles, he began to howl and a search party began to ascend the stairs. We did not have the bottle to hide in the Mother Attic where the demonic monkey lived in the darkness so we were apprehended. What we thought was ancient Japanese samurai armour was, in fact, ancient corsets that were too small for Auntie Lil, who was gravitationally challenged. Only at her funeral did we find that she had 'Keep Left'

45

tattooed across her ample shoulders. She battered us both, obviously viewing us as junior perverts. We saw ourselves as two of the seven samurai getting a bashing from the dragon of Waterloo.

One day we were at war with no one and so decided on an adventure. We went to the Seven Ponds, a vast rubbish dump with large water filled areas in which several children had drowned. The Seven Ponds was an Aladdin's cave full of treasure. It was also out of bounds to Dave and I, but so what? We found an old flea-ridden settee that the snoggers used: some one had set it on fire and inside were several large springs. With great difficulty I removed two of them and began to look for some rope or string. To an observer we were a group of tatty kids scuttling round a rubbish tip, in reality I was about to become 'Spring-heel Jack'. Jack according to Liverpool folklore, was able to jump over a house and was an unsavoury, anti-social being to boot. Jack had red eyes that glowed in the dark, the brightness of which being directly proportional to the volume of draught Guinness imbibed by the 'witnesses'.

I fastened the springs to my shoes; on my head I had a rather attractive sheep's skull with one tooth left. As I began my first phenomenal jump from a heap of refuse, one spring fell off and the other distorted on impact. I came down to earth with a bang. For almost a second I made history, now I was just history. I could not walk as my ankle came up like a balloon, so my brave companions dragged me home on a sheet of corrugated iron, my feet higher than my head. Not only had I sprained my ankle and damaged my pride, but worse was to come. To my disgust my Mum binned the springs and the skull.

I had always had an ambition to bounce and defy gravity even momentarily. I was still sore from my attempt to emulate Spring-heel Jack when I found four huge springs in next-door's bin, so I dragged an old orange box home from outside the greengrocers and began construction of a new bouncing device. I fitted the springs to the bottom of the box and made a compartment for myself to crouch in. The idea was to get my brother to push the box with me in it out of the first-floor landing window when I would bounce on the springs across the garden and beyond - where was not too important to me at this stage. A matter of hours before take-off my younger and wiser brother informed my parents of my plans and the box was turned into firewood.

Every Saturday Mum took us to the Liverpool City centre to the cinema. The Tatler specialised in cartoons and newsreels, the Liverpool News Theatre had cartoons and serials; my favourite was Flash Gordon. He always got the girl and saved the world by the end of the serial. I imagined myself as Flash but I was destined to be Dr Zharkov, the guy with brains and beard who never got the girl and had the credit for saving the world taken by the geek who wore his knickers over his trousers. We would pay our money, sit either side of Mum to prevent us from fighting and watch the programme over and over again until we were dragged out into the daylight, blinking like toads. I wondered what the ticket girl thought was going on; people arriving but very few leaving, then I wondered if the ticket girl thought at all. Tramps slept through the performance, snoggers on the back row snogged through it and perverts with coats draped over their knees abounded: yes, the soiled raincoat brigade still attended! My Mum carried a wicked hat-pin with which to dissuade any would-be perv, but she never got to use it.

Each week I was allowed to buy an American comic which I kept for years until I 'grew up' and binned them. Thinking back I had some early issues that would be worth hundreds of pounds now but so what? Flash Gordon was duly replaced by other serials but none had the same appeal. Superman was OK but a bit porky and when he was supposed to be flying a fuzzy cartoon was used, but special effect photography was not like it is today. Batman was quite good but I could never see the point of Robin. I guess we kids were supposed to identify with the little squirt who was slow on the uptake, he seemed to be a total liability. The ultimate golden turkey was 'King of the Rocket Men' played by an actor called Tristram Coffin. He was the only rocket man, so I'm unsure how he could be king: his pièce de resistance was to run down an alley, a miracle in itself as he had a jet engine strapped to his back, then take off by jumping off a load of dustbins. My interest in serials waned for a time, I even went off my cornflakes, but I did try to design a rocket man suit for myself. I was unable to find an unwanted jet engine to tie on my back: the compromise was to consume a four-pack of Heinz beans and wear a pair of roller skates. I failed to achieve escape velocity and almost ruined a pair of St Michael underpants in the process.

Children are definitely influenced by the media as are adults, but there is a difference; children can have problems differentiating between fantasy and reality. As I got older I was allowed to go to the Saturday matinees at the local cinema. These invariably featured cowboy films, we used to all run home with a curious hopping motion. With one hand you slapped your backside, with the other you held the reins, which only you could see. The adults looked at us like we'd flipped, so what, we were riding the range looking for Indians. Like many, we were indoctrinated with Hollywood tripe; it was some years before I realised that the Indians were not the bad guys. Almost invariably the movie would feature Roy Rogers. One Saturday it was not Roy Rogers, I do not remember who it was, what I do remember was that it featured an implied lynching and we all felt it was high time to have one of our own. Tommy Graham seemed the ideal choice, he was small, skinny and had no big brothers only sisters. I recall one of them had a continuous upper lip twitch, which earned her the nickname 'rabbit-gob'. The oldest sister was training to be a nun, was incredibly po-faced and named after Jesus' mother: we were a bit frightened of her.

We threw an old skipping rope over a lamp-post, placed a tea-chest below and stood young Thomas upon it. A few locals saw the noose being adjusted and ignored the proceedings, perhaps they didn't like Tommy either. I drew a grubby piece of paper from my back pocket, words I had treasured when first hearing them on the cinema.

'You will be taken from here to the place from whence you came and from thence to a place of execution where you will be hung from the neck until you are dead.' At this point we were at a loss what to do, we had no intention of really hanging him. My younger brother, attempting to inject some life into the occasion, gave the tea-chest an almighty kick and suddenly Tommy was dancing on air. I suddenly realised the stunt was a little dangerous. By standing beneath him and supporting his weight, we tried to loosen the noose but the rope had pulled tight. We began to panic; Tommy was well past this stage. Tommy's mother informed by a neighbour that her son had the lead role in a pageant of some description, came leaping across the road brandishing a large kitchen knife. For a moment I thought she was going to finish him off, but she sawed through the rope and rescued her child. She always glared at me from that day on, I don't know why. I was not too popular at home when Mum found out what had happened; she was not impressed by what seemed to me a brilliant piece of street theatre.

As a lad I was taken to the circus on a number of occasions; the proceedings seem to entertain and amuse my parents but most of them disturbed me. A red coated fool with a handlebar moustache who did all the shouting; the idiot who made the mangy lions sit awkwardly on their metal stands; the fat old women dressed in scanty clothing, but worst of all, the clowns. Ill fitting, bad-taste clothing and enormous feet, falling over all the time, just like some of my relatives after a night out. Big red noses and white make up, again like the relatives. Once you've seen one bucket of water thrown over someone, then an identical bucket of confetti thrown over some rich twit at the ringside, you've seen most of the act. Then there was the car that crawled round the ring with bits falling off until it finally blew up. What's so funny about that? Most of the cars I have owned through the years have done that. Clowns are sinister and not a bit funny. I recall an Auguste (an unsmiling white faced clown in pierrot costume) playing a clarinet and a saxophone simultaneously. Before your imagination gets you in trouble, both instruments were in his mouth. Later he juggled 3 bean bags. Not exceptionally funny and as entertaining as watching porridge cool down, or am I being cynical?

My first ever visit to a circus was Wilkies' Circus at New Brighton. There were lions, bears, clowns, acrobats, horses running in ever decreasing circles and, of course, the old women in costumes designed for much younger and smaller people. We didn't have a television and this was the most exciting thing I'd experienced. I'd been to a few Pantomimes at the Shakespeare and Empire theatres, but they didn't have lions and bears and they were confusing to me at the time. Still at the time it was a change from watching the grass grow or the paint drying and we always had ice cream. I screamed 'Oh no there isn't!' with unusual aggression along with all the other scallies on their Big Afternoon Out, but I was confused by the rôle reversals used in this art form. The dames were all weird, from the ugly sisters to Old Mother Hubbard; they had bristly chins and frighteningly deep voices, almost as if men were playing the parts. And the 'principal boys' were always thigh-slapping ladies in fishnet tights who we all 'fancied' as much as seven-year-olds could fancy anything. The pantomime heroes were not on my list of rôle models; I have to admit; I always identified with the villains, particularly King Rat. He had attitude and green lights shining on him at each appearance, whereas the 'Buttons' type characters, supposedly likeable, were wimps who had no lives. They never confronted life's situations but sang about them, and I use the word 'sang' lightly. But I digress: back to the day after the Circus.

49

The next day was a Sunday. We had to somehow reproduce the thrills of the previous evening, but how? Lion or cat-taming was not an option, our moggie was feral and singularly un-cooperative; being clowns was only a small step from reality. Looking out from the landing window, the washing still flapping on the line, I thought, 'What a waste of a trapeze!' Our circus career was beckoning. We pushed all the washing together making a large vacant space then I hooked my brother's legs over the line. He dangled precariously like a bat, not exceptionally happy, as I got one of my legs over the line then with a supreme effort, the other one also. The line supported our combined weight for a second or two then snapped like cotton. We landed on our heads but we had only dropped through a metre or so. Unfortunately so did all the dry washing which was now covered in mud; once again I was in trouble for trying to bring the thrills of the circus to our boring Bootle environment.

Incidentally, if you ever think of visiting New Brighton let me forewarn you. It always reminds me of those old vampire movies; you know the scene; where the strangers arrive and it is just going dark; doors are closing and being bolted, the place resembles a ghost town. New Brighton has an impressive sea wall but little else; it's as if the inhabitants, fearing the end of the world, have emigrated to Blackpool or some such place. I once got a cone of chips from a shop that was actually open. The twelve chips cost £1.50 and had been reheated for the sixth time. If a competition ever offered a first prize of a week in New Brighton, you can be sure the second prize would be two weeks. Maybe by the time this book goes to print things may be different. I hope so; the place was brilliant in the old days.

I mentioned earlier the kiosk on the railway bridge on Captain's Lane in Netherton. It was rented or owned by Dolly, a strange old bird who sold all kinds of things with exotic names that sounded more like medical problems than confectionery: for example, sticky lice, aniseed balls and iced buns. 'Sticky lice' was dried liquorice root that you chewed away at and many spat out the juice like a seasoned tobacco chewer. Some swallowed the stuff and waited for their bowels to be turbocharged and thus get time off school. Pontefract cakes, small discs shaped like oversize red blood cells made of liquorice, were more pleasant to eat than sticky lice but had the same effect on the bowels when overdosed. I used to lick some of them and press them on my face where they stuck as the spit evaporated: don't ask me why, I just did. Aniseed balls were foul but addictive. They made your spit go blood red from the dyes they coated them in. If you sagged school for a couple of hours and sucked an aniseed ball before arriving there, you could spit into a handkerchief, claim you'd been to the dentist and get away with it. No teacher in his right mind would look into my mouth to check up anyway; but back to Dolly's delicacies. The iced buns were soft, coated with sticky icing sugar which instantly revealed any latent tooth decay with a short, sharp pain as you bit into them. They were delivered to the shop on a non-too-clean wooden tray and put in the shop window to sweat in the sun and attract wasps and flies.

Dolly's Brew became famous as a place for a new and dodgy craze; face poaching. All the trains passing under the bridge were steam driven monsters puffing out large volumes of white or black smoke. The idiot children used to hang over the side of the bridge to get a face-full of smoke as the train entered the tunnel, then they'd race across the road, dodging the traffic, to get a second dose as the train came out on the other side. The psychos threw things at the drivers or stokers as the train went through. The same lunatics played chicken across the railway line and climbed electricity pylons for no reason other than boredom. Many of them passed on to the railway line or high voltage pylon in the sky, a good example of natural selection. I saw the stupidity of playing chicken with the buses at last and gave up the hobby.

A local off-licence happily supplied all the Juanita cheap wine and Bents brown ale we wanted; 'It's for me Dad' was the password and they never checked our ages. We mixed the brown ale with the wine and chilled out in North Park. The park keeper frequently chased us, sometimes we would return on our bikes, totally off our heads and ride round the park, because to do so was forbidden. The Parky would chase us, he was no chicken and he usually had a red face, gibbering with rage as he staggered after us. I thought he might 'kark' it once or twice, but he didn't. Now and again he would catch someone and give them a good thwack round the ears; I'm glad to say he never caught me.

Mum took Dave and I to see Lonnie Donegan at the Empire Theatre and we returned home with a new vision; to form our own skiffle group. Dave got a classical guitar for £4 from Young's second-hand shop on Scotland Road, it had a label inside showing the maker's name, Manuel Segura. My guitar was just £3 from a second-hand shop in

Seaforth and was a heap of rubbish, always going out of tune and well past its sell-by date. Dave had a friend who said he played in a band and he offered Dave the loan of his Höfner guitar for a few days. The boy came home from school with Dave and as they walked up the stairs to Dave's room I heard this kid complaining about the smell in the house, Mum was cooking cabbage to go with our pies. Also he didn't like the tatty wallpaper in the hall and as he walked into Dave's room he commented how small it was compared to his own. I called him and as he poked his head round the door I grabbed him by the face and threw him down the stairs. I told him he could stick the guitar where daylight was minimal and offered to help him if he had difficulties with the assignment. Later Dave went round to see him and apologise for my insensitivity and returned with the guitar. He is still an accomplished diplomat, something I could never be without a major attitude adjustment.

I once saved up my pocket money to buy the latest Buddy Holly single from a local record shop. To my dismay I found it had a scratch on one side and, what was worse, it had a Jackie Wilson song recorded on the back although the label read Buddy Holly. Maybe it was worth something as freak value but it was no use to me, so I returned it to the shop and was told to shove off as I had no receipt; to be honest I don't recall being given one when I bought it. I gave it two weeks then rode past the shop one afternoon clutching a brick and launched it through the shop window. To my tiny mind it seemed the only way to achieve a satisfactory payback. I certainly was overdue for an attitude transplant, but before I reveal how it happened, it's into the time machine and back to 1952 when I started at Bootle Grammar School.

Chapter 5

Happy days?

It was 1951. The Festival of Britain was over and the Skylon, a 300 foot steel and aluminium structure which I wanted for our back-garden, had vanished from the London scene; I read recently that it now lies beneath the waters of the Thames. Zebra Crossings were appearing all over the country and Bill and Ben appeared on TV; I disliked this potty duo intensely but I hated the wimpy Weed even more. The in-movie to see was 'High Noon' starring Gary Cooper and Grace Kelly. The rich kids in the street had coconut shells to simulate hoof-beats; we still had to use our limited imaginations: smacking our backsides with our left hands, holding invisible reins in front of us, and squeaking, rather than drawling, 'Do not forsake me, O my darling' in a murderous parody of the sound track.

It was a year of fear. The hydrogen bomb was successfully detonated, the Mau Mau were killing anything that moved in Kenya and in London, air-pollution was responsible for the death of four thousand people. Smog masks were the new fashion. Talking about fear, it was the year I moved up to grammar school. I've heard older people moaning about school. 'When I were a lad, school were not like it is today'. To be honest the education system has changed, not necessarily for the better, and there is a lot of truth in the statement. I passed the so-called Scholarship exam, the forerunner of the Eleven Plus, and was sent to Bootle Grammar School for Boys.

The Pembroke wing of Hugh Baird College of Further Education now stands on the site of the old school and Bootle Technical College. It was a traditional grammar school with no 'stupid girls' to distract us from our quest for knowledge. The school had a good record of success in terms of university attendance, degrees obtained and good jobs for the boys. The system was totally results orientated and at an early age pupils were streamed into 'Alpha', 'A' and 'X' classes representing a judgement of pupils as reasonably clever, so-so and thick-as a brick. I suspect most of us were not that bright, religiously carving our initials or names on the desks with the statutory penknife, then being genuinely surprised to be found out and sent for the cane.

The alpha classes tended to get the best teachers, most homework and studied Latin, French, Classics, Humanities (Called Geography and History at the time), Mathematics and, of course, the Sciences. The Science options were Physics and Chemistry, no-one in their right mind would have attempted to teach human or animal Biology to any of the desperate characters in the school. The 'A' classes were judged academically inferior to the alphas, how this was done I never discovered, and did Spanish instead of Latin. The X streams were considered the equivalent to Neanderthals and had the also-ran staff, but did some really interesting things like Technical Drawing, Metalwork and Woodwork.

Years later I saw the movie version of HG Wells' 'The Time Machine' and instantly understood the school's education policy. The Alpha people were the Eloi, the beautiful people who had white collar jobs and fast lane living; the X people were trained to be Morlocks, stuck underground actually keeping everything moving by the sweat of their brows, worker ants and proud of it. The A classes existed to fill vacancies when the Eloi died of boredom or the Morlocks died from hard work. The really crap teachers were generally assigned to X or A so there weren't too many chances of a wrongly streamed pupil improving although, now and again kids moved into the higher stream as they stopped sucking their thumbs or learned to tie their shoelaces. The class I started school in was called Remove Alpha.

Bootle Grammar was a fairly tough school but not as bad as the kids who had started the year before had told us. Teachers did not rip the left arms off the kids that were left-handed. The school doctor did not thwack your bollocks with a glass hammer to see if you had ever 'done it'. The big surprise for me was the staff, most of whom were psychotic; corporal punishment ruled OK. In the years I attended the school I was caned almost daily, hit with a blackboard eraser, cuffed across the head enough to produce a bruise and temporary loss of hearing, kicked and thwacked on the head with a dictionary. I should point out that my behaviour was far from perfect and degenerated as time progressed. I arrived on time on my first day, totally innocent, wearing my new school cap and blazer, and followed everyone into the huge assembly hall. The teachers lined both sides of the hall, humourless androids with 'Great White' eyes. I commented to a fellow new boy on the size of the place and the numbers. I was aware of movement behind me, a gravelly voice informing me, 'No talking, Boy!' then a searing pain on the right side of my face. After this I had no recollection until a fellow pupil helped me up. I found out later that the infamous 'Jack Chisel', not his real name, a skeletal woodwork teacher, had administered his famous friendly cuff round the lughole and I had lost consciousness for several seconds. Before I attended any lessons the learning curve had commenced; intimidation was the name of the game for many of the staff. They weren't all sadistic lunatics but most were eccentric or disturbed in some way. It took years to realise that most pupils would drive anyone over the edge; I now have a lot more respect and sympathy for anyone trying to teach in today's screwy educational system.

School assemblies were long, arduous and a waste of time. In the summer months many fainted, like soldiers on parade for too long. It happened to me once; one minute standing there bored out of my skull, the next being carried out and left to recover outside the woodwork room. As I came round there was the skeletal face of Jack Chisel, grinning like a hungry shark; needless to say my recovery was swift and I returned to the boredom of the talkfest in the hall.

Within a week of my first thwack round the head I was sent for the cane when I'd done nothing to deserve it; here's how it happened As I entered the History classroom, I noticed that someone had written, 'Fuk of dicky the sap' on the blackboard. I sat down and waited to see the reaction when 'Dicky' came in. He looked at the board, rubbed off the message then told me to report to the Deputy headmaster for the cane. I questioned his command, a total waste of time, and went to get my punishment. When I returned, Dicky was grinning like a dog with two dicks. He explained how he knew I had written the message. I was the tallest in the class and the writing was just the right height. I explained that his logic was defective; anyone standing on a chair could have written it and anyway it was not my handwriting and I knew how to spell F**k off! I closed my speech by insinuating that his parents were not legally married. To my surprise I was sent for a second caning. Over the next few months I came to the conclusion that if I was to be blamed for everything, I might as well do it.

My decision to try for the Public Enemy No 1 prize got me so many canings I lost count of them; some weeks I got the cane each day. I was caned for being late, for fighting, for being 'cheeky' to teachers, for breaking things, setting off fire extinguishers and many more. My anti-social behaviour spread outside of school. I took up judo then Chinese

Kung Fu, not to keep fit, but to improve my ability to bully others. I used to plunge my hands into buckets of sand and rice to turn them into weapons as the tutors suggested. I hung around with some sociopaths from the Marsh Lane area who got their kicks from violence and vandalism, some of whom ended up in court and rightly so. Before I tell you how I ended up, a brief section about the staff at the Grammar school who helped condition me. The teachers were interesting people all highly motivated and happy in their work. I jest of course! As I write, two pigs are flying round my shaven pate, trying to find a landing site.

John D Berbiers, the headmaster, was a minuscule Belgian gentleman with a law degree; we called him the Beak because he was the ultimate authority in the school and also a magistrate. If the Beak sent for you it was deep trouble ahead. He always reminded me of Dr Sivana, the tiny bald arch-enemy of Captain Marvel in the American comics.

Wabs was a maths teacher whose sole regret was that the War was over. He could be readily manipulated to reminisce about the Germans he had killed and to bring in bayonets and other samples of WW2 memorabilia. Far from treating him like a hero, pupils used to wind him up by insinuating that he only made tea for the soldiers or found the grenades and bayonets on a corpse. On one occasion he got so mad he challenged the whole of my brother's maths class to a fight outside the school.

Mr. Flood was a ranting hippopotamus employed as a history teacher. Every Empire Day - it was a long time ago, when there was a British Empire - he delivered the same speech, which 99 percent of the audience missed as all the staff and most of the pupils had trained themselves to sleep while standing upright for such occasions.

Mr Guffogg was a science teacher and a hippie before his time. My only recollection of him was the weird brass gizmo he tried out on every class he taught. The artefact was like a blowlamp with tubes, holes and coils everywhere. He would blow through it, launching a jet of soot over the front row of the pupils in the teaching laboratory; he would then make selected pupils have a go. There was a way of holding it that we did not know, consequently all attempts ended up with the pupil getting a face-full of soot. Guffogg would watch impassively like an alien conducting experiments on brain-damaged abductees.

'Jake' taught chemistry. Once, while demonstrating the effect water has on metallic sodium, he used an excessively large piece of the metal which fizzed around the glass vessel then ignited, exploded and set fire to his crew cut. We were of course' highly sympathetic to his predicament. He was good at predicting which topics were likely to appear on the chemistry exam paper and most people got a pass in the subject.

'Piggy' was a rotund little chap who taught French and Religious Instruction. He was basically a good man but his Christian beliefs irritated me. He was teetotal but, because of a circulatory problem, had a big red pin-cushion nose. For minor infractions he would use a bunch of keys as a substitute for the cane. We were told to learn some verses in the Bible for homework; I couldn't see the point of filling my head with such tripe so I made a hand written version with which to cheat. I was caught of course and sampled the keys. A classmate had been to Germany with some youth paramilitary group, the Boy's Brigade I think, and had bought a souvenir; a large bladed sheath knife with a deer's foot handle. I was sitting on the back row inspecting this fine weapon when Piggy noticed I was not paying attention and wandered down to see what I was doing before I could return the blade to the owner. Piggy's ranting about my inattention and the importance of the Bible so annoyed me that I unsheathed the knife and impaled the Bible on the desk, a statement which did not help my case. My friend had his knife confiscated and never saw it again.

I always sat at the back of the class so I had more options: to listen, read a comic, doodle or daydream. Piggy was writing on the blackboard when someone somewhere in front of me broke wind explosively, a real knicker-ripper. I wondered what they had been eating but as I pondered this question, Piggy demanded to know the identity of the pupil with the thunderbum. Each successive row, from the front backwards, claimed it came from behind them until it came to me. There was no point accusing the wall behind me of terminal flatulence; I was about to suggest the use of a sniffer dog, when I was grabbed by the ear and guided to the door. Protesting my innocence I was sent for the cane once again.

'Dicky' was a rat-faced little man: he was the first History teacher I had and, like all the subsequent history teachers, managed to make what is a fascinating subject into a cure for insomnia. He had a widow's peak which gave him a slight resemblance to a certain Transylvanian count and all the pupils called him 'Dicky'. I theorised that he had some kind of genital abnormality, perhaps hung like a hamster or an elephant; careful research revealed the origin of his nickname; when he first came to the school he always wore a dicky-bow rather than a tie. For several years he attempted to pump some history into our class until we had to choose between history and geography. All I remember is that every lesson seemed to focus on the Assyrians, the Sumerians, or the 'Fertile Crescent'; I recall no details. The most useful bit of information that I retained was how to remember to put the 'n' in the word 'government' because his name was G.O Vernon. Dicky had an on-going problem with a boy in our class called Ralph Gunnion, almost to the level of persecution. In one lesson he totally lost control and ran towards this boy who also ran off and dodged between the desks. As Dicky pursued him, an 'anonymous' foot appeared and Dicky fell heavily. Master Gunnion was duly sent for the cane and the lesson continued as if nothing had happened. I had to take off my shoe as my toe was sore.

'Rocky' was an ex Commando who taught Physical Education. He arrived each morning on a noisy ex-War Department motorcycle. Built like the old-fashioned brick toilet, he filled the door space as he entered the classroom. He would tolerate no messing about, so we didn't bother to try. The school assembly hall was also the music room, gymnasium and punishment centre. Now and again there were occasions when whole classes were caned and this was the venue. One day we arrived for PE to find the old upright piano right in the centre with chairs arranged around it. As we discussed what was going on, Rocky arrived. We were told to put the chairs and piano away and so we did. We shifted the chairs and were about to move the piano and pull out the boxes, vaulting horses and similar items of torture when the doors crashed open and in stalked 'Dicky'. He pushed past everyone, grabbed two boys and ordered them to replace the chairs while wagging his head at Rocky. I thought he had flipped or had a death wish; Rocky was almost twice his height and probably three times his weight. The class crowded round, our street mentality recognising the likelihood of fisticuffs. With hardly any effort at all, Rocky grasped the piano and pushed it across the hall at such speed that as it hit the wall, the front cover and some of the keys flew into the air. Dicky stormed out muttering. The cause of the fracas and the outcome were never revealed to us but it knocked five minutes off the PE lesson!

My first Science teacher was a gentleman called 'Bulldog' ; years later I realised he was nicknamed after a pulp fictional character of bygone times. Bulldog attempted to solve the class control problem by carrying a length of rubber Bunsen burner tubing with which he disciplined miscreants; the said rubber tubing wrapped round the buttocks at high speed and definitely had a sting worse than the cane.

After receiving the tubing for some crime I can't remember I decided that payback was in order. One of Bulldog's prize possessions was a glazed porcelain anatomical model of the upper respiratory tract, with the tonsils and other bits held by chromed springs so they could be displaced to view other details. While Bulldog was escorting another criminal upstairs for the cane, I grabbed his model throat and stretched every spring so each bit was dangling in space like a weird vase of flowers. Needless to say, he was not amused and consulting one of the many squealers in the class he sent me for six-of-the-best. One day we had a physics lesson in the laboratory adjacent to Bulldog's. Suddenly there was a loud explosion and the lab steward, Bert the beetle, raced in screaming that Bulldog had been injured. We all scuttled to see what had happened. A bottle of oxygen mixture, left too near a lighted Bunsen burner had exploded and the glass fragments had showered Bulldog. There was a lot of blood but his glasses saved his eyesight; the incident provided first class entertainment for the psychos in the class, of whom I was chief.

'Mad dog' was the deputy headmaster and state-registered cane administrator. Probably the oldest person on the staff, he had a scraggly neck and hooked beak, a vulture who enjoyed his corporal punishment administration. When you knocked on his door and were told to come in he used to peer over his spectacles, smile with anticipation then select a cane, holding it like one of the seven samurai. I got to know him quite well as I was caned frequently, sometimes for being late, fairly often for cheeking a teacher, once for sagging games and most annoying of all, for nothing at all. If an incident occurred there was a pool of possible perpetrators so someone would be punished unless they could prove they were innocent. Alibis given by classmates were not acceptable. Nature does have a tendency to even things out: I deliberately set off a fire extinguisher in the corridor as the masses were squeezing in after the lunch break and some geek got blamed, but later that term someone else did it and I got the blame.

'Ben' was a Latin teacher built like a professional wrestler who earned respect by punching wrongdoers in the chest, kidneys or chopping the back of the neck. I respected no one, including Ben, but I feared him. I did my homework translations diligently and sat in his sessions avoiding all eye contact. Homework generally consisted of working through Caesar's war with the Gauls, 'De Bello Gallico', and producing a reasonable translation. As we arrived in each lesson Ben took our translation notebooks and date-stamped them. He then selected pupils at random to translate paragraphs here and there. While date-stamping, he didn't have the time to read the translations and some wags would write a load of gibberish and just end with the last part of the homework. One pupil with a death wish did this regularly until one day he was asked to stand up and translate part of the passage. He was having difficulties because he hadn't even looked at the work he should have done. Ben called him out and examined his notebook. The boy had written out items from the personal column in the Liverpool Echo and Ben was not amused. 'You've been a naughty boy, Whiskers!' he growled, then hit the boy so hard that he flew through the air into the front desks. It took about ten seconds for consciousness to return, but more was to come. Dragging his 20 stone or so from his chair, Ben prowled round the desks doing a random examination of the open notebooks. Many were the rabbit punches and kidney digs given out in that session. I sat cool as a cucumber; I had done the homework. As I said, I was careful to keep on the right side of my beloved Latin teacher. I got a good grade in the GCE and can still read Latin texts if I have to.

The woodwork teacher was Jack Chisel. Pupils were not allowed to know the Christian names of teachers and I wasn't bothered. Jack was a vicious hard-knock who never sent anyone for the cane; he enjoyed handing out the punishment himself. He had three different shaped pieces of wood he called Faith, Hope and Charity and you were allowed to choose which one you would like to be hit with. He hit you for talking, working too slow for his liking, having an untidy work area in his opinion, but most frequent of all, for failing to produce a good wood joint. At the end of each class we had to line up at the front of the class to present our artefacts. Each item would be banged down on the desk: if they fell apart you got a comment, if they did not you got a compliment, but if they fell apart and the illegal glue and sawdust packing fell out, he took it personally and you had to pick the cane of your preference. One boy, Ralph Gunnion, was picked on by many teachers and one day so annoyed Jack Chisel that he made him stand at the far end of the woodwork room while he threw pieces of wood at him.

All the staff had to wear the traditional black gowns at assembly, Wabs even wore a mortar board. A boy called Dave Andrews, aka Archie, said he would grab Wabs' mortar board and run round the schoolyard if we collected a pound. Twenty pupils volunteered a shilling each and he did it. He got the cane for his trouble but a pound was a lot of money then: I got the cane frequently and was paid nothing.

The school introduced a prefect system and the authorities decided that these worthies would wear black waistcoats made of the same material as the teacher's gowns. We promptly named these garments 'monkey jackets'. Almost all of the sixth form pupils were given these monkey-jackets with a notable exception, me! After a few months someone realised that I was the only sixth former not rejoicing in prefect status and I was appointed. I lasted three days as a prefect. One job was to stand in a line with some other prefects and ensure pupils entering the school walked in a single line to their classes. I found delight in pushing them so they bounced off the school corridor walls and was relieved of this duty. I explained I was only doing my job but I got my first public warning. The following afternoon I was assigned to the dinner-time patrol, the main job was to report kids riding their bicycles across the school yard. I had an alternative solution to the problem. A boy rode through the gates and one of the other prefects shouted him to dismount. He continued, waving two fingers in a crude Winston Churchill parody. He still had one hand in the air when the brick I launched at him collapsed the front wheel of his bicycle and he bit the dust, the hospital said he was suffering mild concussion. Just like the guards loading Jews into the gas chambers I justified my action by claiming I was 'only obeying orders'. Instead of a commendation for upholding the Law I was swiftly removed from office and had to return my sartorially elegant monkey jacket.

Before the perils of cholesterol were publicised, all school children were provided with 'free' milk to give us strong bones and healthy teeth, a welcome alternative to Pedigree Chum dog food. To this end each pupil was forced to go to the canteen at break and imbibe one third of a pint of milk from quaint little glass bottles. The result of this was universal halitosis; every milk drinker had badger-breath during the afternoon sessions. I used to pocket my bottle and place it in front of the back wheels of parked cars. Some days I got two bottles so my target for the day had one bottle for each rear wheel. On one occasion I was more peeved than usual. I had been given the cane for something I had not done, quite a common occurrence. This treatment led to a mindset of 'If they punish me for not doing things I have nothing to lose if I do them'. I put three bottles in each pocket and kept them until lunch-time. Instead of going home as usual I went and stood in the middle of Stanley Road and threw my milk grenades at passing cars. One hit a windscreen, but the bottle smashed and not the windscreen.

It never crossed my tiny mind that what I was doing was dangerous to others and myself, there was a buzz in doing stupid things and not getting caught. It was only a matter of time before I was caught.

As a demonstration of my disrespect for authority I threw a bottle of milk through one of the mayoral office windows that overlooked the school-yard, then ducked down as a face appeared. Just as I ducked down so another pupil looked over and was seen. The whole school was made to form an identification parade and the aforementioned pupil was identified. Here was a problem; he was innocent of this particular offence, he also knew it was me that threw the bottle, but the big problem was he was the 'Cock of the school', the meanest dude around. It took me a very short time to make the right decision: I went to the headmaster and explained that I had thrown the bottle, but that the 'rough boys had made me do it.' Not only did he let me off with a warning, but he paid for the window out of his own pocket.

The sound of breaking glass always gave me a buzz and I frequently went for phone boxes and the occasional house windows. Coming home from school I wrapped snow around a rock and hurled it through the window of one of the flats, with no malice towards the occupants but it seemed a good idea at the time. The next day, the head teacher announced that a window had been smashed by a pupil and requested that the perpetrator own up. Of course I did not. He then elaborated; a baby in a pram had been showered with the glass fragments but had not been injured. I actually felt bad about what could have happened and resolved to just specialise in unoccupied phone boxes.

We were just in the teddy boy era but had no money to ponce about in flashy drape suits like the real thing. We all had sideburns and DA (duck's ass) hair styles, we had jackets that were too big for us and ill-fitting 'drainpipe' trousers. Most of the kids wore crêpe-soled shoes, known on the street as 'brothel creepers', although I had no idea what a brothel was. Everyone walked about scowling like a gunfighter's convention and made interesting conversation. Some examples may clarify.

'Who d'yer think youse are lookin' at, eh?'
meaning 'I have an identity crisis!'

'D'yer wanna face full'er gollies?'
meaning 'Would you like me to spit in your face?'

Where the Bugs wear Boots

'D'yer wanna face full'er dandruff?'
meaning 'May I present you with a complimentary head butt?'

The latter was a common form of greeting, also known as a scouse kiss. You grasped someone by the lapels of their suit or school blazer then rammed your forehead sharply between the eyes or the bridge of the nose depending how far apart these places were. As I was not into excessive pain I invented a defence mechanism: a box of three quarter inch blued tin-tacks which I pushed through the lapels of my jacket from the back. I only ever had two people grab me then let go with blood dripping from their fingers, but I frequently scratched myself on my own defence system. Another antisocial fad was the rolling up of the school cap, hard peak outermost to make a rudimentary cosh. These featured in many a schoolyard fracas. In a moment of lunacy I sewed razor blades into the peak of my cap, then fortunately took them out again as I could think of no-one fully deserving a slashing.

It was 1956, well into the Rock and Roll era. My cousin, had a very rich grandmother; whatever he wanted was granted. It was like having his own genie of the lamp. When he asked for the cash to get a motorcycle he got a surprise; she said no for the very first time because she'd only just bought him a brand new racing bicycle which cost hundreds of pounds. He conveniently had it 'stolen', and lo and behold, he received a nice shiny new motorcycle. I first heard 'Hound Dog' by Elvis Presley at his house. The Scotty Moore guitar solo still gives me the twitches, although there are many faster and more skilful guitarists around. I saved up to buy a copy of my own; it was the very first record I ever owned, I didn't even have anything to play it on, but I had the record. I used to visit rich kids' homes clutching my treasure so I could hear it now and again. Eventually, Mum got a second-hand radiogram which had a metal needle, rather than the more expensive diamond stylus, which destroyed my record within a couple of weeks.

Later that year the film 'Rock Around the Clock' was released, or perhaps it escaped. The reactions to the film were to rock the decent public to the core and give Her Majesty's Police plenty of excuses to feel the collars of many young hooligans. In those days I had stopped carrying an old style 'cut throat' razor, mainly because I didn't want to use it on anyone. I sent off to a war-surplus company for an ex-army machete with an sixteen inch blade. It came packed in obscenely smelling grease which took almost a week to remove. I kept it hidden under my mattress so my Mum didn't find it. When I went out to cause trouble I took my trusty blade with me, stuck carefully down my trousers. This meant I had to walk as if I'd a bad leg or had pancaked my underwear; it was razor sharp so I had to draw it out extremely carefully when reinforcing an argument, proving what a retard I really was. I took my machete to the Gainsborough cinema in Bootle where they were showing Rock Around the Clock. Within a short period there was bedlam as everyone started fighting. There was no point trying to watch the film; people were attacking each other for no reason. Two full blown Teddy Boys waving flick knives came towards me as I was getting out but the sight of my machete helped them to change direction and they ran back into the chaos. I was just making my way home up Knowsley Road as the police arrived mob-handed and surrounded the cinema. I've seen the film since and still can't see what made everyone go ape.

A few years later a different phenomenon caused a similar incident although the police were not involved as far as I know. Some 3D comics then films and cartoons had been produced. To view these you had to wear cardboard glasses with red and green plastic over the eyepieces. To compete with 3D films, which didn't really have the continued impact the makers predicted, 'Emergoscope' was introduced. During a scary movie, 'The House on Haunted Hill' if I remember correctly, a plastic skeleton flew out on a rail across the theatre from a hidden recess at the front of the cinema. Some patrons were more than slightly disturbed. On the occasion of the next showing of the movie, it was the skeleton's turn for the surprise. As it began its flight, it was pelted with ice creams, Coca Cola bottles (cans were not in use at this time) and a range of detritus that the enterprising scallies had smuggled into the cinema in anticipation of the event. In a matter of seconds a further element of surprise was introduced. All the material sent into orbit now returned to earth as a consequence of gravity: many bumps on the head were reported. The ice creams, on landing, gave the impression that the victims had been crapped on from a great height by mutant seagulls.

Once a week we had swimming, not my favourite activity as I will explain; the school did not have its own swimming baths, very few did in those days. We had the use of Balliol Road swimming baths, just a short walk down Balliol Road towards the Bootle docks. This Victorian edifice was considered by many to be architecturally magnificent. My memories of the place are far from happy. We always visited the baths at nine in the morning whatever the time of year or state of the weather. Before you even entered, the appetising aroma of chlorine gas and stale sweat assailed the nostrils together with that weird sound common to all swimming baths: immature squeaking distorted by multiple reflection from the tiles. The changing rooms were dark and cold with permanent pools of icy unknown liquid. We were pushed two at a time into the cubicles which had been designed for thin dwarfs. Our class had several obese pupils; I learned early on to avoid sharing with these porkers. The next stage in the proceedings, once the swimming cozzie was worn, was to go into the ice cold showers then march through a trough of cold pungent antiseptic to the main pool. This pool was carefully kept just above freezing point, the water was cloudy from the sporadic dumping of excessive quantities of bleaching powder with shoals of detached sticking plasters moving with the current like flat, dead fish. I used to take as long as I could to get ready; last in and first out. It was worth the occasional cuff round the ear or good-natured kick from the games teacher to reduce the time actually spent in the water. I used to fake the cold shower by wetting my hair and pretending to shiver like the fools who showered, but whatever you did was never enough to prepare you for the trauma of getting into the pool.

Approaching the steps you could see several keen types swimming up and down the length of the pool; the games teacher's pets. Most of the class were clustered round the filter pump intakes like maggots on rotten meat. Their quest was to glean an odd calorie from the very slightly warmer water coming in. All but the fattest were shivering, twitching with wedding tackle shrunk to infinitesimal proportions, slowly turning various shades of blue, apart from their eyes which were bulbous and red-rimmed from the excessive chlorine. Some pupils would be lying on the pool-side like beached whales; flushed distended heaps of human offal, fools who had tried to dive and only belly-flopped from a great height. Should a pupil be stupid enough to forget his swimming kit, usually as an attempt to wimp out of the session, he was provided with a slip; a frighteningly small canvas triangle with side ties. These would have been obscene were it not for the freezing water and the consequent shrinkage phenomenon described earlier. One gravitationally challenged (obese) pupil, claimed by his parents and peers to be virtually unsinkable, hit an iceberg on his maiden voyage. He had ignored the ice warnings and attempted a new speed record. Fortunately he survived with all passengers; his swim trunks however were deemed totally unusable and had to be destroyed.

The water in the baths, although cold, had a strange buoyancy which intrigued me as an amateur scientist. I recalled a magazine article on the Dead Sea with a photo of a man sitting in the concentrated salt water reading a newspaper. With observation I was able to formulate a theoretical explanation of the phenomenon. Every swimmer would frequently clear out his sinuses into the pool. With each class the nasal mucus concentration and therefore, water viscosity, increased; by Friday afternoon the water resembled wallpaper paste and it was almost possible to cross the pool without getting wet. This observation, and the failure of many pupils to use the correct facilities for bladder emptying, resulted in my developing a unique swimming style I called the Terrapin Paddle: a basic dog paddle with the mouth as high out of the water as the neck will allow.

Adjacent to the large pool was a smaller, shallower one, despised by the teachers and the strong swimmers as the 'baby pool'. Some would surreptitiously sneak into the pool and warm themselves in the lukewarm dilute-urine mixture. After what seemed an eternity we were ordered out of the pool, a command which I hastened to obey; probably the only command I always obeyed. The showers by now were almost boiling and could easily poach a slow pupil. I used to race through the spray right into the cubicle and throw on my clothes while still wet, as there was a bonus for the first dozen or so to be dressed. For the sum of one old penny you could buy half an 'Oxo' cube dissolved in hot water. The stuff tasted like salty rat urine but it probably saved me from death by exposure or frostbite of the extremities. The last straw was the return to school. All of us shivering and steaming in the frosty air, with every brain cell screaming 'Run!' we had to walk in an orderly manner, at a pace determined by the sadistic games teacher, two by two, like the animals en route to Noah's Ark.

I've always been sensitive about getting my kit off in public, perhaps a blessing in disguise. I have never aspired to be a stripper, flasher or skinny dipper and this mindset helped me to avoid injury one hot Bootle summer. Some of my street half-friends decided to go skinny dipping in the Leeds-Liverpool canal behind the Carlsberg Brewery in Bootle. The canal never appealed as a place to practise my Terrapin technique, not just because it was full of leeches, but also it was used by the irresponsible public for dumping almost anything: mattresses, dead animals, bicycles and milk crates to name a selection. The largest item we ever discovered was a burnt-out Morris Minor. We had been to school and, overheating from the poorly ventilated classroom, we came home via the canal. While I was still wondering whether to go in or not, Dave Jones whipped his kit off, raced to the edge of the canal and dived in. There was an immediate screech and we ran to see what had happened; I half-expected him to be covered in leeches. For some reason the canal must have been blocked further upstream, because there was only a few inches of water out of which protruded several bicycle frames, window frames, bricks and assorted detritus. Dave lay spread-eagled amongst the 'crud', butt-naked, still screeching and not even wet by the green, evil-smelling water. 'Look before you leap' comes to mind, but remember this incident later when I relate one of my trail-biking experiences.

Another school activity, almost as bad as swimming, was games on a Wednesday afternoon, which took place at the Orrell Pleasure Ground, a scrubby vacant lot where the Savio High School is now situated. It was in Orrell and covered a lot of ground; but I could never see where the pleasure came in. We were forced to play football, cricket and indulge in athletics and cross-country running, to me a form of punishment. One day a football match between Everton and Liverpool was rearranged for the same afternoon as the games lesson. Most of the school missed games to see the match, I just went home. I had a bad feeling about the school's reaction to no-one turning up for games so I feigned toothache and my Mum dragged me along to the dentist. My teeth were gross and I had several fillings but I could also prove that I was at the dentist's. The next morning the registers were brought to assembly and only those who had attended games were allowed to leave the hall. Ten teachers armed with canes stood at the front of the hall and we lined up in classes for a mass caning session. At this stage I produced a note confirming my absence and escaped being caned for once.

At the age of sixteen my value system took a twist. Thanks to my endocrine system, I became Spotty Muldoon and simultaneously interested in the opposite sex, not a symbiotic combination. There was no Biactol as commercial television was non-existent, the BBC was the only option at this time. My nose was big, it still is and when the family sat in a line it was like the toucan house at the Zoo. To make it worse, on the odd occasion I did wash my greasy locks, I used to slap on the Brylcreem when my hair was dry and comb it back over my ears. This resulted in a further accentuation of the 'beak', I was indeed hatchet faced. Brylcreem overdosing also resulted in a comb that was heavy with great wadges of greasy hair fixative. I used to clean my comb by running it through the cat's scraggly fur which killed three birds with one stone. First, it cleaned my comb, second, it gave the cat a neater, glossy appearance but thirdly, the cat liked the taste of it. I often wondered when it was wailing outside to its girlfriend whether it was actually suggesting 'try some of this, man!' Who knows? Anyway, I had this dilemma, proboscis related. You could buy a decent motor-cycle for the price of a nose job, 250 quid and cheap at half the price. What could I do? I would never 'pull a bird' with a snout like mine but neither could I cruise along Queen's Drive on a nose-job. In case you're interested, I chose the wheels.

On my uncle Harry's advice I responded to an advert in 'The Motor Cycle' magazine by King's in Manchester and bought a 250 cc Panther without even seeing it. I sent off the money and after several weeks while they searched for a machine bad enough to send, I got a postcard informing me that it was arriving by British Rail at Bootle Station. Bathos is not one of the Three Musketeers; it is what I felt when I saw my dream machine. The magazine description was recommended for Porky-of-the-Month at the Liars Institute. My motorcycle had both tyres flat as an M6 hedgehog. It was supposed to be blue but there was so much rust I was tempted to re-register the colour as reddish-brown. The battery was in the same state as the tyres - dead flat. I pushed the thing home - a nose, a nose, my kingdom for a nose. With help from a motorcycle mechanic who lived up the street, I got the engine started, with great difficulty as the engine compression was considerable even with the exhaust valve lifter which was supposed to make kick-starting easier. Yesterday I was a geek with no chicken, today a biker with L-plates.

It was a Thursday morning and I decided to go to school on my mean machine. This sad excuse for a Harley Davidson looked better than when I got it - all the chrome had gone to the electroplating centre in the sky, so I painted over it with aluminium paint, which never completely dried in the two years I had the bike. My mother shouted, 'Be careful!' as I shot out of the driveway and down the road. The bike was riding me, rather than the reverse. At the end of the road, I attempted to slow down and then found out that neither of the brakes worked, so I shot into the traffic. Motorcycle yob - prejudices confirmed. I could hear the upper lips curling in the bus queue as I accelerated towards the roundabout at Fernhill Crescent: it's still there only now it's called the kidney island. The throttle stuck open, the brakes once again failed to obey me, so I banked the bike over sharply to take the curve. A footrest stuck in the ground, then snapped off. As I hit the ground something shot past me and into the railings outside the shops - it was the missile I used to call my motorbike. I lay there, my trousers changing colour, with blood, I hasten to mention. The impatient motorists were weaving past me as I lay in a heap. No one stopped, no one even beeped me to get out of the way - I had temporarily cloaked and was now invisible. A red face with beer bottle bifocals loomed into view. A fat priest, probably wondering whether to pass by on the other side, do the last rites or go for the Good Samaritan of the week award. He chose the latter, helping me to the side of the road and together we got the bike upright. It was the first of many such events (crashes that is, not meetings with priests), but you always remember the first time, so they say.

My friendly neighbourhood mechanic came over later and examined the bike closely. It was a real grid with twisted forks, badly worn brake shoes and a worn swinging arm bearing that guaranteed problems for any rider. He made a list of things that were wrong and we returned it to Kings who promised to fix it. This they did, but presented me with a bill for doing so. I travelled to Manchester on the train with my cousin Jack. He demanded a road test of the work and drove off on my bike while I stood outside the shop waiting for him. The sales assistant went into the shop for a moment and Jack appeared, I got on the bike behind him and off we went home. I heard no more from Kings so I think they got the message.

I still had the matter of passing the motorcycle driving test to deal with; I chose Liverpool City Centre test centre, I'm not too sure why. I demonstrated I could read number plates at a great distance then prepared to move off at the examiner's command. As I operated the clutch to move into first gear the cable snapped and the test was over before it had started. No bike, no test! I managed to get a cancellation and passed the test a few weeks later on a mate's side valve BSA C11. The test has changed a bit from 1959. Unlike the car test where the commands to turn or stop were communicated directly, you had to keep stopping to get new instructions all the time. Eventually the crunch came; the Emergency Stop. During the car driving test the examiner thwacked the dashboard when you had to stop in a imaginary emergency; for the bike test I was told to drive round and round the block in the Grove Street area until the examiner jumped out: I then had to stop in a safe manner (not run him over). I know this sounds a bit obvious, but several examiners had been injured because they jumped out on the wrong motorcyclist, or the right motorcyclist who failed to react quickly enough. I failed to run over the examiner and so passed the test. This meant I could carry passengers, i.e. ladies, so I thought, but this was not to be. No one wanted to ride on the back of my bike or let me ride theirs. I guess I was slightly crazy at that time and had many crashes, eight of them in the space of a year, before I wrote the Panther off totally. I never had a single broken bone, although I shed quite a bit of blood and occasionally observed my bones through abrasions. Many years later I tripped over my stupid knee length boots in the house, fractured a bone in my leg and snapped the cartilage on my left foot. My bike was in worse condition than I was. One fateful day I was stopped by a police patrolman. I tried to outrun his machine which was a waste of time. He tried my brakes - the front one was useless. He asked where the horn was and I showed him the piece of wire taped to the handlebar which I pushed against the bar if I needed to sound the horn. We sat on the roadside and he explained the stupidity of riding uninsured on a heap of crap and convinced me to legalise the bike and I did.

Many years later my affection for motorcycles led me to meet the girl who ultimately became my wife. It happened like this: a friend, Pete, had a Royal Enfield Crusader 250 and I was working on his bike one day when his sister, Viv, brought us a cup of tea and a McVitie's digestive biscuit. From that instant my priorities changed; Viv was (and still is) what is commonly called a Babe, a rather exotic beauty, not just beautiful outwardly, but in personality and temperament. I began to lose interest in getting black fingernails from oily motorcycles, and worse, I began to rapidly lose interest in Chemistry and the detailed study of the latter. Viv liked me a little, which is more than could be said of her parents. As far as they were concerned, I was an oaf who was encouraging their son to ride his motorcycle, and was now interested in their daughter. I received a letter from her mother to the effect that she was unable to understand how a seemingly intelligent person at university could speak with a common Liverpool accent. I was informed that I was forbidden to see Viv unless I was prepared to have elocution lessons. My reaction was to confirm her prejudices: I returned the letter in tiny pieces, suggesting that she kept the bits to use as confetti at our wedding and the 'Cold War' continued.

Viv was sent to elocution lessons, even though she spoke properly: her younger sister went to the same woman for singing lessons. As I accompanied them to the elocution woman and sat there like 'One of Lewis's' while they performed, I decided to get a bit of elocution myself. To assess my vocal non-talent I had to read a short passage with Mrs Woman correcting me as I went. Our first confrontation was on the word 'tongue'; I was informed that it was pronounced 'tarng' not 'tung'. The next problem was the word 'bath'. There has never been an 'r' in the word, so I objected to having to pronounce it 'barth'. Similarly, glass became glarss, and class became clarss. To this day the addition of a virtual 'r' still bugs me. The basic problem was that she taught southern style English, posh but also affected. Sacks, pronounced 'sex' was what the coalman brought the coal in. She finished the lesson early; the next day she had a heart attack and the elocution lessons were over. But I digress; back to the Grammar school.

Opposite the old Bootle Grammar school was a big old house they called the Annexe. This dump had several rooms full of old-style desks with inkwells. Unless your family was rich enough to get you a fountain pen, you had to write with wooden sticks with metal nibs attached which you dipped in the blue-black ink in the inkwells. Creeps known as ink monitors made the ink from powder and water and filled up the inkwells as good boys should. We used to cut a cross in the end of the pen and fit a crude flight to make darts to stick in the door when the teacher left the room for any reason. The inkwells had a fatal fascination for some pupils; looking into them was like having your very own Black Hole. One kid 'nicked' some calcium carbide from the laboratory and dropped it into his inkwell. As he went to ignite the acetylene coming off there was a loud explosion which nearly cost him an eye. Before the ambulance arrived I tried to comfort him; he was griping about the possibility of ending up blind in one eye. I pointed out that he had nothing to moan about because he had a spare eye. After a week off school he returned with his damaged eye resembling a fried egg.

One dinner time in summer someone noticed that the girls from the telephone exchange next to the annexe were sunbathing at the back of the building. Some of the baser types stuck their heads out of the windows and made rude comments, to be told to clear off in less than ladylike terms. Each of us took two or three inkwells and threw them at the unappreciative bags that had rejected our immature advances; many were splattered with ink and were not amused. This was duly reported to the headmaster and the whole class was called to task, even those who took no part in the atrocity. The punishment was to hang from the wall bars in the assembly hall/gymnasium under the watchful eye of the games teacher until we cheered up and he felt we were suitably repentant. Those who dropped from exhaustion were whacked with his spare training shoe.

Where the Bugs wear Boots

As I mentioned, I lost count how many times I got the cane. With my Dad being the way he was and my Mum looking after him full time, my behaviour inside and outside of school got worse. I stole anything that wasn't tied down for the buzz of being chased and vandalised anything that was breakable. I sometimes visited a bookshop on Brownlow Hill near the University and stuffed books into my pockets so the staff could see. I then ran out of the shop to be chased by the security person. If he was catching up I dropped a few books to slow him down and avoid capture. Very sad but exciting at the time! I once attended a Christian Union meeting in the chemistry lab, the teacher in charge thought I had 'seen the light', in fact I only did it to get hold of the laboratory keys and make an impression in a bar of soap. Later in the week we raided the outside chemical cupboard and removed some dangerous chemicals. A car was set on fire by smearing white phosphorus on the tyres.

On the day the A level exams finished, we tanked up on cheap wine in the park then returned to school to look for trouble. Wash-basins and toilets were smashed, doors ripped off their hinges, any coats in the cloakrooms were ripped from bottom to top, and then we went looking for staff to harass. The outcome was that three of us were suspended then expelled from the school; the others in the wrecking spree turned states evidence and grassed us up. My reaction may surprise you; pride in having achieved fame at last! How sad can you get?

One day I was standing with some kids from school on the corner of Oxford Road when an invalid carriage came slowly up the hill. It was my Dad on his way home from the town hall where he had a part-time job. Three of the kids started shouting abuse and running after him. I fished out my home-made knuckle-duster and moved forward; a split lip each was in order. I stopped for an instant to consider what my peers would think, by which time my Dad had started down Breeze Hill and the three heroes had returned. I let the incident go. It haunted me for years that I was ashamed of my Dad and I often wished I could reverse time for an instant and give the insensitive bastards the smack in the mouth they deserved. Despite Professor Hawking's theories, time does not reverse. There was to be no easy atonement for my failure to stand up for my Dad; I had to live with that.

Chapter 6

Time for a change

Conversions were happening everywhere. Many people replaced the old gas lamps with electric lights. Some pulled down the old outside toilet with its million spiders, icy draughts and screams for 'paper' when the last remains of the Liverpool Echo had run out; they converted to an inside toilet. Ours was just inside the back door next to the coal cellar. The air pollution was getting beyond a joke and a law was passed. Many had to convert from coal, with its amazing light-show as it burned, to boring old coke or over-priced anthracite.

I myself had three distinct conversions. First I swapped my old bicycle for a motorcycle. I saved a lot of time and energy but who cares? The move to two motorised wheels was the third best thing I ever did. Secondly I underwent a conversion in musical appreciation. I had been part of the Classical Music society, and still enjoy some now, but much of it I found depressing. A great deal of it, of course, was written by very talented people who were depressed out of their skulls, and some by people just out of their skulls. Someone lent me the Disraeli Gears album by Cream and I was converted, first to Underground and Progressive Rock, then Hard Rock and ultimately Heavy Metal - but that's another story.

The third conversion turned my life totally upside down and inside out. I'd not long been expelled from Bootle Grammar School and was still basking in the street credibility this afforded me: this was the level of self-delusion I was wallowing in. The reality was that I had been accepted to read Chemistry at the University of Liverpool; I had got a provisional acceptance the year before as I did my A-levels in one year. I had never once thought what the expulsion from school and the revelation of the kind of loose cannon I was would have on the powers-that-be at the University.

Only my Mum knew the truth, and she was shell-shocked. I told my Dad that I had finished school early because of my achievements and he never questioned it. We deliberately spared him the truth about his golden boy (me!) because the succession of cerebral haemorrhages had damaged him greatly; the information that I was actually a scumbag could have harmed him. Unknown to me, my Mum had asked some of her friends from church to pray for me. As I regressed socially and morally these people were regularly asking Mr Big to do something about it; and He did! Mum was so devastated by my suspension then expulsion that I tried to be atypically nice to compensate. She asked me to go to church with her; although what she hoped to achieve from this I had no idea. Many people only attend church when someone is born, married, or snuffs it. Churches are so varied with different doctrinal biases, different ways of doing things etc. I had no interest but agreed to go with her for a couple of weeks.

Some older readers may recall the song, 'Green Door', immortalised by another son of Scouseland, Frankie Vaughan. My mother was probably his greatest fan. 'Green Door' captures the atmosphere of the private club and the futile attempts of the singer to gain entry although he tries every means. I'm going to open the green door on my first experiences of church; it was, as I suspected; full of people in suits and boring as watching paint dry - a waste of time as far as I was concerned. It was the same dump I had experienced many years earlier, but at least then I had been bribed to attend. The varnish on the pews had still not set properly; it still made a ripping sound as you stood up and left a perfect bum print: so little had changed, it was like being trapped in a time warp. I amused myself by counting the panes of glass in the windows, light bulbs, and then people, male and female, with and without hats. Every one that came in sat down then slumped forward as if the hard pews had induced a stroke. Apparently they were praying so I did the same, leaning forward, counting to five then sitting up again with a beatific grin. The hour and a half felt like a whole day. I'd had a bellyful; I'd done my penance by attending as I'd promised, this was to be the last time I would waste my time in this church or any other. I was also afraid of contracting 'evangeloids', a nasty condition induced by hard pews and long sermons.

They did not believe in fresh air and the radiators had been on all day. They had a choir elevated above the masses, that was full of people whose sell-by date had well expired and in the corner was an 'orchestra', two or three violinists who played totally out of sync with each other, a cellist and pianist. The speaker for the evening was small, pixilated, wizened and Welsh. He had bifocals that seemed very wide apart enabling him to resemble a chameleon; this wasn't a bad start, I like chameleons. His worst characteristic was his voice, a sing-song Welsh screech as he got excited, accompanied by the dull thwack of his fist on the huge pulpit Bible as he punctuated the screeches. My first thoughts on seeing this Bible was, 'Wow! You could kill someone with that!' As the sermon dragged on I began to visualise the little Welsh bluebottle as the victim of a pulpit-bible-from-a-great-height accident. I have always had the ability to switch off, to retreat into a mind shell while those around accuse, threaten or lecture me, very useful during a long sermon. This sermon was long; I noticed several choir members nodding off.

Eventually he shut the huge Bible with a dull thud, a good sign that the torture was nearly over. With his head scanning the congregation he couldn't see, his scrawny neck and prominent Adam's apple wobbling, he pointed across the auditorium in my general direction. 'There is a young man here who is a sinner.' His voice rose in pitch as he said 'sinner': this was nothing new, I knew I was one. 'You need Jesus!' he screeched. 'Like a hole in the head' I thought to myself, but even as I thought it, I could feel my eyes watering. 'Hay fever', I explained as I borrowed my Mum's handkerchief. I was annoyed with myself; this horrible little Welshman had invaded my agnostic cool. Theologically I was neither a believer nor an atheist. I could not imagine how the world around me with all its complexity could have come into being from a piece of snot from outer space and a few million years. The obvious design in nature implied a Designer; religion may well have some truth hidden behind the boring people that embraced or propped themselves up with it, but it was irrelevant to me. It didn't bother me that this old goat called me a sinner, but the idea of Jesus loving me enough to die for me was like a kick in the belly. My eyes were now running like a glassblower's ass: I now know it was God's Holy Spirit laying into me. I once again chickened out and claimed immunity on the grounds of hay fever. I don't recall anything else about the meeting other than a driving urge to get out of it.

When I eventually got to bed I couldn't sleep. Hammering at my subconscious was 'Jesus died for you'. But I didn't ask him to! What relevance did a Jewish martyr from almost 2000 years ago have to me, a would be scientist waiting to see if the university would kick me out before I'd even started? Suddenly I saw the situation without the filters of delusion, stupidity and arrogance. I had taken advantage of my Dad's illness to go completely off the rails. I was getting a buzz from terrorising others. My years of vandalism and violence had all but finished off any chance of a reasonable education. I was just a sad lonely fool. I sat up and said to the wall, 'God, if you're real then do something with me. A crazy thing to do? Yes, even crazier because He did!

If you are a Christian reading this, it may make sense. If you're not, it probably won't. All I can say is that what happened next changed my life, my thought processes and my motives. A sense of peace flooded over me and I fell asleep. The next morning it was still present, I felt different; the truth is I was different; I still am after fifty years. My mother was pleased and so were her group of praying fishwives. My peer group of fellow bikers and scallies were not; most of them feared me as a loose cannon, a 'nut job', but they were unable to cope with me at all as a Christian. One positive thinking acquaintance informed me that it wouldn't work as I was such a bad dude. More than twenty years later I visited a heavy metal 'disco' at the Black Tulip pub in Batley, Yorkshire. The place was packed, mainly with a chapter of the local 'Satan's Slaves' motorcycle club. As we were leaving someone noticed the 'Jesus Saves' on the back of my friend's leather jacket. He remarked to me as I passed him, 'Been there, done that, didn't work!' I quickly replied, 'Been there, done that, still working after 20 years!' He walked away, scratching his head and blinking like a toad in a sand heap.

My peers first of all had no idea what a Christian was. They thought everyone that lived in Britain, a nominally Christian country, was automatically a Christian. Wrong! Others thought that people who went to church were Christians; again possibly, but going to church doesn't make someone a Christian. If you sat in a garage with a mouthful of antifreeze and a dipstick up your ass, would that make you a car? I don't think so! So how does living in the UK or sitting in church make a person a Christian? Short answer, it doesn't! Christians are those who have realised that their behaviour is unacceptable to the God who made them; the Bible calls this 'sin'. This sin makes any relationship with God impossible, but by accepting the death of Christ on the cross on their behalf, the relationship is restored. There is a lot more to it than this but I'm not about to attempt to brainwash you or ram my beliefs down your throats. The fact is, I changed radically in outlook, behaviour, motivation and attitude to others but am still far from perfect. Jesus being your Saviour implies that His characteristics and attitudes will be displayed in your lifestyle. Consequently Christians should be loving, honest, trustworthy, caring and hospitable: if not you have every right to question their faith. A hypocrite is anyone whose life is a sham: I agree you'll find some in the church, and as many in the factory, the university, the school or the pub. All humans have a body to enable them to live in our global ecosystem, a soul giving the ability to think, express emotion and make decisions, and a spirit capable of contact with God. Christianity is not a religion, rather a relationship with Jesus that provides access to God and starts a process whereby you can have a new start in life and begin to resemble Jesus in thought, word and action. This takes longer in some than others. Religion is Man's efforts to contact God; Christianity is what God has already done to enable Man to find the way to God, which was sending Jesus.

Even atheists are religious. They have a set of beliefs, or creed, which they follow like any other religion. They believe that humanity is the result of chance evolution, that the universe as we know it came into being because of a Big Bang, or a series of Steady State changes, that there is no God: but have no more proofs for their theories than any other religion. The atheist says 'Big Bang', the Christian says, 'God did it', the X-File people say,' The aliens did it' but most ordinary people say,' Who gives a monkey's toss?' It is interesting that the atheistic evolutionary theory is taught in schools and accepted as fact, yet there is no more proof for this view than any alternative. Like the soap powder and cosmetics ads on TV, if you get pseudo-scientific with people, or show some geek wearing spectacles, the implication is he must be clever and therefore reliable. So the gullible buy into the lie or half-truth. I have great respect for Professor Dawkins as a fellow scientist but I disagree totally with his atheistic evangelism. He states that 'there is probably no God', but that's because he's never had a relationship with his Creator. I could have buses printed with 'There is probably no Professor Dawkins' because I've never met him and the photos could be anybody!

I've heard people say it doesn't matter what you believe as long as you believe something. With respect, Bollocks with a capital B! What you believe determines your thought processes and behaviour. Beliefs are intensely personal and in any free country you can believe in the flat earth or the tooth fairy. There are many parts of the world where the religious authorities do not tolerate alternative beliefs; places where discrimination, persecution and even execution occurs if anyone attempts to defect from the state religion. But does it really matter what you believe? I think it does, because your belief system will be the 'glasses' through which you view the world and affects the way you think and act.

A genuine Christian will see others as God sees them and will respect life and want only the best for them. They won't be perfect, but they will be working at it. If at the end they are mistaken and God does not exist they will still have lived a good life, enjoyed peace and joy and will have contributed positively to the good of others. Similarly a person who believes we are all a product of chance, basically pieces of meat with eyes, is likely to have no qualms about abortion of the innocent, euthanasia of the elderly or manipulation of the simple to their own advantage. They will answer to nobody but themselves. But if at the end of their lives they are mistaken about the reality of God, they stand neck deep in the brown stuff. I make no apology for making you think about these things for a short while. Most of us live in total unreality. We think one day we'll win the lottery, we think we'll go on forever, we live our lives through TV soap characters and either file God along with Santa, Rudolph and the tooth fairy, or see God as a geriatric idiot who has a bad memory. My recommendation to you as an ex-thug and bad scally changed by God, a Christian of 50 years, is at least to look into it. Don't make the mistake of judging Christ by his imperfect followers, seek the God/Man himself. Get a gospel of John, read it and get a life!

So I was now a Christian. I started going to church to learn what being a Christian was all about. I still met my old mates but they were freaked out by the new me, not that I was Bible bashing them; I didn't know enough to lay anything on anyone other than something weird but real had happened when I asked God to sort me out. I guess they found me boring because I no longer wanted to steal, fight or cause trouble. I found others suspicious because I tended to arrive on time, work hard and I no longer bullied others; almost 'wussy' although no-one risked saying this to me. I realised later in life that anyone who does the right thing will automatically be a prick to the conscience of the layabouts, the dishonest and the disobedient. Try dieting, regulating your drinking or giving up smoking and see how your peer group try to get you to reverse your decisions and be like them. In view of this I decided to spend more time with the people in church, not the best idea I ever had but it seemed the right thing to do. They had some weird rituals, like eating dry bread and very dilute Ribena. They called it 'Communion'. Later I learned the significance; to celebrate the sacrifice Jesus made and to remember that he will be returning to earth some day. Trouble was they all had citrus gobs when 'celebrating'. When I was asked to take the bread and wine round some years later I used to smile at the recipients. Big mistake! I was told off as I was supposed to look as miserable as everyone else. To my way of thinking, celebrating the Good News that

Jesus died for us is a time to be happy, not to have funeral gobs.

To many of them I was a trophy, a bad-ass changed for the better and I was taken around other churches to tell my story of my life before and after what they called 'conversion'. I hadn't been a Christian for more than a few months when Stan, the youth leader, invited me to join a team visiting a large youth club in Moreton on the other side of the river Mersey. I'd heard of Moreton: Cadbury's chocolate factory was there. On the way through the tunnel they informed me that I was to speak for ten minutes or so on how I became a Christian. It was a large place, with over 150 kids of around my age, and we were to 'perform' on a large purpose built stage. I waited at the back of the stage for my turn to participate. My brother's band, 'The Ambassadors', was top of the bill and a bloke called Ralph was due to speak before me. There was a lot of noise from the crowd and I peeped through a gap in the backdrop. Each time Ralph said something there were hoots of derision or laughter from the crowd. He was trying to explain how someone at work had so impressed him with their Christian lifestyle that it got him thinking about life, death, the Universe and everything. The way he put it was, 'There was this guy at work who had something I didn't have.' Before he could qualify his statement with, 'He had peace and joy, even in difficult times' the hecklers went for him. The merciless crowd turned everything he said into a crude double-entendre.

To date, each time I had shared my experiences so far was to older Christian people who were sympathetic. As I told them some of the things I had done and how God had changed me, there were sharp intakes of breath and a few 'Hallelujahs'. But this audience was the real world, and they seemed highly antagonistic. I was slightly nervous, but highly annoyed with the way they had received Ralph. When it was my turn I stepped up to the microphone and announced, 'If anyone wants a fight, let's do it now!' The place went quiet. I was told later that our youth leader had his head in his hands, no doubt regretting selecting me for the evening. I waited, like they do at the 'lawful impediment' bit in the wedding ceremony, but there were no takers. I then explained that if anyone chose to interrupt me while I was speaking I would leave the platform and personally 'kick their teeth in'. I didn't know any better and never took that approach again but it worked on this occasion. After I finished many of the would-be hard knocks spoke to me and said they'd look into Christianity. I suspect God was being kind to me as a learner.

Unknown to me God had a plan to sort out many of my unacceptable attitudes. At this time the Liverpool and Bootle docks were extremely busy with ships from all over the globe unloading and picking up stuff to take back. I was introduced to another guy called Stan who visited the ships in the Bootle docks every Thursday evening to talk to the different nationalities about his faith and offer help or hospitality to those that wanted any. To crack the language problem he played them records of songs and short sermons in their own languages on wind-up gramophones that you could see in museums; other communication was in pigeon English or by sign language. Before I became a Christian I was a racist yob, even though one of my good mates at school was Chinese. I caught this viewpoint, not from my parents, but from certain family members who had been involved in the War. As a Christian I had to rethink my motives and attitudes; because God loves all nationalities and sees us all as equal, I had to. I now do. To work with the ship visitation team was a good opportunity to get to know and help people from other cultures and ideologies.

We visited Russian ships where handing out Christian literature was to push your luck; the sailors seemed eager to receive it but the officers carried guns and were scary. On one occasion, Stan was thrown down the steep gangway and his case full of booklets pitched over the side into the oily waters of the dock. The Indian crews were very hospitable, but their accommodation was cramped and full of steam flies and cockroaches. You couldn't kill them as the Hindus believed in transmigration of souls; a roach might be a relative who'd been a bit of a bum in a previous life. I remember a song we used to march and sing along to: 'Be kind to your web-footed friends, for a duck may be somebody's mother.' I recall drinking tea on many ships with Indian crews. The cup was in fact a bean tin with the lid cut and folded back to make a handle. They always splashed condensed milk into it whether you wanted it or not and when you got to the bottom there was an extra surprise. It is almost impossible to clean a tin can without the right equipment; the bottom of the 'cup' invariably had antique squashed bean bits in the crevices; mmm tasty! On another occasion I was having tea and stale cake when a cheeky cockroach raced across the table intent on having a bite of my cake. I picked the cake up and continued to eat, then out of the corner of my eye I saw something familiar on my shoulder. I began to sweat, I couldn't knock it off in case it was someone's grandma. Fortunately it stayed where it was. When we got off the ship I looked and realised it was not a cockroach but a large blob of oil from my motorbike.

Many ships' crews were friendly towards us; they called us the

'Padre Sahibs'. One time the whole ship visiting team was invited to a meal on a Bibby Line ship called the Derbyshire. The meal consisted of a green cabbage curry, ice cold physically but chemically vicious; we all had burned mouths and lips. We had stale bread with the meal and bean-tin cups of cloudy water. What rattled me most was the tiny weevils that lived in the bread and scuttled round the plates. Our policy was to eat anything we were given and like it so as not to offend our hosts in any way. We usually never suffered any ill effects from eating all manner of weird and almost fresh delicacies. On this occasion it was different. Every team member was violently challenged, gastronomically speaking. I myself was unable to leave the house or the vicinity of the smallest room for over two days.

On another occasion we visited a ship with a Nigerian crew where a party was in progress. We were invited in and we joined a group of men playing cards. My companion asked if he could preach for five minutes if he won. The Nigerians were amused by this and let us play; we lost but they invited us to speak anyway. One of the crew had won a lottery, only a few hundred pounds or so, but better than a kick in the head. My companion, certainly not anticipating the reaction, commented, 'You could buy Lagos with that!' Big mistake! He was grabbed by the throat and thrown out of the cabin; I got up and suggested I join him. As we left the ship we heard the party restarting. John still was not too sure what he had said to offend them; perhaps the concept that their capital city had a value of a paltry few hundred quid had upset them. I made a mental note not to repeat the mistake!

The church I attended was determined to reach their neighbourhood with the Good News. Once a year they marched around the streets with the local Salvation Army brass band; they also held open-air meetings in selected streets in the vicinity of the church. The music was provided by means of a knee operated bellows organ which required a professional contortionist to operate the bellows and play the thing at the same time. This was eventually superseded by a piano accordion which gave a nice French café sound to the singing. We were singing songs that Noah would have recognised and few of us were musically talented. At a given signal from the pastor people would come up to a loud-hailer and shout out bits of the Bible, usually positive, encouraging things like, 'The soul that sinneth, it shall die!' or 'Beware your sin will find you out!' While this was going on some people knocked on the doors to distribute leaflets, some of which were an insult to a dog's intelligence. After being serenaded with, 'Bringing in the sheaves' and threatened by Bible verses promising hell and damnation, not surprisingly, very few dragged themselves away from the television and opened their doors. The next stage was the mini-sermons; two older men always said something and both had continuously running noses. Once they had pressed the microphone under their snouts, there weren't too many others wanting to follow. Christians should be prepared to tell those that want to know how to find peace in God, but shoving it down unwilling throats and ears didn't seem to be the way to go about it.

One Sunday morning a couple came to the church who looked totally out of place. Most of the congregation were done up like pox-doctor's clerks, that is Sunday Best; this couple were hippies. The man was long-haired and bearded, his wife was wearing a voluminous home-made poncho. Not quite the pork pie at the Bar Mitzvah, but different enough to have most of the congregation hyperventilating. They were definitely my kind of people: I invited them for a meal and sometime later the invitation was reciprocated. They were great people, slightly mad, which is why we got on so well, and heavily into conservation, recycling and healthy eating, well before these things became fashionable or popular. We sat down at the table. The first course was wheeled in; large bowls filled with onion rings, raw herring and vinegar. As I peered into my bowl the stench of the herring nearly made me puke. My wife grinned at me from across the table; she knew that fish was to me what Kryptonite was to Superman. I quickly devised a cunning plan; I would wait until none of their family was present so I could pocket the offending filth, pretend that I'd eaten it, then throw it down the toilet later. The opportunity never presented itself as they all sat down with us. I poked about in the bowl, digging out bits of onion, but the smell of the fish was too much. Everyone had finished and waited for me to do so. I had to confess that fish was the one thing I can't and won't eat. After a brief lecture on the benefits of oily fish, which failed to convince me, the bowl was removed and the next course arrived. At least it wasn't fish! A huge bowl of grated raw vegetables was placed in the centre of the table. the lady piled food onto my plate, explaining how cooking wrecks the vitamins. I tucked in, feeling not unlike Bugs Bunny, my jaws aching with the effort of chewing. We overdosed on raw cabbage, and as a consequence were all farting like parrots for days. The final course was also edible and different: three fig biscuits and lukewarm custard; it sounds weird but it tasted good. I had a second portion, not realising the dangers of overdosing on fig biscuits after eating raw vegetables. I am proud to confess that I did manage not to compromise my underwear, but you've only got my word for that.

When the church leaders were sure I was trustworthy, I was invited to join the youth-work team. One advantage of co-leading a youth group was the availability of help. Help with babysitting, help pushing dead cars, help with household jobs; I really should have screened the people I used though. For example, while making a concrete base for a garage we ran out of sand. A young lad helping out had a plausible alternative; he reckoned his dad often used garden soil instead of sand, claiming that soil is only worn-down rock like sand is. The idea sounded OK; it was cheap, no dragging bags of wet sand about so we tried it; big mistake! In due time a significant part of the 'concrete' base grew weeds and crumbled. Another time, two of the youth group offered to help wallpaper the kitchen. They started at different places and when they arrived together I noticed there was no match in a conspicuous place; a close inspection revealed that one of them had pasted the paper upside down. I thanked them, gave them a meal and then they went home. I had to strip the paper off while it was still damp, buy more paper the next day and do it myself. The most traumatic time was experienced when one of the group offered to help me fix the bedroom window and re-glaze it. The top of the bay window frame was rotten, so we cut it out and removed it. As we lifted it out, the ceiling of the bay collapsed and covered us with bird's nests, dead birds and living spiders. We were chasing spiders for weeks even after the job was complete. The worst part of the job was fitting the huge plate glass window, which was very heavy. We placed two ladders in position then tried to climb the ladder at the same speed while carrying the glass. Halfway up my 'helper' had a laughing spell, which set me off doing the same. How we managed not to drop the glass and chop our feet off or some other significant portions of our anatomies, I don't know.

Working with young people is very much like working with people in general: you come across the good, the bad and the ugly. Some you could trust with your life, others who would whip the gold out of your teeth if they got the opportunity. Most people are amateur psychologists; listen to most pub conversations, we all know what others should have done or expected. The truth is you think you know somebody and how they will react under certain circumstances, but life is full of surprises. The youths we worked with were mainly from Bootle, a mixed bag of backgrounds, personalities and temperaments. I often wonder what they are doing now, some forty years on and if the care and support we gave them in their teenage years made any difference to their lives.

I know all too well what one of them was like. A woman with a difficult background met us in a local supermarket many years later and told us that she had moved into the area and was having difficulty getting her son into a school. As I was a parent governor of a local school I asked the head teacher to give him a place, and so he did. Some months passed then I received a nightmare phone call, in a weird screeching voice, 'They've taken my child, so I'm going to take yours!' I recognised the voice and drove round to her house. Her mother opened the door, snarling at me, 'You've got a cheek coming round 'ere!' Before I could explain that I had no idea what had happened, the woman came running from the kitchen waving a bread-knife, but her mother, a gravitationally challenged soul, promptly sat on her and I removed the knife. It appeared that her son had turned up at school with considerable facial bruising, not for the first time, and the deputy head had phoned the 'Social' and he was taken into care. My only part in the drama was to have helped to get the kid a place in the school. Once again she promised that she would get my children and that I wouldn't get them back again. I contacted the Police, who informed me that they could do nothing until she did something; I felt totally reassured with this news; I made sure that I was early to pick the children up from school and told the teaching staff that no one else was authorised to collect them.

As the days drew on, the stress began to tell; I couldn't sleep and jumped at every knock on the door. I often drifted off to sleep, sitting on the stairs with my machete on my knee in case the mad woman broke in. A week later she 'phoned to tell me that my problems were over, she'd decided to overdose on sleeping pills. One half of my over-stretched brain said, 'About time!' but the responsible half prompted me to go and help. When I arrived at her house the door was open so I went in. She was capering about on all fours like a rabid dog and as she saw me she spat out some fifteen tablets like a hailstorm. She sat down laughing; informing me that I wouldn't get rid of her that easily. Every instinct was to kill her there and then. I was playing football twice a week and weightlifting at that time, I could have snapped her scrawny spine in seconds and I moved towards her. She stopped laughing. Then I realised what I was about to do. It wasn't that I didn't know what to do with the corpse, a drunken Hell's Angel once told me about 'the bottomless pits' on the Denbigh moors where, he claimed, the 'Government dumped nerve gas'. True or not, that wasn't the problem. I was a Christian and doubted that God would be pleased with my even considering that option. I walked out of the house to the accompaniment of more crazed laughter. My wife and I prayed, and God sorted out the problem! There is a lot more to this situation that I'm not going to reveal, but it was a trying time for all of us.

Part of the youth training strategy was to show young people that they were not the only living species on the planet. We put on parties for orphan children, helped to landscape the gardens at a large children's home and began an Old Age Pensioners project. The youth group had anyone over forty written off as useless old farts, and most of the older people in the church thought the youth were all yobs or scallies; there was some truth in both opinions! To bring a degree of age-tolerance we started visiting pensioners at home in twos, a leader with a young person. I had Harry, a sharp young man, who knew the old lady we were visiting quite well. The smell as we entered the living room was almost tangible - like the elephant house at the Zoo. We exchanged pleasantries, listened to her catalogue of ailments, aches and pains while her son, who was definitely crazy, went to get us a drink. The weather was hot and we asked for something cold. The glass was grubby, the orange squash was turbid, and strangely viscous, one sip confirmed the worst - it had not been diluted. Several choices were available: we could ask for water to be added; rather embarrassing. We could each drink a pint of water when we got home and jump up and down to dilute it, or drink it as provided; we chose the latter.

Her son, although a nut case, was a talented pianist and sat at the piano belting out some jazzy tunes of yesteryear. While musing on how to get round the undiluted drink problem, the pensioner droning on about her veins, piles and other areas of malfunction to piano accompaniment, Harry tried to change the subject and asked the pensioner, 'How's the dog? The piano playing stopped instantly. The old woman stopped like the coin-op television that runs out of credit. The atmosphere was charged. Had we been in a Western bar-room, the clients would have rushed out. She began to tell us how the beloved mongrel had gone to the dog's home in the sky some months ago. She recounted, down to the last graphic zoological details, its symptoms and final moments. Have you ever wished you hadn't asked that kind of question? Tearfully, she continued: how she missed her canine companion and how she couldn't bear to lose him, then lurching from her chair, she reached under the sofa on which we sat and pulled out the stiff, decomposing body of the dog, seething with happy maggots. 'I couldn't bear to let him go', she informed us. She let us have a good look, while we held our breaths, then she slid the corpse back underneath us and carried on with her medical history. At least it wasn't sitting in a small rocking chair like Mrs Bates à la Psycho. We let others visit her the next time, but we did warn them to ask for tea rather than orange squash!

Another way we tried to improve the relationship between old and young was to operate pensioner's days out and arrange OAP parties in the church hall. The outings to the Botanic Gardens at Southport and similar places were popular, but the organisers always took a huge tea urn and consequently most of the pensioners overdosed on tea and so needed continual visits to the toilets. The parties were less stressful in some ways but we had to provide entertainment as well as the refreshments. One year they tried community singing, which went down like a lead balloon with the pensioners. We decided to organise some humorous sketches and formed a committee to look into it. One early attempt was most successful right up to the conclusion. a friend and I were dressed as painters and decorators and set out to renovate the church hall in which the audience was seated. We swung from ropes and ladders like mad primates and amused everyone apart from the pastor, who wasn't easily amused at the best of times. Tomato ketchup butties were thrown, water splashed everywhere but we could never have predicted what happened at the end. A volunteer agreed to have a bucket of water thrown over him but as the water left the bucket, he had a change of mind; he ducked and the whole bucketful drenched a poor pensioner in a wheelchair behind him. We were no longer entertainers but ageist ruffians persecuting the disabled; we were warned by the church leaders not to make any future attempts at entertaining the aged.

I did not get where I am today by doing what others told me. The next year I had a brainwave. I had seen the old skit where a mock operation is performed shadow-style behind a white sheet and all kinds of things are apparently pulled out of the patient from bras to sausages. I devised my own version to move the old sketch into the 20th century, no sheets, no shadows, but the real thing in glorious Technicolor before everyone's eyes. A friend agreed to be the patient and I found two willing helpers from the youth group. I wore a stained white coat which became spattered with fake blood as the 'operation' proceeded. I gave a running commentary as I made the first 'incision' and a jet of red ink squirted up in the air and splattered the white coat. To simulate the cracking of the rib cage I snapped some thin pieces of wood. The intestines I removed were white balloons filled with water then covered in ketchup, most realistic. I dropped them into a white plastic bowl and they quivered convincingly. I got so carried away with my work that I failed to notice the audience reaction, which is best described as 'terminal nausea'.

Some of the pensioners had to lie down to recover, nowhere near me of course! In the course of the skit the patient 'stopped breathing' so my assistants began to inflate a large polythene bag hidden on his chest. The sheet began to rise as the bag filled with air. When it was fully inflated I was to plunge a wicked looking cooking knife into the bag and deflate it. The bag was taking so long to inflate that my 'patient' pushed it up in the air to look like it was full. Unfortunately he failed to inform me of this fact so when it looked full of air I jabbed the knife through the partly inflated bag and it went right through his hand. As a good trouper he didn't jump up and spoil the sketch, but whispered to me that I'd stabbed him. I told the assistants to end the sketch and I pretended to collapse on the floor. Instead of stopping they threw eggs and milk over me and completed the sketch at high speed. I jumped up, explained that an accident had occurred and threw a towel over Johnny's hand, which was pouring with blood. The pensioners with stronger stomachs went wild and applauded, thinking it was part of the act and screeched for an encore. I drove Johnny to the A & E department at Walton Hospital where he was duly stitched up;

fortunately the knife had passed through his hand in the same direction as the tendons without severing them. He was physically back to normal in a few months, his psychological state took a bit longer. From that day to this we refer to that particular knife as 'the Johnny knife!'

Almost a year later to the day I was asked to perform the now infamous sketch at a youth event at another church. I decided to do it with no assistants. My previous 'patient', now an ex-friend, was not interested so I recruited another lad who liked a challenge and didn't know about the accident. I added some new special effects, including a sponge soaked in a mixture of tomato ketchup and red ink, which had just the right consistency of blood. David, my new 'patient', lay on a bench with this sponge next to his head. The idea was that I explained to the audience how I was going to anaesthetise him with a mallet, then I would hit the sponge, a spray of 'blood' would appear on my coat and the patient would scream then go silent. Once again, my patient decided to ad lib and turned his head to face the sponge just as I hit it. The ink/ketchup mix splashed into his eyes and the vinegar in the tomato sauce caused him to rush from the hall to wash his eyes with water, screaming like I'd cracked his skull. My 'patient' no longer had delusions of fame as an actor and there were no takers to replace him so the show ended before it really began.. There are still people who think I really hit his head with the mallet, but some people will believe anything.

Why sail across the Atlantic? Why climb Everest? A favourite answer is 'Because it's there!' While staying in a guest house in Wales with the youth group, we visited Aber Falls. While the group admired the view and ate their sandwiches, two of us decided to climb up the waterfall, which is fairly sheer in places. Having achieved our objective, to climb that which was there, we had to get down again. To the left of the falls there is a steep scree and rock slide; we decided to descend by this route, basically because it was there. At first it was like skiing, the scree was uniform, and then came the rocks. Suddenly, I was running unable to stop, then I tripped and began to bounce down the rocky slope. I could see drops of my blood flying into the air as I rolled, with a long way to go below. In the blur I saw a sapling: I grasped it and slewed round, two fingers dislocated, and crashed into a friendly boulder - I had stopped! At first I thought I was blind, but it was just the blood in my eyes.

Instantly, I recalled a scene from my past. I was standing on the opposite side of the road hurling abuse at a 'yobbo' who was holding a large piece of slate; I concluded by informing him he was dead if he threw it. Big mistake. The dude probably did share a brain cell with his hamster, but the hamster had run off with it. As I turned, the slate hit me on the top of the head and stuck there. As I pulled it out, a torrent of my own blood flooded my eyes and as I made death threats the perpetrator escaped, but that's another story! On another occasion a kid standing on the other side of the road had a handful of dry dog turds and was throwing them across the road at us. The traffic was heavy so I couldn't run across the road and 'gob' him. I warned him what would happen if he threw any more; but he threw some as I was speaking and a large piece hit the elm tree outside our house and broke up into fragments. Most of the crappy shrapnel missed me but several bits went in my mouth. It tasted like mouldy rust so I ran into the house to swill my mouth out with water and when I came out he had gone. All I can say is dog food must taste bad if they lick their asses to take the taste away. Let's go no further down that road and return to Wales.

I cleared my eyes eventually, to see Andy, my companion approaching, white-faced. He could see what I looked like, I couldn't. My tie-dyed T-shirt was in tatters, and was now red, not multi-coloured. I spent three hours in Bangor Hospital waiting to be seen, a borrowed towel around my head. To the staff I was not an adventurer but a long-haired lout who was stupid enough to fall down a rock face. I refused the injection of anaesthetic in my scalp because I wanted to appear 'well hard', then wished I'd had it. Sixteen stitches in the scalp are not the most exciting way to spend an afternoon. The curved needle they were sewing my head with was a dead ringer for the needle I used to join a carpet at home. The various gashes on the rest of me they left to Mother Nature - just as well. The final indignity was the anti-tetanus injection. A big fat nurse, whose dislike for me sparkled like a McDonald's badge, slammed the needle high in my right buttock - right into the sciatic nerve. I had walked into the hospital but limped out, dragging my 'dead' leg behind me. When I got back to the guest house I was in trouble. The manager informed me: 'You're late for dinner.' Quite true, four hours late in fact. There were no microwaves to heat up my dinner, in fact, there was no dinner to heat up and I received almost-fresh ham sandwiches as punishment for my stupidity. I felt I'd had a bad deal although the whole incident was my own fault.

There is a tendency in most humans to shirk accountability; everything bad that happens is someone else's fault. Psychologists help to reinforce this mindset. They tell us that criminals aren't responsible for their actions: their behaviour is due to their genes or dodgy upbringing. In other words it's the parents of criminals that should be jailed, not the criminals themselves. I read somewhere that a serial killer's behaviour was possibly due to his not having had a teddy bear in his infancy; what a load of codswallop! To even things up, we are now told that badly behaved schoolchildren have Attention Deficit Hyperactivity Disorder. So it's not the kids' fault, it's not even the failure of parents to discipline or teach decent values to their offspring. Obviously parents gladly accept such a diagnosis rather than be accountable. I'm not saying every diagnosis of ADHD is spurious but it is a great get-out clause. This is my opinion but, as a chemist, I am aware of the effect of food additives like tartrazine on susceptible individuals and the way alcohol changes personalities.

Anyway, off the soapbox and on with the story. I once blamed an innocent dog to save my own neck when I was the guilty party. Several of the youth group visited a girl who was sick. As soon as we arrived the dog came in and the others made a fuss as you do. I am a cat person, not crazy about dogs unless they are cooked properly, so I just sat there. One twit found the dog's tennis ball which was covered in dog dribble and matted dog hair and launched it at me to test my reactions: my reactions failed the test and the ball smeared my T-shirt. Being a mature forgiving person I hurled the ball back at him, missed, and the ball bounced a few times then knocked over a vase containing flowers on the sideboard. The water shot over the polished surface then dripped downwards, creating a dark wet patch on the orange carpet. I stood the vase upright and replaced the flowers, then I heard big mamma coming in. 'Naughty dog', I said severely. She saw the wet patch on the carpet and believed the worst. The dog took the fall: two swipes of a rolled up newspaper and banishment to the yard. It cost me ice creams all round to keep the secret and preserve my teeth from big mamma's wrath.

One Saturday we were looking for something for the youth group to do and saw a newspaper advertisement for a 'Western-style Rodeo' taking place in North Wales. After a long search, with no directions posted, we found a field full of people. It was not exactly a western style rodeo as described; the main attraction appeared to be a huge beer tent and a few carthorses providing expensive rides to local children. The event was crowded, probably the high point of their year. Just over the field from the beer tent was a rickety pen with some cattle grizzling noisily. At a given signal the locals took it in turn to climb on the back of one of these beasts and be thrown to the ground almost instantaneously. The crowd cheered loudly as each contestant bit the dust. It can get a bit boring after a while watching idiots falling over, you can see that anytime at the circus, outside most pubs and in some churches.

I decided to visit the toilet, but where? There aren't too many bogs in the fields in the backside of Flintshire. I asked a bulbous, red-faced local and he pointed me towards the pen where the cattle were stationed. The idea of relieving myself along with the cattle did not really appeal, but as I approached I noticed a vast black polythene structure behind the pen. The 'toilet' consisted of four wooden posts laid out in a square with the black polythene stretched and tied to them. I am not too slow on the uptake, I grasped the basic principle; you had to enter the black enclosure and urinate against the plastic wall. It was a risky procedure as the 'wall' was flapping wildly with the wind, but I achieved my objective without warming my feet. To my left was a beefy cowboy resplendent in a light tan fringed cowhide jacket and western boots. I'd noticed him swaggering about earlier with a pint glass stuck to his face: the excess fluid was obviously overloading his system. As I began to move towards the exit, there was a loud cracking sound. I turned round to see one of the corner posts give way under the wind pressure. Immediately the dripping wall of plastic moved forward at high speed and totally enveloped our cowboy chum who was seeing how high he could pee when the polythene hit him. His light tan jacket was now a range of shades, so was his face as he let forth a torrent of Welsh profanities. We didn't see him swaggering around after the incident.

Some time later we had a Bible study in a mid-terrace house in Bootle. It had been foggy and very cold all day and I was surprised how many had turned up. One of the girls decided to visit the toilet, which was down the yard outside the house. As she opened the back door the fog billowed in, then there was an almighty shriek from outside. Several of us ran outside to see what was happening. Floating in the mist above us was a headless man; a closer inspection revealed a pair of long-johns, old fashioned underwear, swinging stiff as a board from the clothes line in the freezing fog. Our would-be visitor to the toilet now no longer needed the facility and had to borrow the necessary replacement clothing from her cousin who lived there.

We took many of the young people on one week holidays as most of them had poor home situations. Many guest houses and holiday centres at this time were family orientated and refused block bookings of 15 to 18 year olds which was the age range of our group. Those that did accept us were often very suspicious. One guest house in North Wales had the girls' dormitories on one floor, the boys' on another with a big dog patrolling the corridors at night. We stayed at another place where the dormitories were in adjacent buildings with the doors facing where the people in charge of the place slept. One night I saw the camp manager watching from his window, so four of us went into the girl's dormitory making a lot of noise. We then dressed up as girls and ran back into our own dormitory and got into bed. Within five minutes he arrived, searching in vain for the boys in the girl's dormitory and vice versa. As the group became older and more responsible we travelled a lot further for the youth group holidays. Devon was a popular choice as the weather was almost invariably better than it was in Liverpool. One year we took several cars and a 12-seater minibus to Ilfracombe. Several of the girls were travel sick and the paper bags they puked in had holes in them; guess who had the job of swabbing out the minibus when we arrived. It was really hot and after registering at the guest house we went for a short drive to Lee Bay before the evening meal was served. It seemed a good idea to me to walk into the sea till it came up to my neck and I did so to cool off. Each of the group decided to do the same: some Americans must have thought we were a suicide cult and scuttled to record the action on their movie cameras.

On another day we went mackerel fishing but I caught nothing; I did provide regurgitated bacon and egg as ground bait though. One lad caught three small mackerel, which he kept in the washbasin in his room all week: after a few days they smelled grim. He made some 'Out of order' signs which he fitted to all the toilets. One of the other guests, a lady with minimal sense of humour and even less tolerance of Scouse scallies, saw him fitting them and reported him to the manager. The day we were leaving he went up to this lady's room with the now rotten fish to hide them under her bed as she was staying on for an extra week. As he knocked on the door to check no one was there she opened the door. Having to think quickly, he spluttered, 'We're going home now, hope you have good holiday'. She was overcome with emotion and gave him a sloppy kiss, failing to notice the rotten fish he was still clutching behind his back, unable to read his mind or discern his real intentions.

The first time Viv and I travelled to Devon was in a beat-up old Mini when there was no M5 or Severn Bridge: it took over twelve hours to get there. Some of the hills were so steep that my passengers had to get out while the car crawled up in first gear, screaming like a banshee. When we finally arrived, totally knackered like our transport, we parked the car and went to inform the hotel manager we had arrived at last. As the visitor's book was proffered for us to sign, in a crazed moment I wrote in the book, 'Lord Russell of Bootle and party'. Tittering to myself as sad people do I went to get the cases as the girls were shown to their rooms. The girls had slept part of the way but the travel had tired me so I had a short sleep to recharge. I was rudely awakened by frenzied shaking; Viv had overheard the proprietor telling someone that they had a special guest for the week, a certain Lord Russell from the North of England, and she was worried that I might be in trouble for impersonating an important person. Some nice people are gullible, I suppose it never crossed his mind that I might be joking, but worse was to come. I went to see him before dinner and apologised for what I had written in the visitor's book. He understood that I wanted to travel incognito and promised not to make a big deal and treat me like any other guest. I think he so wanted to entertain someone of significance that I wasn't able to convince him it was a hoax. They even served our table first each night so I left him to his fantasies.

Another place in Devon we visited with the group was Exmouth. The weather was far too hot and we were all badly sunburned on the first day. We came down to dinner with shirts unbuttoned to keep cool and were informed we had to wear ties. All the lads trooped off and came back with no shirts on at all, but each wearing a necktie. The proprietors had delusions of grandeur, expecting young people to wear ties in the middle of a heat wave; the place wasn't exactly the Ritz either. One evening meal consisted of a single slice of ham that was so thin it was translucent, a single dollop of mashed potato and twelve peas. I hoped the pudding would be more substantial or it would be off to the fish and chip shop after dinner. A waitress brought in a plate with a mound of chopped red jelly flopped onto it. 'Who wants some jelly?' I shouted to the people round our table. Before they could answer, I picked up the serving spoon and struck the jelly dead centre when almost one third of it shot in every direction. All of us looked like we'd been struck with measles, with gobbets of red jelly stuck to our faces and clothing. The management were not amused. There was another youth group staying at the guest house and we got on well with them. They were in a coach with a driver, who stayed in an outhouse rather than in the main house with the rest of us. I'm not sure what he did to deserve this. One night we filled plastic 'squeezy' bottles with water and squirted him through the open window. He had a hosepipe set up all ready and soaked us, the girls, of course, were screeching as the water was cold. The noise woke up the manager who sent his wife out to tell us to keep quiet. As she came through the trees we all hid, but the driver, thinking we were returning, poked the hose through the window and totally soaked her: she was not amused.

Viv and I visited a guest house on the edge of Lake Windermere and mentioned to the management we were looking for somewhere to take a group of young people for a week's holiday. They assured us that their premises were ideal and that they were trying to get more young people to visit. The following year we booked the group in and travelled by train. We put all the cases in one taxi with one person accompanying them and the rest of us walked the mile or so to the guesthouse. After the evening meal we were informed that 'a time of fellowship' was to take place and this was a condition of staying at the place. We had to introduce ourselves then people who had a 'party piece' could share it. Some of the guests who'd been there on previous occasions persuaded the manager to sing a favourite hymn. As he belted out the words of the highly repetitive chorus, ' Nearer, draw nearer' a huge spider began to cross the room towards the part of the floor where most of the girls in the group were sitting. They began to move about and react to this large creepy crawly and eventually ran to the other side of the room. None of the other guests appeared to have seen the monster. Mr Jones warbled on, but he totally misinterpreted the reaction to the spider as reaction to his singing. He now had a problem with the younger members of our group and treated them without respect or consideration.

Where the Bugs wear Boots

One night they were all outside eating fish and chips and one of the kids saw him putting the clock forward by fifteen minutes so we were late entering the house. He grabbed Brian, my co-leader and informed him he wanted to see him first thing in the morning. I knew nothing about this until the next day. Brian looked like he'd not slept: he hadn't thanks to this bitter old git and I managed to find out what had happened. I went to see the man myself. I had all the kid's cash for the holiday in a bag and I took it with me. Before he gave me the lecture I accused him of lying when he said he wanted young people to stay, that someone had seen him adjusting the clock and if he persecuted anyone else in the group I would burn the holiday money in front of him. He took the message and kept away from us. I found out they had three canoes that they lent to guests, but never mentioned it to us. We never found the canoes but we did discover where he kept the oars. At 2.00 am one morning we crept out, got the oars and found a skiff abandoned on the lakeside. We pushed it out into the lake and assigned the first shift of rowers. It was very dark and one of the lads had a torch which he placed under his chin to make a spooky face. There seemed to be a lot of water in the bottom of the boat and I asked the lad with the torch to shine it downwards; the water level was rising rapidly then I realised that the skiff had been abandoned because it had a hole in it. We were well out in the water and Windermere has some very deep spots so we turned around and headed for the shore. By the time we sank the water was only chest high and we scuttled back to the house with the oars.

So much for the lunacy of youth work. The kids accepted me; most of the church accepted me, but what about the University? Everything worked out OK: the headmaster hadn't told them what had happened, and I was now a Christian and no longer the lunatic that had been expelled anyway. It was a few weeks before I was due to start a Chemistry degree course at Liverpool University. My best mate Dave was going to study Engineering, also at Liverpool, and our other friend Johnny had been accepted by Cambridge University. We were the only kids in the school with motorcycles and were good mates. For a week or so Johnny had been having difficulty getting his bike on the centre-stand; his doctor sent him for blood tests which indicated he had leukaemia. He went into Walton hospital and towards the end he was getting transfusions almost daily. He knew he was dying but reckoned he didn't need God. It was a Sunday morning and I was lying in bed recovering from flu when Mum answered a knock at the door. It was Dave and I knew there was something wrong; he'd just heard the news that Johnny had died. The funeral was harrowing, but funerals for seventeen year olds are always going to be. His family wanted me to see the body; I wanted to remember him on the motorcycle with his quizzical grin and love of speed, not in a wooden box coated with corpse make-up. Right at the end of the ceremony the headmaster read out a letter Johnny had written a matter of days before his death. In it he revealed he had decided to accept Christ as his saviour and embrace Christianity for the very short time he had left. Few of us are in a position to know when life is going to end; perhaps we would live differently if we did. So Johnny never got to Cambridge University, still he made it to Heaven. For Dave and I life went on, considerably emptier than before, in a matter of weeks we were first-year students at Liverpool University.

Chapter 7

University challenge

My first reaction to University was 'Welcome to the freak show!' What a collection of weirdos. Apart from a few longhairs, most had Beatle haircuts and Manfred Mann chinstrap beards, and the women were no better. We were given a pep talk informing us that we were potential makers of the future, the cream of society, individualistic geniuses. So individual that virtually every bloke wore a blue or black roll neck pullover and an Afghan coat, probably the most evil smelling clothing known to man. The camel, yak or whatever skins the coats were made of had not been cured properly, consequently the coats and the wearers smelled like a gorillas armpit and this is being very kind about it. For some students this was a distinct improvement on their normal stench. Looking at my fellow students in the faculty of science it was obvious most had swallowed the crap that we were a superior species with the world as our oyster. I saw my University education as a means to an end, to get a good job and help the family survive: since my Dad's stroke, life had been difficult. At this time there were plenty of jobs to choose from and the big companies regularly visited universities to get the pick of the so-called élite. Many students came in flashy cars and spent a great deal of time in the Students Union bar drinking, womanising or 'just floating, man!'

My GCE results were good, so good I was allowed to take my A-levels in one year instead of two. This I did and got provisionally accepted at Liverpool when I was too young to start. I chose Liverpool firstly because it was one of the best in the country for physics and chemistry (so they claimed). This choice also enabled me to live at home and help Mum cope with looking after Dad. It never crossed my mind that living at home would also mean being fed and looked after. How I envied my fellow students who wiped their noses on toilet paper, played hypothermia roulette every winter, suffered the fun of abuse by crooked landlords and had bread and Marmite for every other meal. The canteen, or refectory as they called it, was almost clean but the food was terrible. The chips were so soggy that you could see the shape of the serving scoop in the chips on the plate. The church leaders said I should be different as a Christian, including my appearance, so I wore a big black coat and black leather gloves all the time, even when I was eating. Before eating I stood up and said grace loudly: not surprisingly I sat by myself for most of the first term and was considered a total nut case by all I met and why not?

I had chosen chemistry because I was good at it and my chemistry teacher at school recommended it. For reasons discussed earlier on, I was not the most popular person in Bootle Grammar School; the staff were not queuing up to help me achieve my full potential in life. Because my A-level results were good I was allowed to miss the foundation year and start in Year 2. Big mistake! I coped but only just. As quantum theory, relativity, statistical thermodynamics and other scary topics were laid on us I realised that we had not covered large slices of the necessary mathematics that our lecturers assumed we knew. I coped by parrot memorisation and sheer luck until my mind caught up. At least the course taxed the brain. There was such a concentration of information that I began to doubt if my brain could absorb it all. Our organic chemistry textbook was written by Louis Fieser, an American chemist who was the inventor of Napalm. Nice to be famous! For inorganic chemistry I had to buy two enormous volumes, Sidgewick parts 1 and 2, which were unbelievably heavy. These books were useful as steps when I needed to get things from the top of my wardrobe.

Most of the lecturers were brains on legs, acknowledged experts in their fields, but many could not communicate for monkey nuts. We listened, we made notes and we read the notes, wondering what it was all about. In all my years at school and university, no one ever taught me how to study; I had to devise my own way of assimilating information to cope with the amount we had to learn. This became the basis of the Structured Learning course, which I published many years later and is described in Chapter 12.

The Donnan Laboratories at Liverpool University were fairly new: clean, bright and well stocked but at the beginning of term you had to pay a deposit which was used to pay for any breakages of glassware stored in individual 'glass cupboards'. We were issued with flasks, beakers, condensers etc. and now and again I found certain items missing or broken. I realised that amongst my fellow students there were thieving bastards. I do have a vigilante streak and at first decided on a witch-hunt to find the missing items and punish the miscreant; this was a waste of time because one beaker looks very like the next one. Another option was to coat all my glassware with a fluorescent dye and test every student, ninety in my group, with a ultra-violet source: quite a big job. I even considered trapping a rottweiler in my glass cupboard and performing a finger count if anything went missing: again not very sociable or practical. I ultimately devised a method which was 100% effective. I decided not to wash any glassware I used and left it encrusted and suppurating in the cupboard. If I wanted a piece of equipment I cleaned it before using it. This masterpiece of psychology worked, most students are lazy, why bother stealing dirty glassware then having to clean it when others keep their stocks nice and clean? I applied the same psychological technique to the security of one of my cars. It was old and scabby, not unlike myself, it had been sprayed with a contrasting colour, had wipers and aerial removed, it had been scratched and even shot through a headlight, but it was never stolen: it was too mangy to steal.

There were loads of societies one could join; the bell ringers, debating, chemical, various sports and some Christian ones. Maybe I'm just antisocial but after spending all day with chemistry students, the idea of spending my 'spare time' with these berks was as attractive as eating candy floss in the elephant house at the zoo. I was at University to get a meal ticket, not to socialise with a bunch of misfits from every corner of the globe. I did once attend a Debating Society meeting but left after less than thirty minutes; the ramblings of self-opinionated tosspots did my head in; I remember thinking, 'If these are the future of the country, lets emigrate now!' This viewpoint was further confirmed by the rag week behaviour. One group of idiots sabotaged the Tommy Steele pantomime at the Empire Theatre, full of children and enraged parents. Our faculty just walked out of a class in a long line and down the hill into the Liverpool City centre, round the shops then back again. Such creativity and over-the-top behaviour so impressed me that I went home to fix the gearbox on my motorcycle.

When I could afford it I visited the Golden Phoenix Chinese restaurant on Leece Street. The meals were cheap and always hot and tasty, which was more than could be said for the waitresses. After every meal I was always high as a kite thanks to the mono-sodium glutamate and tartrazine they spooned into the food. MSG is a so-called flavour enhancer, it works by making the salivary glands work overtime; it also causes headaches, nausea and breathlessness, the symptoms known as Chinese Restaurant Syndrome in the medical profession. Tartrazine is an azo dye used to colour food and it causes allergic reactions and asthmatic attacks in those sensitive to it.

Two memorable occasions come to mind in the Golden Phoenix. I was tucking into my lunchtime special one day when a bearded Captain Birdseye look-alike entered and ordered a meal. As soon as it arrived he gobbled it up, ordered apple pie and custard and disposed of this at speed also. Within seconds of his last mouthful he was out of the door and running down Leece Street towards the city centre. Within a few more seconds three of the kitchen staff came running out of the kitchen and raced down the street after him, each one waving a sharp instrument. By the time they got back I had returned to the university chemistry laboratories, having paid for the meal but not the entertainment. The second memorable occasion was the first time I experienced the Golden Phoenix's custard. For some reason they never used any milk when making it, so it appeared as a transparent golden fluid: it tasted like custard but looked like Shell Viscostatic motor oil.

My Dad died a few weeks before my first year exams. I found the funeral difficult; I loved my Dad, but the state he was in after the second stroke convinced me he was better off dead. The real problem was the relatives and other parasites that attended the funeral and the nosh after it. As I indicated earlier, we were not exactly besieged by helpers in the difficult times after my Dad was no longer able to work. It annoyed me to see these patronising leeches eating their ham and tongue sandwiches, with little fingers raised and their Crosby accents, saying the right nice things - but where were they when he needed them? I stood up as if to make a speech and everybody stopped eating. I informed those who never came to visit or help out that I hoped they'd choke on their free nosh! I sat down sharply as my Mum pulled at my jacket. I passed my first year exams, not as well as I would have liked but they did allow for my state after the bereavement.

In the summer holidays I applied for a number of temporary positions and spent summer 1960 as an analytical assistant in the laboratories of a local factory. On my first day I was asked to report to the stores to get a 'long weight'. I instantly realised it was an initiation rite, a mickey-take. I happily played along, called at the canteen to get tea and toast then came back twenty minutes later so my 'betters' could have a cheap laugh at my expense. In the afternoon I was sent for a bucket of steam so I got a bucket, put some hot water in the bottom and dropped a piece of dry ice (solid carbon dioxide) into it. When I returned with a bucket of 'steam' the cretins were mystified and forgot to send me for the statutory left-handed screwdriver. After the stringent safety standards and almost clinical cleanness of the university laboratories, I was in for a shock in the real world of industrial chemistry. Rubber gloves, safety spectacles and correctly fastened protective clothing were alright for wimps; but real men had fingers missing, and eyes like fried eggs with pirate patches. I was the temporary lab rat (a euphemism for an assistant) and as such got all the good jobs: making tea for the chemists, clearing up spillages, carrying hydrogen cylinders around and taking the blame for other people's omissions or mistakes. The factory premises were dusty, dirty and dangerous, but the factory inspectors never called during my eight weeks sentence: apparently they always informed the company when they were coming so that any condemning evidence could be disposed of. I know a number of people who trained as teachers, then changed career direction after seeing what teaching in the real world was like during teaching practice. My two months of vacation work made me question the wisdom of a career in the chemical industry. Before I could think too much about it the first term of the second year had started. I wondered if I had taken the right course; the english and media studies students seemed to have a good time, like watching movies then writing essays about them. The only part of the course that I enjoyed was organic chemistry. All the lecturers were good communicators and the subject was interesting. As you might expect, the subject I liked most was the subject I was best at. Every job I got after I graduated was based on some aspect of organic chemistry.

I was and still am what my American friends call a rat biker. Improperly dressed in anything waterproof and insulated, riding old motorcycles with oil dripping from every orifice, I'm talking about the motorcycle of course! I never cleaned my machine from day one, but I did put a drip tray under the engine to catch the oil slick that formed daily. What mattered was that I was on two wheels and not four, not that I subscribed to this philosophy when pushing it all the way home from Southport with a flat tyre in the dark. My mate, Dave, had an old BSA C11, the bike I passed my driving test with. The paintwork was drab maroon but the bike was in good condition. The seat cover was ripped in several places so the bike was kept under an overhang with a tarpaulin over the seat to keep out the rain and avoid wet bottoms. Dave had transferred to the same course I was on so we rode into Liverpool together on most days. One morning I called for him and he wheeled the bike out of the back yard. Unknown to us, the local tomcats had got under the tarpaulin in the night and used his sponge seat as a pissoir. Dave kick-started the bike, moved off then braked sharply. I caught up with him, his face was a mask of anger and horror. As he had sat down, his weight had compressed the sponge and released several pints of ice cold TCP, or tomcat urine, through his denims and into his boots. We were running late as usual so we had to continue our journey. He sat by himself in the lecture hall that morning; isn't it strange how something that amuses one person can have totally the opposite effect on someone else?

One very cold morning I was on my way to the University and approaching the weird kink in the road opposite the Princess Cinema on Southport Road. The cinema is now a Bingo emporium and the bend in the road has long been straightened out. A scooter was slowly spinning to a stop on its side and the rider was sitting on the floor holding his head. My brother Dave had a scooter so I had no real animosity towards owners of squeak machines. I considered stopping to help but I was running a bit late so I accelerated as I hit the patch of invisible black ice which the scooter rider had found. The bike went over, the petrol cap came off as it bounced along and petrol spewed out. The bike was spinning on the footrest and throwing up sparks; I slid along the ice, right through the petrol until I ended up against the kerb. I was soused in cheap petrol and fully expected to do a Buddhist monk routine. Whether an angel extinguished the sparks, or the ice cooled the petrol to below its flash point is a subject for discussion. I decided to return home and not push my luck too far as most of the students in my group were fag-heads and I was highly inflammable.

When the motorcycle was indisposed I travelled to the University by bus, the 57, 58 or 59 to the Old Haymarket, by the Mersey Tunnel entrance. I then walked up St John's Lane past Lime Street station and the Adelphi Hotel on the left, and the fabulous Palais de Luxe on the right. The Palais was a favourite cinema which put on special 'seasons' like the 3 Stooges, Abbot and Costello and Norman Wisdom films. It had an amazing metal sculpture of a film camera man outside, when the place was pulled down I wanted it for our front room, but it vanished, possibly to Riversdale College. From the Palais I had four options depending on whether I wanted to visit specific shops, or if I was bored with any particular route. Copperas Hill was a bit out of the way but taking this route I could visit Auntie Gertie's shop for a cuppa then turn right at Russell Street, named after me, then left at Brownlow Hill and up the hill to the Student's Union. This also meant passing Tong's fish & chip shop, a favourite stop around dinner-time. Some days I'd just walk up Brownlow Hill, quite a boring ascent but probably the most direct. The last alternative was much longer but more entertaining. I used to walk right across from the Adelphi and walk along Renshaw Street.

On University rag days, the statue outside Lewis's sported knickers or painted privates instead of being exceedingly bare. It occurs to me that some readers may not be local so I'll explain the statue reference. Lewis's is a large store and many years ago had a sculpture of a naked male ship's figurehead erected outside the store; I'm not too sure why. Some years later a popular song celebrated this fact, along with the two cathedrals and Scouse accent. For your interest I reproduce the only verse I've heard, in its Scouse phonetic version.

In me Liverpewl 'ome.
In me Liverpewl 'ome.
We speak wiv an accent exceedin'ly rer,
Live under a statue exceedin'ly ber,
If yer wanna cafeedral, we've got one ter sper
In me Liverpewl 'ome

But I digress: at the top of Renshaw Street I then went left up Leece Street. In summer it was advisable to stay on the left-hand side of the road because the public toilets on the right were a major health hazard in hot weather. Anyway, the restaurants, car sales showrooms and coffee bars were on the left side of the road. Then it was right at Hope Street past the Philharmonic pub with its impressively large, antique urinals which always flushed at the exact moment someone was using them, past the large building containing the synchro-cyclotron up towards the metropolitan cathedral and on to the Students Union. For two long years most of my time was spent in the Donnan laboratories, later renamed the Robert Robinson laboratories, why I don't know.

Maybe Dr Donnan upset someone.

Auntie Gertie's shop was a tall two storey building sticking up like a tower on a piece of waste ground almost opposite Tong's fish 'n' chip shop. It looked weird because the shops on either side had been knocked down. Gertie's shop was spooky. It had gas lighting, very bright but unflattering to the human complexion; Gertie and her sister Ivy looked undead, a whiter shade of pale. In the basement was a wizened dwarf of a man, Mr Smee, whose large head and hairy red nose always made me feel the Christmas spirit. He was a joiner but I never saw right inside his workshop; I imagined him making toys for the children with the help of his fellow gnomes. On darker days I wondered if he used the toys to attract daft kids into his shop where he pickled them in malt vinegar and sold them to Tong's chip shop. At street level there was an entrance to the shop with rails and hangers everywhere. There was never anyone there, but a bell rang when the door was opened and they could see into this part of the shop by means of two huge mirrors clamped on the spiral staircase. This part of the shop smelled like a public toilet; on one happy occasion Auntie Gertie explained why. Many of the customers were incontinent; others choosing not to wear underwear and consequently presenting horribly skidded trousers for alteration or repair. She and Auntie Ivy had to repair or alter them in the state they arrived in. She invited me to sniff a few samples but I insisted that I believed her story and scuttled upstairs to eat my dinner.

Whenever I was near the shop at dinner-time I got a pie and chips from Tong's and climbed the stairs as quickly as possible, firstly because I was hungry, secondly to escape the toilet atmosphere and thirdly to avoid meeting the old goblin in the basement; even though I was eighteen, tall and fairly tough, he scared me. One night I was delayed at a meeting, the bike was off the road and I decided to walk down Brownlow Hill. As I passed by Tong's I observed a large ginger tom-cat sleeping on top of the pies in the window. I suppose it was to keep the pies warm and keep the mice off them at the same time. Clever! I determined to find an alternative chippy.

The sewing machines in Gertie's shop were the antique treadle type; on a rush job my Aunties' knees went up and down in unison, like a machine gun. They were so proficient they could run a seam at high speed and hold a conversation as well. One day Auntie Gertie was hammering away on the machine and turned towards me like Winifred Attwell used to do when playing the piano, to ask me to put the kettle on. Suddenly something went wrong, the machine came to a halt with a jerk and Gertie was squealing like a pig. The needle had gone through her thumbnail and was sticking out of the fleshy part on the other side. Ivy was swooning and retching while Gertie, cool as a cucumber after her initial screech, told me to borrow a screwdriver from Mr Smee. Fighting my fears of the occult I descended the stairs into the workshop to borrow the screwdriver that would free Auntie Gertie from the machine. She went off to hospital with the needle firmly fixed in her thumb. She told me it had happened before and they would get it sorted. I returned to the laboratories for the afternoon practical sessions.

Throughout my spell at university I was sneezing and wheezing. Every time I caught a cold I ended up with a sinus infection; sinus headaches don't help study overmuch. My doctor blamed this on the new germ pool I had entered and prescribed a few nasal sprays, all of which failed to work. He decided to send me ultimately to the ear, nose and throat hospital for a sinus wash. I often sit and think, but sometimes I just sit. Thinking about the 'sinus wash' and the ENT hospital I wondered if the urology section in our local hospital was in fact called the Willy Ward. Apart from my BCG inoculation, and a short spell of treatment when my brother had para-typhoid, this was my first in-depth experience of the medical profession. It sounded harmless enough; I didn't think too hard about where the sinuses were and how one would wash them. I arrived at the Ear Nose and Throat hospital on the day appointed and was shown into an open hallway where thirteen people sat in line on a set of benches, each one with several chromed wires protruding from their nostrils. It reminded me of a book I had read about the ancient Egyptians. The embalmers used to remove the brains of the deceased via the nose with a metal probe: some of the characters in the queue looked like they had experienced this treatment in the past. Minutes later I was in a side room having the wires holding a Novocaine-soaked swab shoved up my beak also. The people in the queue in front of me were summoned one at a time and I never saw them again; I assumed there was an alternative exit or the Aliens had abducted them. In time I too was ushered into a room with beds where people were lying horizontally, the wires still sticking out of their nostrils. An oldish guy in a white coat came in, probably a doctor, and did something to each of the others in turn, but I couldn't see what. Then it was my turn. The silver wire was removed and a gadget resembling a knitting needle was shoved up my nose, so far that I could hear it crunching into the bone, but at least I couldn't feel it. The middle bit was removed and a large syringe full of white liquid was attached to the metal tube still protruding from my nose. He operated the syringe, I could feel the warm liquid sloshing around inside my head and face as it raced through the sinuses; suddenly it started pouring into the back of my throat and I retched. The doctor was looking for this reaction and quickly pulled the syringe and fitting from my nostril, shoved a shiny metal kidney dish under my nose and the nurses heaved me into a sitting position. With a slurp all the liquid plus a load of unwholesome greb shot into the dish.

I had a flashback: I recalled a party where someone made me laugh while I was eating trifle and a load of it went up the back of my throat. I suggest you don't try this at home, it's very painful. About an hour later I sneezed into a handkerchief and, lo and behold, a small portion of sherry trifle; slightly more palatable than the contents of the shiny dish still pressed against my face. The treatment was effective, I had no sinusitis for three or four months then back it came. The doctor informed my Mum that we would need to move to somewhere like Florida to solve my sinus problems, but he refused to give us a prescription for the treatment.

As the second year ended I began a temporary job in a local laboratory. The conditions were much better than the grim laboratories of the year before. The labs were better equipped and I was treated as a chemist and not the tea boy. Nevertheless I was treated to one of the initiation rites that most laboratories used to operate. As I entered the laboratory on my first morning, I noticed a crowd of white-coated people standing in a circle watching a scruffy youth who had a large cork balanced on his forehead which he was attempting to catch in a plastic funnel stuck in the waistband of his trousers. After many pathetic attempts he succeeded and someone else had a go. It seemed rather juvenile and so, when they asked me if I wanted to have a go, I accepted the challenge. The funnel was placed in my belt, the cork was placed on my forehead and simultaneously a beaker full of ice water was poured into the funnel. Gotcha! I knew I was going to enjoy working there!

In the second year at university we had been studying wave

mechanics, atomic physics and the kinetics and mechanisms of organic reactions; this stuff seemed almost transcendental. My vacation work was basic analytical chemistry, very repetitive but important to the company, and it brought me a wage for several months.

This company had one member of the laboratory staff who was a weightlifter and a bit of a bully. He left me alone for several weeks, but it annoyed me to see him pushing other people around. One day he decided to show me what he could do. Grasping me by my shirt, and another member of staff in the same way he straight-lifted us both up without any effort at all. He let us go and as we landed, four or five shirt-buttons bounced round the floor. This guy was six foot six, built like a brick toilet and mean with it. He grinned at me as if to say,' What you going to do, about that, college boy?' I tucked my shirt back in, borrowed a safety pin from one of the girls and got on with my work. It was my turn to make the tea and coffee and this I did, even for the bully boy. He was most impressed with my servility and never saw the payback coming. Two days later we were told he was in hospital with suspected dysentery. When he returned to work he was white as a sheet and had to perch on a rubber ring for comfort. His mysterious symptoms had begun with diarrhoea, but eventually he was passing large quantities of blood. The symptoms were not a mystery to me! His face was a picture as I explained over coffee that he'd been my guinea-pig for a day and that I'd doped him with a mega dose of an interesting organic laxative. Before he could grab me I got the other side of the bench and explained quickly that there was a world of interesting chemicals he would be sampling if he gave me any more grief. He got the message. I had no more trouble with the dude but he never let me make his coffee again. Like the previous year, the vacation work seemed to be over very quickly and the final term was about to commence; my interest was flagging at a rapidly increasing rate. I played football for a team that demanded I attend a practice during the week in order to be picked to play. I was also playing the guitar and practising with some other musicians with a view to forming a band and I wanted to spend as much time as I could with my girlfriend.

The Final Exams were held in a cold gymnasium on Grove Street, which was originally a church. One student walked into the hall, looked at the paper for a few seconds then walked out: three years of his life down the tubes. No re-sits or similar second chances. At the degree ceremony I had to hire a 'gown' which might have fitted a smaller person but so hunched up my shoulders that I looked like Quasimodo receiving his BSc, consequently I refused to have my picture taken. I had done the bare minimum of work in my final year at university and, not surprisingly, I did not obtain the grade of degree I was capable of, but I could now get a job and make some money.

Chapter 8

Work, Work, Work!

All the big companies visited the universities to interview prospective graduate staff, the only company that I fancied working for was Kodak Ltd. I had an interview which was unsuccessful. After a number of application rejections I was offered an interview with a company I'd never heard of. The job description was Development Chemist; the salary was £900 a year to start, some £400 less than the Kodak starting salary, but they promised increases in pay and status if my work was satisfactory, so I took the job.

The company had an interesting structure; directors, senior staff, staff and workers and each of these levels had their own toilets, cloakrooms, canteens and locker rooms with strict rules of segregation applied. The staff toilets were ten minutes away on the far side of the factory but the senior staff toilets were just outside the laboratory in which I worked. I got hold of a key, made a wax impression and had my own key made: I could now relieve myself when I felt like and in relative luxury. This was only to last for a few months. A senior staff spy reported my presence in the 'Holy of Holies' and my line manager sent for me. He informed me that I'd made a bad start. I was not servile enough, I was pissing in a place reserved for my betters and I was mixing with the wrong kind of people: he was referring to the fact that at lunchtime I played football with the builders and electricians in a field just outside the factory site. No mention of the significant development work I had done for the company, but there was a reason for this. Apart from misuse of the toilets and associating with riff-raff, another factor was evident. I answered to the assistant chief chemist who selected the projects I worked on, supervised my work and took all my reports and had my name replaced with his own, quite a common procedure in Research and Development. He was the very first person to take credit for what I had done, but was certainly not the last. It became obvious that the promises of pay rises and promotion were merely figments of someone's imagination.

Where the Bugs wear Boots

I started looking for a better job and found that most jobs similar to mine were paying at least £500 a year more. Once again I had many rejections without even an interview or a 'we regret' letter, then I got an interview at the Adelphi Hotel. Any decent company would have hired a room at the hotel and conducted interviews therein, but many cheapjack companies had another, cheaper method. The interviewers hung about in the vast lounge, bought an overpriced coffee now and again and conducted the interviews in the lounge. I arrived ten minutes early and reported to reception as instructed in the letter. People came and went but no-one called out my name. After an hour I decided to go home and got up to tell the desk clerk. A bloke in a suit was in front of me and as he was being attended to I heard my name mentioned. I told him who I was and we went into the lounge for my interview. I'd noticed him coming and going with others, but several companies were conducting interviews that day and no one had called out my name. He explained what had happened: my rate of pay was so poor for my age and qualifications that he was 'expecting a coloured applicant' and not seeing one had assumed I was late or absent. This says a lot about society at that time, the whole equal rights thing and the company I was working for.

Now and again my girlfriend and I would go into the city centre for a meal, usually at the Squealing Dog in Victoria Street. In case you are interested, this is not the real name of the restaurant. The meals were edible, cheap and not excessively dosed with monosodium glutamate. We had a favourite table near the entrance, not so we could do a runner when the bill arrived, but to eat in a stream of relatively clean air as there were no 'no smoking' areas at this time. One evening we arrived to find a scabby couple sitting at our table; the woman was eating like she had a Guinness record to defend, the bloke was eating and smoking at the same time. I was so impressed with these dudes that I wrote a poem about them, but you'd have to buy one of my poetry booklets to read it.

My first thought was to eat somewhere else, but it was raining heavily, so we found an alternative table against the back wall, parallel with the swinging door to the kitchens. We ordered and waited. The demon fag-head was now eating his sherry trifle with his cigarette jammed in the corner of his mouth. Suddenly our attention was diverted as a waiter dropped a glass on the floor just as he kicked the kitchen door open and we saw into the kitchen for the first time since we had been patronising the place. There were no dogs hanging up waiting for currification or kebabbing; although there were urban myths of hygiene inspectors finding dog corpses in some restaurant freezers. The kitchen looked fairly clean; the 'chef' was another story: he was stripped to the waist, from the neck down I'm glad to report, with a sack tied around his waist with string. He was built like a zeppelin and resembled a poor man's sumo wrestler. Just as the waiter picked up the last glass fragment and the door was swinging shut, we saw our bulbous chef scratching his considerable tits then wiping his greasy hands on the sack round his waist. We had lost our appetite, and that's unusual for me, so we went back to Viv's for cheese on toast.

Viv lived in a cul-de-sac off a cul-de-sac with her parents. There was a short cut through a green door by the Sefton Arms which was kept locked, but privileged residents had a key. The door led through a dark, leafy pathway, a real mugger's delight and few used it at night. We were coming home from Aintree station at about 10.30 one night, trying to beat the 10.00 curfew imposed by her parents. As we opened the green door I heard a noise behind it. We had been to see an action movie and the thought of bashing a would-be mugger appealed greatly. I swung the door open with a bang, pulled it shut then slammed it back again for good measure. Unfortunately there was no mugger, just a harmless young couple having a quiet snog. As I jumped through the opening I found them lying in the nettles where the door had knocked them. As we were late we just kept going and hoped they would recover soon from their earth moving experience.

At university a big deal was made of recognising toxic or hazardous chemicals and understanding how to handle them: many of the chemicals used on my employer's premises were extremely dangerous. I noticed how many of the women in the factory were pale with purple blotches on their arms; my Auntie Clara used to call them 'dead men's pinches'. When I found they were cleaning with a solvent mixture including trichloroethylene and benzene, I reported this to the department manager and was told in no uncertain terms to mind my own business and warned to stay out of the department. Other areas of the factory were equally hazardous. All the dyestuffs and resins were blended in a filthy dump called the Mixing Room. The atmosphere was always heavy with solvent vapour and dust; the workers were given primitive dust-masks which were virtually useless in protecting from very fine particles or solvent vapours. Many had a scary cavalier approach to safety and did not wear safety equipment; on the few occasions I visited this department I was frequently greeted by process workers quacking and doing chicken impressions. I often wondered how many of them ended up in hospital as a reward for their stupidity.

One of the dyes used was Rhodamine B500, which was used for years as the colouring for the lettering and outside coating of Blackpool Rock. This material is highly carcinogenic, specific to the lips, tongue and bladder. Fortunately a bright doctor in the Fylde area observed the connection between lip and tongue cancer patients and workers in the rock factory and a safer alternative was found. Whenever it rained at five o' clock you could recognise mixing room personnel by the fluorescent pink streaks running down their faces as the rain dissolved the dye on their hair and faces. It was not uncommon to hear what sounded like thunder, but it was only a minor explosion somewhere in the factory. For some reason I could never understand, the Factory Inspectorate always told the company when they were coming, when there would be a mad panic to clear away the crud and dodgy materials.

There were several unpleasant initiation rituals for newcomers in the engineering department which, in reality were gross disregard for the Health and Safety at Work Act, non-existent at this time. New apprentices were stripped naked, dunked in used motor oil, rolled in sawdust then hoisted from a crane and left swinging some twenty feet in the air for a given length of time. The previous ritual, insertion of a compressed airline up the rectum of the happy newcomer, went out of fashion when several initiates suffered ruptured bowels as a result of the stupidity. Humouring such people was not an option: I made it plain from day one that jokes at my expense would result in severe injury for all those involved and it worked, but I was then considered a misery guts and spoilsport; so what's new? The working conditions were bad, the pay was poor for all but the process operators and they only got good money by working every hour they could, but something kept them happy.

It was, of course, the social club at the far side of the site which had an impressive bowling-green, a large outdoor area set out with tables and, more importantly, subsidised (cheap) beer. At the back of the bowling-green were the storage tanks where the solvents were stored. One fateful day a tanker driver connected his vehicle to one of the tanks and left it pumping hundreds of gallons of solvent into a tank that didn't have enough room for it all. The driver was sitting at the back of the social club imbibing the amber nectar as the overflowing solvent poured across the bowling green destroying the grass in minutes. It was several years before the grass grew back, even after the topsoil had been replaced. This gave the workers a real problem, they'd have to go home to their families or find somewhere else to get drunk on the cheap; what a calamity!

The stools in the laboratory were four legged with a carrying slot in the seat. Someone rigged up a hosepipe under the stool used by the oldest female assistant who was pregnant and generally miserable. When the water was turned on, the range of expressions through which her face passed were amazing. Then, without warning, she leaped off the stool and the jet of water hit a lamp which shattered and rained bits of glass everywhere. She ran off to the boss and told him what I had done; there was a slight problem with that - I hadn't done it! It was like going back in time to school. Being blamed when you have done something is bad enough; to be blamed when you haven't is a lot worse. I decided I owed her one. The general low morale extended to all the female staff. They were creatures of habit; you could set your watch by the precise time the four of them went to the toilet or visited the canteen together. When they went off for dinner I entered the women's rest room, placed all the toilet seats upright, which in itself was guaranteed to get them in a great mood, then applied a quantity of moist nitrogen tri-iodide to the seat pads. This material is a very unstable explosive, just-about stable when moist, but explosive when dry: I've seen a small quantity explode at the touch of a feather. When the women returned thirty minutes later the explosive was dry. They all trooped into the toilet, then there was an outcry. One of them shot out of the toilet like a Ninja to identify the male desecrator of their hallowed premises, but before she could demand an explanation for the upright seats and consequent violation of their khazis, there was a succession of loud explosions as several of the seats were lowered. Several of the lovely ladies now no longer needed the toilet anymore and were not thankful at all. I was threatened with the sack and worse for this one; they knew it was me because no-one else in the laboratory knew any real chemistry.

One day I was writing up a report in the main laboratory when I heard a shout from the adjacent development lab. The operator of a huge slow moving machine had dropped his pen into the machine and had removed the safety cover to retrieve it. As he fished around, one of the moving rollers had gripped his finger and was slowly pulling his hand into the machine. The 'Off' switch for the machine had been cleverly positioned on the other side of the machine so I ran round to the far side and switched it off. He continued screeching, began to sway then passed out. I had to grab him to prevent his whole weight, which was considerable, from dangling from his hand which was firmly gripped. I called out for help but it was a tea break and no one was around. He began to come around and started squealing again. I could hear a slow dripping sound and at first thought his bladder was taking the easy way out, but as it splashed down slowly and seeped from the machine casing I could see it was blood. I raced back into the main lab, picked up a Stanley knife and returned to the captive who fainted again as he thought I was going to amputate his hand. By now I had found an assistant to support his weight while I cut through the drive belt that powered the rollers and then reversed them to get his fingers out. Three of them had burst with the pressure and were now spouting blood everywhere. I 'bandaged' them up with duck tape, threw him over my shoulder in a fireman's lift and took him to the nurse. His fingers were saved and although I didn't expect a medal, I thought my actions might have been appreciated. This was not to be: the drive belt I had chopped cost several hundred pounds and the management informed me I should have called out an engineer and left him there bleeding. I went from hero to zero.

Lunch time was far from a welcome break from work. Some days it took all my self-control and concentration not to kill everyone in the canteen. The food was horrific, the chips so soggy that the heap on the plate was moulded to the shape of the shovel they served them up with; it was like being back at university. The atmosphere was smoky: some sad addicts ate their sandwiches with a cigarette stuck in the corner of their mouths. I sat at a table under an open window with a group of boring 'anoraks', but at least they were non-smokers. One office worker had two irritating topics of conversation. He would recount everything he had done that morning, like any of us gave a monkey's toss, then update the continuing saga of his catarrh and sinus infections in a graphic way. He had no life, so I decided to help him. His wife always made his sandwiches yuppie-style; no crusts and cut into triangles, so I prepared some expanded polystyrene ceiling tiles to fit. He entered the canteen, sought out the cleanest plate he could find, placed his sandwiches on the plate then went to the serving hatch for his cup of weak tea. I quickly fitted the polystyrene supplement to his sandwiches. Not surprisingly he was not too happy with the sandwich quality but ate them without opening them. As a would-be yuppie he would never inspect the interior of a sandwich, or lower himself to open one up to add potato crisps or inspect the contents like lesser mortals. Worse was to come: because expanded polystyrene is a cellular matrix of gas bubbles it is unsinkable, as his next few bowel motions would be. The thought of his unsuccessful attempts to flush the floaters round the toilet S-bend kept me amused for several days.

He, however, showed no improvement and continued to spoil our lunch breaks by grizzling on about work: it was time for the Full Monty. I had some trade samples of hydroxy-ethyl cellulose, an additive used in the food industry to thicken catering products; a spoonful in a cup of hot coffee made it set like rubber. The industrial grade was used to thicken emulsion paint and was the basis of most wallpaper adhesives, but the pure grade was used to thicken salad cream and mayonnaise. By careful adjustment of the water content and amount of green food dye I created a quantity of synthetic but edible 'nasal mucus'. Just before dinner I filled a rubber bulb with the stuff and connected the bulb with rubber tubing to a nozzle wedged under my watch strap. I waited patiently for Sam to get round to his sinus report then complained I was having similar problems myself. As he picked up a sandwich I feigned a sneeze and pressed the rubber bulb sharply. A jet of pale green gelatinous greb splashed onto the plate in front of me. 'Sorry', I remarked then put a spoon into the 'mucus' and ate it. There was not a dry pair of knickers at the table, three of them from laughing as I had forewarned them. Sam however stood up, regurgitating his dinner in what is known on the street as a 'four-finger-split'. I never knew if he stopped discussing work or his sinuses because he stopped sitting at our table. Fait accompli!

The main part of the factory consisted of rows of 10 metre high machines. Highly paid operators continuously manned these machines. If an operator required a break for any reason, he was not allowed to move until someone replaced him at the machine. The operators were a wild bunch. They all carried vicious knives made from ground-down power hacksaw blades, ostensibly for cutting tangles free and keeping production flowing. The rows of ovens were connected by interlinking gantries and an exceptionally dangerous endless belt lift that one had to jump on and off as required. The operators capered about the structures like the inhabitants of the primate house at the zoo. Office girls walking through the factory were the prime target for their simian behaviour; shouting obscenities, screeching and banging their metal cups on the metalwork. One day one of the female lab assistants got an electric shock from one of the old test ovens. I heard the crash as she dropped the glass desiccator she was carrying. The laboratory assistant next to me saw her twitching before she collapsed and reckoned she was doing a dance called the Monkey, a current variation of the Twist. I rang the works nurse who refused to come over to the laboratory as she was having her tea break, but suggested we put the unfortunate assistant on a stretcher and bring her over to the surgery. We found a stretcher eventually and placed her thereon. The quickest route to the surgery was through the enamelling shop so we set off to get her to the nurse as soon as possible. All the operators were banging their cups and chanting, 'Parrot's dead!' Remarkably she survived the shock.

I owned a pair of boring tan slip-on shoes, but I'd bought a mustard yellow suit and fancied shoes to match. Viv found a suitable shoe dye and I took the bottle to work, wearing my tan originals. At lunch time I removed my shoes, coated them with the dye and waited. They were still not dry after half an hour, then I had a flash of inspiration. We had ovens running at different temperatures, so I put my shoes in the one with an empty shelf without checking the temperature. I had a report to write so I left them in the oven for several hours. Just before home time I removed my shoes to cool them down before putting them on. I found myself holding the uppers; the soles remained on the oven shelf. They must have been cheap with no stitching and the heat had softened the adhesive. They were now dry, mustard-yellow as required but I now had a pair of spats, not shoes. I wrapped wire round the two pieces on each foot to get me across the car park, but as shoes they were a write off.

With time we all put on a bit of weight, that's my story and I'm sticking to it. As I write I'm over sixteen stone; when I played football regularly I was more like twelve. Playing in winter with minimal blubber to insulate me was grim: cold feet, cold hands, cold everything. I recall the exciting slap of a blocked shot on the inner thigh from a waterlogged football at 70 mph plus. A friend suggested rubbing horse liniment on the exposed areas, so I obtained some and decided to improve it. I added a fair splash of methyl nicotinate, a chemical used in most embrocation products that opens up the capillaries and heats the skin, making it bright red. Just before going out from the changing rooms across the shopping centre to the pitch, yes we are not talking big-time soccer, I coated my arms and legs with the mixture which began to heat up immediately. I went to wash my hands; the only sink in the place had no water supply so I wiped them on my shirt. The fumes made my eyes sting so I lay horizontally until just before Kick Off. My brother Dave decided to try some as well: he applied some to his legs and arms then went to relieve himself. In seconds a howl came from the bogs and the sad wail, 'Me willy's on fire!' The effect wore off after five minutes or so with no after effects other than he scored twice during the game. I'm thinking of making a new batch to sell to the managers of football clubs facing relegation.

I played football for a number of teams in different leagues through the years; probably the worst was the Sunday School Union. The teams were supposed to consist of members of church Sunday Schools, possibly the odd one was, but many were made up of free range psychopaths recruited on the day to make up the numbers. The game plan and philosophy was varied also. Some had a policy of 'Kill 'em all and let God sort 'em out' but the team I played for had a weird idea: 'It's not about winning, but taking part!' I don't recall ever playing with more than nine men, or ever winning a game. Year by year I decided to hang my boots up, but kept on playing while increasing in bulk and decreasing in speed. I changed from a fleet-footed winger into a back four cruncher. I was the right weight for a seven foot basketball player, but I was only six foot one. I needed to do something about my weight but what? I thought first of DIY liposuction but our vacuum cleaner was on its way out and not long for this world. I didn't want to be the person to send it to the dusty old carpet in the sky. Cutting down on my food intake was not a viable option. There were so called slimming pills on the market, but I suspected they were just gelatine capsules containing voracious fat-eating beetles. When one of our cats 'went thin' my Mum explained that he had been eating beetles. True or not, I lost the will to take slimming pills.

Mum showed me an ad in a women's magazine for slimming garments. Playing football in a glorified wet suit sounded a bit pervy but the principle was sound. Before the next game I slit two black polythene bin bags, stuck them together with duct tape and embalmed my abdomen. I looked in the mirror; I looked slimmer already. There was one slight problem: I could hardly breathe, but I was prepared to suffer to be beautiful. No pain, no gain or something equally inane. Within a few minutes of Kick Off the sweat began to collect. By the end of the first half there was a considerable amount of fluid squishing around inside the polythene, with a sound very similar to that of a vomiting cat. As I approached opposing players from behind with the sweat wobbling and slopping, the sound was a total give away and removed the element of surprise that I needed. As the whistle signalled half time, I slackened the tape to breathe for a while and a torrent of fluid poured through my shorts and on to my boots. I won't pass on the comments, as most were rude, but everyone was highly amused with one exception: me.

Viv's brother Pete and I frequently went to watch Everton play and, of course, travelled on our motorcycles. As we parked up an army of scrofulous kids usually offered to look after the bikes for a shilling. This was small scale crime: if you didn't pay up they'd pee in the petrol tank, let the tyres down or push the bikes off the centre stands. If you did pay them, as soon as the game started they'd bunk into the ground anyway, leaving the machines unattended. We always stood in the Gwladys Street end and ritually bought a cup of tea and a pork pie before the game. I regularly had to bite off a piece of the crust then squeeze the pie to squirt out the gelatine filler, which resembled infected nasal mucus, before it solidified again. It was a cold day so we kept our leathers and helmets on; this kept the ears warm but must have irritated the people behind me as I'm six foot one without helmet and boots. A further advantage of wearing the motor cycling gear was puke protection. If anyone vomited on you, which happened now and again, you could stand in the garden when you got home and get a friend to hose you down. Younger readers may not remember how it was before the modern all-seated football stadiums.

Everton FC had seated areas, strangely called the stands, and areas where you stood called the ground. There was also a hell-hole called the boy's pen, I suspect to get the local kids acclimatised to borstal or prison life. This held the throwbacks and trainee hooligans who, throughout the game, fought, screamed obscenities and threw things into the crowd. The missiles did show some vestigial originality, varying from sharpened pennies, cheap wooden darts, bricks etc. and on occasions, handbags when the goalkeeper, Gordon 'Honey' West had offended them in some way. A particularly offensive ritual was the drinking of tea, then recycling the bladder contents back into the cup. These cups of fresh urine were then shared with those stupid enough to stand in front of the boy's pen. Eventually a wire mesh was fitted to screen out the missiles but all it did with the urine was to filter off the cups and produce a fall out area of fine droplets. At this time the toilet facilities left much to be desired. Many fans tanked up with ale before, during and after the game and weren't prepared to make the effort to reach the bogs. A favourite dodge was to roll up a newspaper, usually the 'Football Echo', to form a tube then channel the bladder contents to the floor and the feet of others. This was a distinct improvement on using someone's pocket; another good case for wearing motorcycle gear!

Where the Bugs wear Boots

At half time a large number of fans went to stretch their bladders further with even more ale and I noticed two familiar figures some distance away; two teachers from the school I had 'left' some months earlier. I started making my way towards them, Pete behind me. My aim was to tell them that I was now a different person, I had become a Christian. They say it's good to try to see things from other people's point of view. What my ex-teachers saw was a known troublemaker and recent expulsee racing towards them accompanied by another biker. They vanished into the back of the ground at high speed and I never got the chance to tell them my good news.

On another occasion, Pete and I stood waiting for the game between Everton and Newcastle United to begin. We'd all been given a small sample of Ultrabrite toothpaste on the way through the turnstiles; it was a new product and worth a try when I'd used up my current tube of toothpaste which had at least two more years left in it. The game started and I forgot all about it. I forget which half of the game the following incident occurred, but not the incident itself. Alan Ball was sent off for arguing with the referee once too often. Two Newcastle supporters, who must have had three Shredded Wheats that morning, were standing just over to the left of us. They loudly expressed their agreement with the referee's decision; the crowd did not and a hail of literally thousands of tubes of Ultrabrite flew into the air and onto the pitch. Some scallies leapt over the fence and grabbed handfuls of the samples. Having seen the green teeth of some of these worthies I doubted they intended using the toothpaste for themselves, maybe they thought it was pile ointment or ugly cream. Our Geordie neighbours applauded loudly as Ball walked off the pitch: they were still shouting as the noise of the crowd subsided. Suddenly a steak and kidney pie came whistling through the air from the Gwladys Street stand and struck one of the vociferous Geordies on the side of the head. The steaming contents burst out and showered his companion. Both of them screeched as the contents were hot, or perhaps they were Vegetarians. It looked like a cow flying overhead had taken short and targeted them from a great height: it certainly was the most entertaining event of the afternoon.

Some of the characters I worked with in my first job deserve special mention for their deeds beyond the call of duty that helped us to forget the lousy pay for a while. Derek and Dudley had worked in the laboratory for a long time and I learned a great deal from them. They were keen photographers and introduced me to the hobby. Dudley's spare time occupation was driving a hearse for a funeral company based in Lark Lane. He offered to get me the odd Saturday but I tended to sleep in then get up in time to play football, or watch Everton, a more appealing prospect than transporting stiffs to the boneyard.

The staff turnover in laboratory assistants was surprisingly regular. On one occasion they advertised, took on eight people out of twenty applicants, all of whom left within a year, then contacted those they rejected a year ago and offered them employment. The work was repetitive, boring and underpaid and they got the kind of staff they paid for; highly unskilled, many with considerable experience in attending juvenile courts. Several of the assistants had the ability to dematerialise and phase into other dimensions for several hours, or so it seemed. The enigma was solved when a member of staff was sent to take samples from the top floor storage bay. A growling sound from some sacks of resin, at first thought to be one of the feral Kirkby cats, gave the game away. The rogue assistants had constructed an igloo from resin sacks in which to hide during working hours and would have got away with it longer if they had not been loud snorers. Appropriately each was given the sack as a souvenir.

Norman was a laboratory assistant with a razor sharp brain and personality. As you might expect, he was a staunch Evertonian. We often went to the chip shop near the Kraft factory because their curry and chips were excellent: a further reason was that the nearest chippy was crap. All the shops were open but permanently boarded-up and completely covered with graffiti. Vandalism ruled OK. I recall when a new Co-operative store was built in the Roughwood area of Kirkby: ninety percent of the windows were ritually smashed on the evening before the scheduled opening. Returning from the chip shop one day, Norman couldn't wait to get back to the factory before opening his newspaper wrapping and attempted to drive and simultaneously dunk his chips in the polystyrene cup of hot curry. It toppled over and curried his crotch; he screeched, 'Me willy's on fire!' as he leaped out of the car, jettisoning his trousers as he did so. Now when did I hear that before?

Dennis' previous job was writing down the measurements shouted out by the manager in Burton's the tailors. He seemed ideally qualified for work in the laboratory; a transition from inside-legs to chemical analysis which he achieved very well. At tea break he had the peculiar habit of letting his tea go cold then drinking it like a yard-of-ale-contestant in one big gulp. It was my turn to make the tea and as an experiment I half filled his cup with glycerine and floated the tea/milk mixture on the top. He didn't even notice the difference as he swallowed it, but for two or three days his hair was extra-greasy and he blamed the increase in bowel movements on cheap ale. Another person with an even meaner streak than myself placed a hundred gram weight at the bottom of his cup; he did notice that bashing against his front teeth as he swigged the cold tea.

Arthur has his place in my history because of his amazing self-image. If you knew someone, he knew him or her better; if you'd been somewhere great, he'd been somewhere greater; if you'd done anything, he'd done it faster, underwater or upside down. After a while I stopped believing that a genius was trapped in this junior laboratory assistant's body and started to catch him out. I told him I'd played a rare Reissburger guitar (non-existent) in Hessy's music shop; amazingly his brother had owned one! I 'recalled' seeing a band called Amphibious Delicatessen, a further figment of my imagination, on American television. Arthur had all their albums but had lent then to someone so I couldn't borrow them. In the end I left him to wallow and possibly drown in his own unreality.

Tom lived on a farm with his parents. He once replaced the engine on his car by a most ingenious method. Having no A-frame or block and tackle he pushed his car under a large tree, tied a rope to the suspension lugs on the engine, threw the end over a sturdy branch and then fastened the other end to three fat pigs. He was able to remove the dead engine for repair by persuading the pigs to move as required.

The chef, and I use the term loosely, was a gay caballero whose wrists rotated rapidly as he spoke. He claimed to be qualified, perhaps this was so, but most of the meals were gross; over half the people in the canteen brought their own sandwiches. I liked a hot meal at lunchtime and frequently risked a canteen dinner. I made a habit of writing comments on the meal quality on a table napkin and leaving them for the clearer-uppers. I once filled an empty pint bottle with obscenely greasy chips with the message, 'I always wondered how they get the chip in the bottle'. The staff replied with an ornate certificate with which I was awarded the Public Pig Award for the year.

The chef prided himself on his home made hamburgers which he claimed had beer in them. A colleague tried one and found a large piece of gristle and a cow's eyelash embedded in the burger. He tried to chew it but gave up after a while. He spat out the grisly piece, put down his knife and fork and marched up to the till, demanding to see the chef. The chef arrived on the scene with his towering hat and put out his hand. A kitchen assistant placed a knife and fork in his hand like nurses do when a surgeon is operating. He marched down to the table, sat down and cut the piece containing the gristle in half. He chewed, swallowed and informed my colleague that there was nothing wrong with it. I wished I'd had a camera to record the look on his face when my friend told him why it was tender: he had been chewing on the same piece for almost five minutes! Now and again the chef arrived at the lab for a few simple colour-change chemicals. He wasn't only a chef but also an exotic dancer and amateur conjuror. He always brought a little box of cakes he had made which I gave to the more expendable of the junior laboratory staff. Chef was eventually dismissed for stealing four big turkeys one Christmas-time. His story was that they had been accidentally burned and he had taken them home to prevent the cats from raiding the rubbish bins.

Old John was part of the refuse collecting team that swept through the factory on a daily basis. He was ancient and wrinkly, apparently he had lost his birth certificate and didn't know how old he was; he looked well beyond retirement age or sell-by date. One of the areas of the factory he covered was the wire drawing department. All the machine operators were female and most of them were desperate characters. The unit was hot and stuffy and they tended to wear very little beneath the compulsory overalls, so I was told. They decided to give John a treat on his birthday and lined up along his route' then presented him with a group topless flash as they sang 'Happy Birthday'. John had a heart attack as a result and was rushed to hospital never to return to work; a truly tragi-comic event, but what a way to go!

One of the strangest characters I crossed paths with was the Milky Bar Kid, so called because of his physical resemblance to the precocious little twerp on television at the time. His personality was more like that of an expired stoat, not excessively flamboyant. I suspect he was a train spotter or even a paint-drying spectator. He started working in the engineering section and finding that I lived quite near him, offered me a lift into work. Where he got his information from I never found out, but it was totally incorrect. He lived in Crosby and his route to work was nowhere near my address. I had to walk for 20 minutes to the rendezvous point, when, whatever the weather, he would say 'Good morning' and I would reply. Then we would sit in silence as he steered his ego towards work. I am not a morning person at the best of times, but a twenty minute odyssey with this boring dude made me pray that the aliens would abduct one of us. One fateful morning he picked me up and said nothing and, not feeling particularly chatty myself, neither did I. We drove to work in silence then, as we arrived, he informed me that he had not said 'Good morning' to see if I said it first because he always said it first. Because I had failed his little psychometric test I was to be deemed rude, uncouth and undeserving of a lift in future. I was so gob smacked by the whole thing I failed to express my true feelings for him: a boring git that needed to get a life.

There were a limited number of drinks dispensers scattered around the factory but the one near the offices was frequented by some of the crazed machine operators on their infrequent rest periods; they just lay around ogling the office girls. One nut-case was throwing his hacksaw-knife at a fibre drum some two metres away, trying to look hard and glean some attention. This sad behaviour caused most of the office girls to use another drinks dispenser. Not put off in any way the cretin threw his knife a bit harder, it bounced off the drum, turned through 180 degrees and went point first into his shin. As he pulled it out, with expletive accompaniment, the blood started spurting out, making his overalls flutter as if a mad hamster was having a fit inside his trousers. It couldn't have happened to a nicer chap.

I bought a BSA 650 cc motorcycle, optimistically called the Golden Flash, from the head joiner, whose name was George Wink. He explained that he frequently got letters with his surname deliberately mis-spelled; I can't imagine why! The motorcycle had a Busmar Astral sidecar attached to it, a huge two seater which meant I had to learn totally different cornering techniques than I used on the solo machine. The first time I turned right with the combo I instinctively attempted to bank the machine over which had the sidecar floating just below my left shoulder and the passenger screaming for mercy; but I soon got the hang of it. I told you earlier about visiting the ships in the Bootle docks. Most of the ship visitation team rode bicycles, which were frequently stolen from under the gangway where they were parked. When I bought the motorcycle combination four of us could travel in comfort and get round a few more ships in an evening. I was driving downhill towards the docks at Miller's Bridge with Stan on the pillion and two other lads in the sidecar with the top open. Suddenly I grasped my head, told them I was blacking out and flopped across the petrol tank. It was my idea of a joke, there was no other traffic on the road and I was steering with my elbows and watching the road ahead. The lads in the sidecar were in a panic and I was about to let them know it was a joke when I felt pressure on my back and looked over my shoulder. Stan was standing on the footrests, eyes skyward, arms above his head like a goalkeeper shouting, 'I'm coming Lord!' They were not too happy when I shouted, 'I'm OK. It's a miracle!' Funny how people react when they think their life is coming to an end. I was impressed with Stan's calmness - he really wanted to meet Jesus. I do, but not just yet! My passengers were not impressed with me and chose to walk the rest of the way.

Viv didn't like being in the sidecar apart from when it was raining. I had to stay in lines of traffic like a car, getting soaked and asphyxiated by the exhaust fumes. The fun had gone out of biking with three wheels; I considered getting a car, but took the sidecar off instead. We got around a bit but stepping out to go for a meal was tricky: we would smarten ourselves up then put on the gear and arrive with our clothes wrinkled and our faces spattered with dead flies and crud. I couldn't afford a car and a bike so the bike had to go: I put it up for sale. No takers right away, then a month or so later a young lad knocked on the door; the kid next door had told him I had a bike for sale. When I took the tarpaulin off the bike he looked sad, I asked him what was wrong, I expected him to be pleased with it. He explained that he didn't know it was in such good condition and beyond his means. I was asking £100 and he only had thirty quid which had taken him months to save. He reminded me of my brother when he was that age so I let him have it for thirty pounds.

My brother, Dave, was the first in our family to own a car; I was still into motorbikes. He bought a black Morris Minor with the registration RUG 95, most significant as I will explain. After a while he got to know the various idiosyncrasies of the vehicle, like how to start it first-time from cold or how to use the foot and hand brakes to stop it in time. He reckoned the brakes were good and developed the habit of braking late. Once I was in the front passenger seat and as we approached the lights they changed to red. It looked like he wasn't going to brake so I slammed my foot down to 'brake' for him. My foot went right through the floor of the car. We drove to a quieter place and I got my foot free to find that the floor of the car was non-existent. The metal had rusted away and the space had been fitted with tongue and grooved wooden floorboards with a rug glued on top. I replaced the rotten floorboards with new ones and re-glued the rug in place. The same car had another exotic feature which developed with time; something came adrift in the windscreen wiper mechanism causing the wiper blade to wipe across the car bonnet instead of the windscreen.

I learned to drive a motor car with a private instructor called Mr Till, who was the spitting image of William Hartnell, the actor who played the first Doctor Who. I had to travel to his house in Crosby and had an hour's lesson at the end of which I was returned home. This procedure was most inconvenient but he only charged four quid per session and after ten lessons I passed the driving test first time. This was probably because I had been riding a motorcycle for four years and had road sense, but also because my instructor was good at his job. At the first session he explained that learning to drive was something I would have to do for myself, but he would teach me how to pass the driving test. Many years later I adopted this approach in teaching computer literacy in a college; you can't teach all there is to know about Word Processing, Spreadsheet workbooks and graphs and Database in thirty two-hour sessions, but you can teach them enough to pass the exams. One of Mr Till's gimmicks was a paper clip fastened to the top of the rear seat. The car he taught in was a Triumph Herald; when reversing round corners all you had to do was align the paper clip with the kerb-side rear wing and the turn was perfect. Another technique was to set the rear-view mirror correctly then just offset it so you had to move your head to see before moving off. As he explained, its not enough to look in the mirror, the driving test examiner has to see that you have done so. I was so impressed with the Triumph Herald that I bought one when I had saved the money. On the second day of ownership I went to reverse round a corner and realised the car I had bought had a serious defect: there was no paper clip on the back of the rear seat. As the man said, I'd passed the test, now I had to learn to drive.

Morale at the factory was low for as long as I could remember. A new chief chemist was appointed, a man who appeared not to like graduates, he certainly didn't like me. To be fair, at this stage I was totally frustrated with my employers who never credited me with the good work I did do, was still having no luck getting a job elsewhere and was virtually working to rule. I was working on an interesting project using a breakdown tester. This intrigued me; by merely twisting a control knob the voltage could be increased up to more than 100 thousand volts. I took two copper rods, joined them at the base with some silicon rubber to insulate them from each other and clamped them to the terminals of the breakdown tester. As I increased the voltage, an arc began to flash across the lowest part and then moved up the rods until the gap was too large to maintain the arc. It reminded me of the old Frankenstein movies which always had several 'climbing arcs' in the laboratory. Years later when the police were investigating the use of stun guns and tasers, I tried to obtain one to experiment with, not as you may think to zap scallies or miscreants. In the USA many shops sell them, they are banned in this country although they should be issued to the Police and nurses in hospitals to control drunks and nut jobs. I decided to make my own using the electronic control unit from a deceased Vauxhall Cavalier as the basis for the invention. Having constructed my 'taser', fully insulated as I thought, I connected a spare car battery. I have no recollection of what happened next but I woke up on the floor of the garage with a bump on my head and shooting pains through my forearms: I gave up that line of research from that moment as there is no realistic future for a taser that shocks the user and requires one to carry a car battery to power it.

Anyway, back to the breakdown project. I wrote up the research report, and knowing how fussy my boss was, I got several people who were qualified electrical and electronic engineers to OK it first. I then submitted it to the boss and in due time I was summoned and the work criticised. I'd had enough. I was subsequently given three months in which to get another job, great timing as I was due to be married in a matter of a few months.

Chapter 9

Birth of a Salesman

It was 1969. Richard Nixon had become the 37th President of the USA. Concorde with an E and a bent nose made the first supersonic flight, apart from Superman and the movies to see were 'Easy Rider' and 'Butch Cassidy and the Sundance Kid'. It was mid-May, I was due to be married in a matter of weeks and I still had no job. There were plenty of positions for chemists; this was pointed out to me by many nosey-parkers who assumed I was skiving because I was unemployed and they weren't. Most of the jobs were for chemists with different kinds of training and experience, for example analytical, dyestuff, food, pharmaceutical; my experience was with polymer coatings and the treatment I'd had in this field was not an incentive to look further. While looking through the newspapers I noticed many vacancies for representatives: sharp young chaps with the gift of the gab who sold things. I knew several, they had plenty of money and a fairly new car but were thick as a donkey's digit. I thought to myself, 'I could do that!' I started looking and applying for technical representative positions in a number of fields; selling steel doors, commercial weighing machines and even contraceptives, all with no success. The wedding date was looming and I applied for progressively crazy jobs. About a month before the wedding date I received a letter that did not say 'We regret...' It was from a company looking for a medical representative for the North West area. The interview was in Manchester in a hotel near the Free Trade Hall. There were twelve others there, all in similar circumstances, all dolled up like 'pox doctor's clerks' and eager to impress. During the following week I received a further letter from the company - to my amazement I was asked to attend a further interview and medical at their main centre.

After a long train journey I arrived at Euston, totally nauseated by travel sickness and apprehension, as they say 'sick as a parrot'. Fortunately it took so long to get to Victoria, jumping from tube station to station, that my green complexion was virtually now back to off-white. The old steam train from Victoria was a bone shaker but at least it was also non-puke-inducing. Leaving the train at I noticed several of my rivals for the position whom I'd met at the second interview getting into a minibus with the hotel's logo on the side. I did likewise and was amazed to find all twelve prospective employees sitting within waiting for me to get in. The laboratories and production plant were right on the edge of the sea; it felt like being on holiday. I realised as the day progressed it was no holiday; to be cross examined by three 'misery gobs' with less than zero sense-of-humour, a long medical including being poked, prodded and made to cough while a suspicious character held my plums was not my usual experience on holiday, but then I have never been on a Club 18-30 vacation or had any wish to do so. In less than a week I knew the outcome; I had a job! The conditions were that I had to attend a six week intensive training course before joining the North West sales team. Being away from home was not something I relished: when I looked at the dates I realised our wedding was booked for the second weekend of the course. The company kindly let me come home on the Friday night and get married on Saturday, as long as I was back for Sunday afternoon. All heart, but at least I missed out on all the pre-wedding boloney; I also missed having a honeymoon.

Everyone who had attended both interviews turned up on the training course. This motley collection consisted of desperate characters; some had flunked college courses, some had been medical reps before; all were full of crap with their brains securely installed in their Y-fronts. I instantly nicknamed my respected colleagues 'The Dirty Dozen'. The hotel was a magnificent establishment set in acres of land with a helicopter landing pad and a vast golf course. The restaurants were of the highest standard; the clientele I saw in the six weeks included Graham Hill, Sid & Dick, the writers of the Morecambe and Wise Show, and others whose faces were familiar. We dined like royalty on generous expense accounts; unfortunately most of the trainees couldn't hold their ale and frequently fell asleep in the afternoon sessions or relieved themselves every twenty minutes. The training was intensive; the company had a large range of products, about sixty at this time, and we had to learn how they worked and be able to sell them effectively to doctors and chemists. The first part of the course was theoretical and I got high marks in the frequent tests, then we had to role play and pretend to sell particular products to 'doctors' who asked awkward questions. I found this hard going as I knew it was only make-believe and couldn't take it seriously. As we approached the end of the training several participants began to come apart at the seams, hitting the bottle in a big way. Exam week was traumatic but we all passed and were assigned our cars and drove home to begin our assignments in our various regions.

The area I was to cover included South Liverpool, Warrington, Haydock, Wigan, Frodsham and Runcorn. On an average day we would spend all morning visiting doctors to arrange a future appointment, or informing them of the products we were pushing to the chemists in their areas and trying to persuade them to write our particular product name on the prescriptions. If a doctor didn't specify the company product, and used a general name, the chemist could supply any make, usually a cheaper foreign alternative product: so our company didn't get the sale, the rep didn't get the bonus; but the chemist got more profit. Hence in the afternoons we visited the chemists to try to persuade them to supply our particular brand and order direct from the factory when the prescription gave the option. On many occasions the doctor's appointments I had made were cancelled or I was made to wait an hour or so. This would mean there was little chance of reaching the daily target of seven or eight doctor visits per day before 11.30 am. Many of the doctors I visited were ill mannered and arrogant. I could understand their dislike of medical representatives, as many of the medical reps I met were full of themselves and cocky with it. It also occurred to me how annoying it must have been to have some unqualified twit telling you what to prescribe on the basis of a six-week training course, but a few manners wouldn't have hurt. Most of the doctors did treat me in a better way when they found I was a chemistry graduate. I asked to have my BSc printed on my business cards; this request was refused on the grounds that it would make the others appear unqualified, which they were!

People tend to think of doctors as paragons of virtue; worthy of a permanent stance on a plinth or pedestal, I thought that way until I finished the training and went on the road. Like any other member of the human race there are the good, the bad and the ugly; and I met them all. I visited practices where the receptionists filled in pre-signed repeat prescriptions using a pill chart on the wall. Many doctors I met wanted to know what gifts I had for them. I discovered that many of our competitors gave away cameras, bottles of wine and other goodies to persuade, or bribe, the doctors to prescribe their products by name. When hospitals were approached key people were invited to weekend breaks thinly disguised as 'teaching seminars' on Majorca or beyond. In any other business this would be called bribery. My employers were a good company with an excellent range of products and believed that the product quality and service was enough to persuade doctors to prescribe the best. I was given a few magnets and blotting paper with the company logo to supplement my approach to our customers.

In one 'surgery' I visited in Liverpool city centre the doctor's desk, filing system, patients and dogs all co-existed in one small room. It sticks in my mind like a nightmare; people I told about it did not believe me, but it's true. The doctor sat in his pyjamas wearing a tatty brown dressing gown and listened to each patient with all the other patients waiting, able to hear every word. As I stood at the door two huge dogs appeared from behind one of the sofas comprising the waiting area, snarling and snapping at each other. The larger of the two animals then proceeded to mount the other one in the space between the doctor's desk and the waiting area. The doctor continued to deal with his patient of the moment, taking no notice of what was going on. The purpose of the demonstration escaped me, I must admit, and I decided to leave the scene. The job, at first enjoyable, began to worry me. Part of the job was to push the use of antibiotics for children, although I believed then, and still do, that childhood illnesses strengthen the immune system if left to run their course. I asked a doctor at a health centre how he justified prescribing chemicals like pentobarbitone sodium in sleeping pills knowing it metabolises into toxins which remain in the body. His reply; 'Most of my patients are old, will probably die soon and need to sleep' kept me from sleeping for night after night. These factors, plus the general pressure of achieving the visitation quota, began to affect my health. Life working in research was far more stimulating, rewarding and restful.

One afternoon I walked into a chemist's shop and the pharmacist, hearing the bell on the door, came out of his Aladdin's cave and smiled as if he knew me. It was then that I realised that something was wrong. The grinning balding dude in front of me was vaguely familiar but I had no idea why I was standing in this particular shop. As I explained this, he reached over and flipped up my tie with the company logo. I was still no wiser. He reminded me that I was a representative, gave me a cup of tea and suggested I go home and see a doctor. I had no difficulty finding my way home or recognising people I saw, but by the time I arrived home, everything I had ever learned in Grammar School and beyond had leaked away somehow. O-levels, A-levels, Degree and the content of the medical representative's training course had all gone, or were certainly inaccessible at that time. My qualifications were just pieces of paper. I arranged an appointment with my doctor who explained that the stress I had been under had overloaded my brain and it had effectively short-circuited. He had no idea how long it would take me to recover if at all. He consulted his copy of Monthly Index of Medical Specialities and wrote out a prescription for Librium and Triptizol. The tablets caused me to sleep a great deal of the time; when I was awake I was higher than a kite. After two weeks, the Triptizol ran out and I was on 'cold turkey' - down to earth with a bump. I had only lost my memory but was unofficially classed as 'mental' by those around me who knew no better. The truth was that I had lost some of my memory, that's all. It can be painful to see yourself as others do. What I saw in most people's eyes was fear and pity: in Viv's, when I bothered to look, was sadness and pain. People who came near, and there were not too many of them, would speak louder than normal as if I was deaf or stupid, but deafness was never a problem. People kept their children away from me, yet cannibalism was furthest from my mind. I know this sounds a bit tacky, but as a Christian I had peace with the situation. I read somewhere in the Bible that 'everything works together for good to those who love God' and I believed it.

Some people tried to make me feel better by telling me to 'Look on the bright side of Life'. This meaningless platitude assumes of course that there is one. Frequently I have found that the light at the end of the tunnel is in fact the midnight express, or at least a gorilla with a flashlight. Friends told me things could only get better, then the company repossessed the car and I received my last pay cheque. The bills began to accumulate and the money dwindled. I still expected God to sort out the problem but had no idea how. I became so objectionable once my antidepressant 'happy pills' were discontinued that we had virtually no visitors. A notable exception was a mate called Harry who regularly came to see us, despite the abuse I gave him when he did. Viv was a tower of strength as usual. I got a book of crossword puzzles to see if I could stimulate my brain to normal activity. Within a short time I could do the average crossword in the book in five minutes or so, but potential employers were not impressed with this. Meanwhile, I signed on the dole and explained what my doctor had said; they sent me to their own doctor who informed me it was 'all in my mind', that I was 'a big strong lad' and capable of work. The work I was trained to do was specialised polymer research but the dole doctor couldn't grasp it. I applied for any job I saw, had a few replies but when they saw my CV and realised I had a degree, they lost interest.

A local motor company was looking for assembly line workers; when they found I had been to university they equated this with 'having some intelligence' and accused me of being some kind of anarchist or troublemaker. Other potential employers just wrote me off as a 'bit of a nutter' because I had lost my memory. Then I saw a job advertised in the Liverpool Echo for a laboratory assistant at Kodak Limited in Kirkby. I wrote a letter explaining all that had happened with a copy of my CV; To my surprise I got an interview with the chief chemist. He informed me that they couldn't give me a laboratory assistant position as I had a degree and eight years experience in Research and Development, but were prepared to give me a three months probation period as a technician. If my memory returned I would be promoted to full research chemist: if not I would unfortunately have to go back into the unemployment pool. In less than two weeks my memory began to return and the company kept their word, but that's another story and is the subject of the next chapter.

Our neighbours in Aintree were interesting; to the right were an older couple who had both been made redundant from the Courtaulds factory on Dunnings Bridge Road. I shared a plot with them by the Girobank in Netherton, not far from where the seven ponds rubbish dump used to be. We grew potatoes, tomatoes, leeks, onions and other vegetables. The highlight of each trip to the plot was the tea break in the little shed built on each plot of land. Growing our own vegetables was back breaking work and frequently, just as the crops were ready to be harvested, some thieving rat would kindly harvest our goodies, but we never caught them. I considered dusting particular items with a chemical mix which, if swallowed, coloured the urine deep blue and induced vicious incontinence, but I didn't fancy a dose of the same if I forgot which items had been doctored. If you do happen to be reading this and remember 'nicking' our crops I hope the aliens abduct you, or at least your right ear falls off into your left pocket.

On the other side was an Irish couple; for many months we never saw the man of the house, as he was at sea. He was truly an old sea dog, so I guess that made his good wife an old sea bitch. She had a special place in my heart as she frequently reported us to different authorities for imaginary misdemeanours. Our washing machine outflow pipe occasionally emitted a small amount of spray which produced a small damp patch on her side of the shared driveway. She telephoned the relevant authorities, in due time the man from the public health arrived and was more than a little embarrassed at her pettiness, but that was nothing. On another occasion I removed a wall in the house and piled the bricks neatly on the patio at the back of the house in the manner of the Tate Gallery exhibit. No-one offered me twenty thousand pounds for it but my Irish neighbour reported it; she must have been hanging out of her bedroom window to be able to see it. The Rat Man came to see the heap of rubbish which had been reported as 'likely to breed rats'. I showed him the neat stack of bricks, so tightly packed that woodlice would have found a leg-over difficult, never mind rats: the rat man duly apologised for troubling us and departed.

Eventually the old sea dog returned from the sea. I was sitting watching a patronising infantile programme on TV when I became aware of a sawing noise from high up in the front garden and being nosy I looked to see what it was. There was my neighbour up a ladder sawing at a branch on one of the large trees in the garden, but sawing through the branch that was supporting the ladder. I called to Viv to have a look and tried to find my camera; this I did but there was no film in it. Viv convinced me that the neighbourly thing to do would be to stop him rather than to let him fall and photograph the event. As I called to him he stopped, the 'penny dropped', and he came down the ladder. He called me a 'Gentleman and a Scholar', applied a two handed handshake and invited me in for a cuppa, leaving the tree surgery for another time. He was frequently the worse for drink but his personality was such that it was hard to tell. On this occasion he was well plastered, embarrassing his wife by calling her his 'little budgie.' I finished the tea and made my excuses. The front door was stuck and I had difficulty opening it. I have a reputation for breaking things so I was trying to open the door carefully. As I struggled, Phil tapped me on the shoulder and pointed to a 'holy picture' on the wall, a pale faced Mary and fat baby Jesus both with 'golden bananas' suspended over their heads. 'If you need help, ask Him', he said in a side whisper like Robert Newton's portrayal of Long John Silver in the Treasure Island movie, 'And if He won't help, you can always ask his Muvver'. With this lesson in Roman Catholic theology I escaped. They've gone now, their son was left many acres of land back in Ireland by a rich relative and is probably still trying to swap every last cow for a bag of magic beans. All I remember now is the tree, the pile of bricks, the invisible rats and the time I saved their son's life.

It happened like this: we came home one rainy afternoon and found a bedraggled heap of clothes sat in our porch. It was our neighbours' son. We invited him in out of the rain until his folks returned and gave him a cup of tea and a few biscuits. As a reward for our generosity he arranged for some of his scabby friends to break in some days later while we were out. Returning home I noticed a broken window with blood on the fragments of glass remaining in the door frame. Thinking the perpetrators had harmed our cat I raced upstairs, the 'red mist' ruling, with a lump hammer to welcome the intruders, but they had gone. The thieves had stolen my hard-rock album collection and a few books of Green Shield stamps. I told the police I suspected the lad next door had something to do with it; he squealed on his buddies who were actually sharing out my records on a table when the police called. How did I save his life? I didn't kill him!

Our neighbourhood was no better or worse than any other. The guy in the house next-door-but-one had his windscreen expertly removed and the old sealing strip left neatly coiled on the roof of his car. Such care and consideration is a hallmark of certain Liverpool people. Visiting friends in the nearby Orrell Park area I found the same level of neighbourhood care: returning to my car I discovered that someone had snapped off my radio aerial, formed it into an interesting metallic halo and left it on the bonnet of the car. I just wanted to thank the artistically inclined vandal personally but like all true heroes, they wished their anonymity and health to be preserved.

At this time we had a car that had seen better days and was now beginning to suffer from senility. Returning from a visit to a company in Peterborough the car suddenly lurched to one side and came to a halt accompanied by a horrific screeching. Before I could get out and see what was wrong, one of the back wheels overtook the car and then flipped onto its side and also stopped. I would like to report that we all moved to the opposite side of the car and drove home on three wheels but that would be lying. Once again the AA had to tow us to a garage for repairs to take place. We decided not to spend any more on it and I left it out on the road outside our house with several months' tax and MOT, all the doors unlocked and the key in the ignition, thinking if they'll nick a windscreen, surely they'll jump at this. I was wrong! Even car thieves have some pride and there were no takers.

My wife and I were returning home through the Orrell Park area one night at around one o' clock. As we approached the bridge by the station we could see a group of around 12 guys with sticks blocking the road. They made no attempt to move so rather than ploughing through them, not generally accepted by the Law, I stopped the car. A sweating red-faced oaf started banging on the car bonnet with his stick and demanded that my wife and I got out of the car. I considered his proposal for a nanosecond then decided against his suggestion. I operated the car door locks, selected first gear and began to move forward with my finger on the horn push. Several more would-be heroes then began to whack the car. I accelerated and most of them moved; one didn't and flew into the air screaming. I stopped the car and was about to reverse over him, once again the 'red mist' ruling. Viv reckoned it was not a great idea so we drove home. Eventually she slept and I rang the Casualty department at Walton Hospital to see if any one had been admitted with a fractured pelvis; no one had. I'm ashamed to admit I was not concerned about the man's welfare - I intended to visit him and apply some lump hammer therapy to the fracture. Since then God has been changing me but I couldn't guarantee that any threat to my family would cause me to treat any would-be perpetrator with excessive benevolence.

We lived near the Aintree Racecourse for almost 40 years and stayed at home for most of the Grand National races, not because we like horse racing, but to protect our property from the criminal element that infest the area on such occasions. The National may be a Grand Day Out for the punters, but it is a pain in the butt if you live near the course. For many weeks before the event we were awakened around six in the morning by the construction crews erecting the stands etc. If you happened to sleep in the back bedroom you would be lucky to get to sleep at all because of the intense brightness of the security lamps protecting equipment overnight. On race days our road became a virtual 'no go' area which made coming and going of residents or visitors a most irritating experience. Then there were the floor shows. It is an occasion for many to strut their stuff and the ultimate opportunity was the so called Ladies Day, or the poor man's Ascot. Whatever the weather, they minced down the road wearing enormous ornate hats, tottering on high heeled shoes. Unfortunately many of them couldn't hold their ale and a few hours later they returned, some carried by friends, puking, 'leaking' and throwing their wet knickers into the residents' gardens. Nice! 'Ladies?' - my left butt-cheek! This strange ritual has recently stopped and we sure are glad.

But what about the gentlemen and I use the term loosely. Many of the crowds arriving at the course are already drunk as newts, shouting, swearing and being clever. Each year some clowns pick up the traffic cones and place them on their heads, on their crotches, on their upper torsos emulating Madonna, or shout through them like they are the first people to think of something so clever. What a sad unimaginative collection of losers staggering along the road, the happy lobotomised stopping to use residents' front gardens as temporary pissoirs. A further use of the front gardens is as receptacles for their litter; irresponsible scum bags throw their beer cans, bottles and glasses into resident's gardens: the better behaved place their junk on the hedges. Then there are the geeks trying to get over the back fence to get in for nothing. I once chased three dudes with a hammer when they appeared on the roof of my garage when I was working on it. A policewoman let the miscreants go and bravely stood in my way so I had to stop or flatten her.

Realising how much inconvenience is suffered by the residents, the organisers kindly put a voucher through the letter box which gets you a free ticket if you pay for a ticket. Their kindness is amazing but I have no interest in horse racing. The races do, however, represent a wealth of material for anyone studying sociology or abnormal psychology, with an interesting mixture of social groups. At the top of the heap are the mega-rich; in Rolls-Royces, their own or rented for the occasion, or stretch limousines, they arrive in style and migrate to the exclusive paddocks or stands away from the other sub species.

Close followers of the rich are the wannabes, going into debt to rub shoulders with their betters, massaging their flagging self images by knocking back Martinis with the chinless wonders. One of my students paid a small fortune to get into one of the exclusive paddocks and never left the beer tent for the duration of the afternoon's racing. She didn't win anything and the only horse she saw belonged to a mounted policeman. The food and drink vendors offer goodies at exorbitant prices, but have little option to do otherwise when they are paying thousands of pounds for a place on site. This year, the situation was greatly improved with better behaviour from the punters and less detritus to remove from the hedges and gardens.

Chapter 10

The golden years

As I mentioned earlier, Eastman Kodak was a company I had wanted to work for since the interviews at Liverpool University. I was assigned first to a research unit developing novel photoresist systems; these are special chemicals used in the production of printed circuit boards at that time. I answered to Ray, a southerner with a most creative mind and with whom I got on well most of the time. Returning from a meeting at Harrow Research with Ray and my line manager, Paul, we were walking along the platform at Euston station trying to find a dining carriage that was not reserved. At last we spied one that looked hopeful and Paul boarded the train and we followed him. As we went to sit down, a short-assed cockney waiter with a distinctly simian look appeared as by magic and announced that this carriage was also reserved. He began to place 'Reserved' cards on the tables. I shouted down to him, 'Sod you then, monkey face!' and left the carriage to continue the search. I found a suitable carriage then looked for the others but there was no sign of them. I walked back down the train and found them still being harangued by Monkey Face. He thought Paul had made the comment and was regaling him with his sad lot in life; how difficult the job was, how he was horrifically underpaid and that he was only doing his job. We did eventually get seated and presented with a British Rail dinner: the meal was the usual gastronomic atrocity and I spent half the night awake with indigestion. All the waiters had widow's peaks, prison pallor and appeared to be un-dead. Great minds think alike: Paul and I simultaneously mouthed, 'Nosferatu', an old vampire movie if you didn't know. As the food was being served I realised that our waiter was non other than Monkey Face. As he was serving the roast potatoes I asked him to give me 'plenty'. In a superior voice he announced, 'We haven't plenty, Sir, only enough'. All the chinless wonders on the other tables had curled upper lips and nodded their approval at his polite reprimand; I guess I should have chinned the dude earlier when there were no witnesses.

Where the Bugs wear Boots

We frequently had research meetings at the Harrow Research laboratories and in order to get there in time, we had to get the early Pullman train. This was full of suit people with brief cases and superior attitudes, all pretending to read their complimentary Financial Times. I always took a Sci-Fi book or an American comic to read: those sitting near me appeared to think I was defective in some way; so what's new? To escape from the atmosphere of extreme boredom, I always moved to the dining car as soon as breakfast was announced. The British Rail breakfast was filling, extremely greasy and totally overpriced, but my employers were footing the bill. The enormous mutant mushrooms that appeared on the breakfast plate probably grew near Sellafields and held half a pint of warm grease which flowed down the gullet when bitten: this meant by the time the train was pulling into Euston I was about ready to 'throw up'. I worked out that I could get an aeroplane from Liverpool to Heathrow for the same price as the Pullman train from Lime Street to Euston plus the price of the breakfast. From then on that's the way I travelled; the flight only took 35 minutes and I arrived feeling well. When Graeme Souness left Liverpool Football Club to play in Europe, I was on the same flight to Heathrow when he was flying out with his family. Although a staunch Evertonian I wished him 'All the best' in his career move as we disembarked at Heathrow; he nodded but failed to pull his forelock or genuflect.

Eastman-Kodak was the best company I ever worked for, not just the money but the conditions of work and approach to research. The money was good. My yearly bonus after a few years was considerable: enough to buy a new car for myself and a good second hand car for Viv. After working on photoresists for several years with some success the management decided to change the direction of the whole research programme. I joined a newly formed polymer coatings group answerable to our parent company, Tennessee Eastman, co-ordinated by Paul, probably the most intellectually talented person I had met to date. I learned more about chemistry, theory and practice in these years than I had ever done before. The Eastman group operated Research by Objectives; basically a topic was researched in the literature and a Basic Research Proposal produced, which was only funded when approved. Obviously company research programmes are classified; all I will say is that for several years I worked on different solventless coatings; that is coating systems that cause little or no atmospheric pollution.

Having a decent job meant we ate better and had a car which didn't

138

break down all the time. I didn't bother with sandwiches for dinner, I regularly had something and chips at lunch time and also chips with my evening meal. I arrived home once after a hard day at the lab. Viv was preparing the evening meal having also had a busy day at the office. I sat down to read my latest American comic imports which Paul used to get for me, when she called, 'Tea's ready' and I came and sat down. We had no children at this time so I felt it was OK to read on as I ate everything with a fork, not counting soup of course. As I became engrossed in the adventures of Conan the Barbarian, I thrust forth my fork into the unknown and brought back a mouthful. It was tasty, one might even say delicious, but there were no chips. For a healthy change she had made Spaghetti Bolognese. Still half engrossed in the comic I registered a complaint to the effect that there were no chips and continued to fight the hordes of Chaos with Conan. Suddenly I felt a burning sensation in my skull despite my long hair, I felt the hot blood dripping down my neck. I looked at my hands, a thick red viscous fluid dripping on to the table, wormy pieces of pasta wriggling down under gravity, then I realised I had not been savagely attacked by a Scythian warlord; Viv had just up-ended my plate of spaghetti on my head! After an equally hard day to my own she had prepared something healthier and different and her reward? 'Where are the chips?' I was tempted to tip her plate over myself in agreement. I was not annoyed in any way apart from the few drops of sauce that had splashed on the comic, and the meal was not wasted; what I could get back on the plate I ate and enjoyed. It was a major step in my learning curve of life: I was the eldest of two boys and never did any household jobs at home. My Mum did all the housework and also held down a responsible job as a solicitor's secretary in the city centre. We didn't even clear our plates after a meal because we thought it was the woman's job to do so. Viv had an elder brother who was allowed to loaf about and a younger sister who was too young to be given household chores. Viv was expected to help her mother because she was female. When we got married we were already conditioned, me to sit around, Viv to work   The spaghetti episode was one of many lessons I learned: marriage is about sharing in all areas of life. Most lessons in life I seemed to learn the hard way.

My brother Dave moved to Maryland, USA, as a professor at Howard University in Washington later in the year. We decided to have a few weeks in Devon and save up to visit Dave the following year. We also bought a brand-new car for the first time. It was a Morris Marina 1.8 coupé that went like a rocket and did 25 miles per gallon in my dreams. It broke down 13 times during the warranty period, the dealer failed to provide a courtesy car, which convinced me to stick to second-hand vehicles in the future. After Christmas we looked at the cost of scheduled flights to the USA; very expensive. We met someone who told us about a travel club that operated charter flights for people with relatives in the USA. We joined the club, paid out the money and waited for our tickets; they arrived on the Saturday morning that we were due to travel. Fortunately the flight was after midnight. The plane was old and every seat was occupied. Had a monster climbed aboard the aeroplane and poured tomato sauce all over me, I would have known exactly what tinned sardines feel like. The in-flight movie was two years old and boring; I paid £1 to borrow some headphones and found a hard-rock-ish channel to head-bang to. After five hours the toilets were overflowing, the fuel was running out and the plane had to land at Gander, Newfoundland, to refuel. It was July but as we left the plane while they refuelled it was snowing. We had been advised to wear light clothing to travel as New York was over 90 degrees at one o' clock in the morning: in Gander we all sat shivering until we could board the plane again. When we arrived at JFK Airport we had to circle for three quarters of an hour: I didn't mind because the views of Boston and New York from the air at night are amazing. Stepping out of the plane we were met with a blast of hot air. Dave said to dress more conventionally to save problems at Customs and he was right; we walked right through but the guy in front of us with long hair and denims had all his bags opened and they even tasted his toothpaste and talc. We got a taxi to the Ramada Inn at the airport for the night: Dave was to pick us up the next day.

The door to our room had been crudely repaired; it looked like the Incredible Hulk had walked through it; when we tried to sleep I put all the cases against it. It was too hot to sleep so I turned on the air conditioning, which was nice and cool but was very loud. We turned on the television, which had more than 40 channels most of which were an insult to a dog's intelligence. At around 3.00 a.m. we decided to phone room service for some sandwiches and Coca Cola; in no time there was a knock on the door and a serf brought in our snack. The next day Dave arrived and I settled our account before leaving; our little snack, four rounds of bread with a little ham and salad plus two bottles of Coca Cola came to £15 which in 1971 was daylight robbery. I tried to keep a straight face and inquired about the state of the door. The desk clerk explained: two days earlier a woman and her niece had been robbed at gunpoint in the room; the perpetrators had burst through the door, taken their cash and shot the older woman in the leg when she raised the alarm. It made me almost feel at home!

Dave picked us up in a white Cadillac, strange as his car was a red Chevrolet Camaro. His next door neighbour had loaned him the Cadillac for a year or so, not because he was generous, but because he 'didn't like living next door to a one-car family.' Dave used the Cadillac daily and eventually sold the Camaro for more than he paid for it. Dave's neighbour drove a quad-cum-lawnmower around his huge garden that he called his 'yard', with cans of Budweiser in a home made carrier. He was a fat arrogant git and the only American I have ever failed to get on with to date.

Washington was very hot and extremely humid. Sitting in the garden under a parasol the sweat dripping from my armpits like a tap with a defective washer, I watched the kids from next-door playing in the pool wearing plastic anoraks with the hoods up. Their parents were neurotics where health was concerned, any skin blemishes like moles had to be removed and the scare of the moment was skin cancer. As I sat there on a stool a large red ant ran across my foot and bit me. I retaliated by reducing the ecosystem by one ant: I drowned the dude in my own sweat! Later we went down Pennsylvania Avenue to call on the President. Outside the White House every political nut had a place: people campaigning for prison release, a woman handcuffed to the railings with a banner reading, 'The FBI killed Kennedy' and a huge procession of Hare Krishnas, gibbering, clicking their finger cymbals and twirling like dervishes. The President was too busy to see us so we just visited the local sights; the Washington Monument, Lincoln's memorial, the Capitol building and the Smithsonian Museum. One day Viv and I wandered downtown. Washington at this time was 75% black: in the district we had entered there was not another white person anywhere to be seen. The houses were terraced with great holes in the walls where the kids ran in and out, the men wearing soiled Bruce Willis style vests sitting in rocking chairs on the verandas. We entered a shop to buy some slides of Washington at night, as we were warned not to wander about in the dark in downtown Washington. After a few minutes it became obvious that the sales person had no intention of serving me; each time I tried to catch his eye he turned away, then served the next black person to enter. It was a weird feeling to be discriminated against on the grounds of my skin pigmentation, as I have never done the same to any racially different person.

Where the Bugs wear Boots

For the final week of our holidays we went down to the beach, in this case Virginia Beach. We rented an apartment near the ocean and got in the water as soon as we'd unpacked. As usual, I overdid things and stayed out in the sun too long. I went to bed with a red back and woke about 4.00 am when I thought I'd wet myself. My shoulders were covered with huge blisters, some of which had burst. The next day I wore a T-shirt but the damage had been done. We were in a self-catering apartment but one night we went to an Italian restaurant where they made pizzas while you waited. We ordered our various pizzas and the chef, an exhibitionist of great skill, threw the dough around, spun it and stretched it, then his assistants added the topping and threw them into an oven. The resulting pizzas were huge, over half a metre in diameter, and were unbelievably hot. They were so tasty that we all had second degree burns on the face and fingers as a reward for not waiting for them to cool. As therapy we moved to an ice cream parlour and cooled our 'gobs' with some bizarre flavoured ice creams.

Each apartment had a local newspaper with details of what was happening and I noticed that Black Sabbath was playing at the Virginia Beach Dome at the weekend. We wandered down to the place and booked our tickets. The Dome, only a twenty minute walk away, was a huge geodesic structure constructed out of metal triangles and looked like a giant silver golf ball from a distance. I recall the considerable police presence on the night of the gig, all with side arms and bludgeons. Many of the young people in the queue to enter the dome were pushing their luck by standing on policemen's toes and making 'smart' comments. The police did well to keep their patience. The support band was 'The Blues Project' from New York. Before either band began, a representative of the management explained that the audience were to applaud at the end of each band's set and not after each number. Maybe they'd had crowd trouble before or were just a bit neurotic, as Sabbath had not played the venue before. It was a great performance and the crowd behaved well enough for the concert to conclude without incident.

Before we returned to Washington and home, we drove down the highway from Virginia Beach to Atlantic City and then Ocean City. These cities are all linked along the edge of the ocean by a massive boardwalk, with the ocean on one side and shops and restaurants on the other. I had to see what it was like 'under the boardwalk': dusty, dirty, smelling like an open plan toilet and full of derelicts, freaks, couples making out and old guys with metal detectors. Even as I was clambering out from under the walkway, a quarter fell through a crack in the boards and bounced off my head. It vanished into the sand. We walked for an hour observing beach life from the boardwalk. All human life was represented; surfers posing because they could, families just roasting themselves and a fenced-off body builders' pen containing a dozen men with boobs, covered with oil and shining like codfish. In the pen next door was a bevy of bimbos, in scanty but expensive bikinis, equally shiny, leaning on the fence and watching the guys exercising till they dropped. You can only hold your stomach in for a limited period!

In 1972 Charles Atlas died at the age of 79; in the same year my Mum died from incorrectly diagnosed ovarian cancer. Some months after her death I developed chronic abdominal pain. My doctor told me it was only wind and that I should eat slower and have less gravy on my meals. The symptoms failed to disappear. To be honest I didn't really trust the medical profession; they had almost killed my brother by incorrect diagnosis and had treated my Mother for obesity when she had an ovarian cyst almost football-size growing inside her. I was given an appointment to see a specialist some months in the future but I wasn't too sure I had a future. I had all sorts of tests, barium meals and IVP (kidney scan) plus X-ray investigation and then had to wait five weeks for the results. A friend who was my Best Man when I got married, suggested we went on holiday to Majorca and it seemed a good idea at the time. Some weeks before we went, another friend who had a big house in Thornton asked me to help paint his house. After some preparation it was time to apply the undercoat. I suggested I paint the extremely high bits for him, and he was quite happy to let me go ahead. The extending ladders only overlapped by two rungs, I secured nothing with rope, including myself and appeared to take frightening risks. His neighbours thought I had nerves of steel; nothing could be further from the truth, I was so convinced that I was terminal that I would rather have fallen from the ladder than slip away a day at a time like my Mum did over six horrific months. We completed the undercoating a few days before we were due to fly to Majorca so I arranged to help with the topcoat when we returned. We travelled by air from Manchester to Palma. As we disembarked, the heat was like opening the oven door and not moving back quickly enough. A coach with no air-conditioning took us to the hotel and arrived an hour before the evening meal, where we met the holiday representative. The hotel was excellent; the rooms all had a view of the pool and the beach beyond. I remarked to my friends that there was no way we were five minutes away, unless they expected you to jump off the cliff. The next day we found out the hard way: twenty minutes downhill and half an hour returning to the hotel laden with beach junk, knackered from swimming and heat exhaustion. The problem with all holiday brochures is that, like job descriptions and resumés, they only contain some truth with loads of flannel and small print, but at least the hotel building was complete.

The brochure promised four course meals and so there were; soup, vegetables, meat and ice cream. The soup was the same every day, virtually clear with four tiny bits of unknown vegetable and floating liquid grease blobs bringing an exciting rainbow effect to the dish; to be honest it looked and tasted like dishwater. The next course to arrive was the vegetables, almost always green beans; a very small portion in an aluminium ice cream dish which effectively radiated the heat away very rapidly indeed making the beans deliciously lukewarm. I waited for the meat to arrive and almost had to fight the waiter who was instructed to remove the vegetable dishes before the meat was served. The next course consisted of obscenely large gobbets of meat in painfully thin gravy which congealed rapidly. I found out later it was bull stew. The dessert was always ice cream, served in an aluminium dish that cleverly conducted the ambient heat into the contents so it was always soft and squishy; camel vomit comes to mind. I never really succeeded in communicating my wish to eat meat and vegetables together: to get the meal reasonably hot I had to conform to their four-course system. The headwaiter was an interesting dude, a six foot six stick insect, with a pale complexion and jet-black hair receding into a widow's peak. I proposed a theory that he was a vampire and proved it by taking Viv's concave make-up mirror and showing that there was no reflection. Sometimes he would help out his acolytes by serving the soup course: as he approach I would hunch my shoulders, whisper, 'Watch your necks!' and snigger with glee at my own stupidity.

The place we were staying at was called Arenal; I renamed it Urinal for reasons I will explain later. It was the cheapest place to stay on the island and we were beginning to find out why. The beach was an exhibitionist's paradise, with those who had it, flaunting it. Of course those who hadn't got it still flaunted it. There were human chipolatas, coated in coconut and other greasy tanning preparations, poaching themselves in the ultraviolet radiation, sand kickers expressing themselves, iron pumpers pumping; swimmers splashing and screeching, others just going through the motions, literally. Sand in every orifice and exotic insects hopping across your body, burrowing

144

into your skin, exploring your tonsils. A total new set of pathogens to which your puny body had not yet developed immunity, giving you dysentery with one drop of water. The beach was also dirty, littered with ice-cream wrappers, plasters and assorted detritus. It was infested by what seemed like several million tourists of the white trailer-trash variety. At least the water was clear, but then so is cat urine. While snorkelling near the posh end where the yachts were moored I thought I'd discovered a new variety of seaweed; a closer inspection revealed a tangled mass of used toilet paper. Nice! After a few days when my companions had enough of swimming in other people's urine and zapping themselves with ultra-violet B radiation, we went sightseeing in Palma, situated further down the coast. We saw the magnificent cathedral, visited a flea market where I was bitten by a flea, but the most memorable incident occurred just outside the cathedral. As we approached the entrance a local beggar cum shoeshine man dived at my feet in a well-executed flying tackle. Why me? He sat on the floor and signed that he wanted to shine my shoes. I tried at first to sign back that my suede boots were not supposed to shine and that if he did not let go I would have to kick him. He wouldn't let go so I dropped him a few pesetas and kicked myself free, as gently as I could.

On one occasion being still hungry after the hotel dinner, I was tempted to treat myself to bratwurst and sauerkraut from one of the many street vendors. I never buy hot dogs from street vendors at home as you don't really know what's in them and for how long they've been floating in brine; for some reason I trusted the grinning German implicitly. I had eaten bratwurst before but was totally unprepared for the sauerkraut. Within seconds of the first mouthful my past life flashed before me: now I understood why the German tourists drank so much; not just to take away the taste of sauerkraut but to remove the memory also. All night, every night we tossed and turned till about three 'o clock until the tourists, bevvied out of their brains on two-and-sixpence-a-bottle 'champagne' had beaten the Guinness Book of Records for singing 'Viva España' one million times. The clubs were full of greasy red-faced cretins, worse for drink, trying to stay upright at least until they 'copped off'. I was amazed at the profusion of night clubs: sweaty, noisy, smoky rooms full of slappers and parasites with the ubiquitous bimbos outside trying to persuade people with full wallets and empty heads to enter and sample the delights of watered down ale. I recall trying to avoid the pools of steaming vomit in the streets: life in the fast lane? I don't think so!

Where the Bugs wear Boots

In the fortnight on Majorca we did visit some nice places; Palma, Magalluf, Cala Bona, Formentor and Pollensa to name a few, all a reasonable drive away and all considerably classier than Arenal. The holiday probably did me good, but I didn't enjoy it much, after all I was under sentence of death, or was I? Less than a week after we came home I went to see the specialist for the results of the tests. To my surprise he informed me that they were all negative, there was nothing to worry about and that the pain was probably a nervous reaction caused by stress. I suggested that maybe I was on my way out and he was just making me feel good because I couldn't handle the truth. I still remember his answer, 'Bugger off and don't come back! If you're dead in six months, you are right and I am wrong!' The shock treatment worked; maybe I was alright. As soon as I grasped it I began to feel better; the power of the mind. The friend in need who had asked for help with the painting suggested we apply the topcoat at the weekend, weather permitting. Weather did permit so I set up the ladder secured to a drainpipe and began painting wearing a safety harness. They all thought my nerve had gone while on holiday: the truth was I was glad to be alive and had no intention of falling off his extremely high rooftop.

In 1973, Britain joined the Common Market, although I don't recall being asked if I wanted to or not. At this time the management introduced company appraisal before pay rises were assigned. These increases had two components, a large percent cost of living raise and a nominal (£50-100) merit rise. I was summoned to the Research Manager's office to hear the worst. He was a man who had worked for a large pharmaceutical company and was a brain-on-legs; unfortunately he had problems relating to people. He went pillar box red if he had to discuss money and seldom made eye contact. He usually cut his nails with a pair of scissors or gazed out of the window while anyone was speaking to him. He informed me that I was a Jekyll and Hyde character: one moment presenting an excellent seminar and the next hanging upside down in the toilets. Actually the way he put it was 'suspended in an inverted position in the bathroom'. Before judgement is passed and I am made to wear that uncomfortable jacket with the restraining straps again, I'd better explain.

A documentary on television suggested that the upside down Yoga position aided meditation by virtue of the increased flow of blood to the brain. The next day at tea break I decided to investigate. With great difficulty I suspended myself from a door on one of the cubicles in the toilet and found myself almost blacking out before I could attempt any

146

mental arithmetic. The door opened and the boss entered, saw me hanging upside down like a bat and walked out again. He had his own toilet adjacent to his office which he seldom left. He was fairly inaccessible, like a techno Howard Hughes, aided by a Gorgon-like secretary. Why he wandered onto the first floor and decided to take a leak I never found out. I chose that time and venue for my experiment because people never visited the toilet in their own time at tea breaks. Needless to say the upside-down experiment totally cancelled out the six months successful research; my merit rise was zilch again. I was quite happy with the cost of living rise but I must have looked a bit sorry for myself. As I was about to leave he took an envelope that had another chemist's name on it, removed a card and placed it in an envelope he had been writing on during my assessment. It was an invitation to a Common Market cheese and wine party at his large house near Southport. My first thoughts were unprintable, but on reflection I thought, 'Free food - party on, dude!' Then I remembered what had happened to my line manager. Paul was a most interesting person, closely resembling the actor Steve Buscemi, with eyes that looked as if he'd been run-over once or twice; I think the medical term is exophthalmia, or pop-eyes. His consuming interest in American comic books and old movies infected me also. He and his wife were invited to a dinner party at the boss's house. The meal was, as you might expect, fairly exotic; fillet steak with vegetables you can only get in the better shops and an array of cutlery that needed his high IQ to work out the order of use. His steak contained a small piece of gristle and to avoid the embarrassment of leaving it on the plate or the ordeal of actually swallowing it, he pulled out a pocket handkerchief and feigned a cough as he spat the gristle into it. The meal completed they retired to one of the lounges for coffee. This room was carpeted with a rich white rug with a pile you could lose a dachshund in. As they enjoyed their coffee the family cat entered. Cats always recognise those who fear them or are allergic to them and tend to approach these people. As the cat zeroed in on Paul he sneezed and instinctively pulled his handkerchief from his pocket. The gobbet of gristle flew into the air and landed in front of his boss's seat. Before Paul could confess the truth, or claim it was something that he found while clearing out his nasal passages, the cat pounced on it and ate it. The animal then assumed he had more tasty morsels secreted on his person and pestered him till his nose was running like a glassblower's ass; his hosts kindly removed the cat from the room.

Where the Bugs wear Boots

As I said, a free meal is a free meal, and a rare occurrence, so we decided to accept the invitation. In each of the many lounges there was an abundance of products from the major EEC wine and cheese producing countries, with his two young children embarrassingly scuttling about dressed as waiters. We dressed rather informally as usual, unfortunately most of the guests were suit people: my boss wore a suit with a pair of matching slippers to help us feel a little more comfortable. It was, to be honest a good do, but with few exceptions it was filled with rich and boring wallflowers. I frequently tend to be assigned to people sitting by themselves because I have the gift of the gab; once you start talking to the wallflowers at a party you soon find out why they are on their own.

In one room full of holiday curios and souvenirs there was a mandolin made from a large turtle shell hanging on the wall. I swiftly unhooked it and began my infamous impression of Elvis singing, 'Are you lonesome tonight?' With perfect timing the boss came in with some guests whose upper lips visibly curled at my crass exhibitionism and limited vocal talents. He informed us that we were going to play some games in the main lounge: this was not an option but an offer not to be refused. The 'games' consisted of a huge circle of guests with the boss in the middle reading quiz questions from a large book. I felt my minimal party spirit evaporating at an even greater rate. It felt like a new kind of assessment procedure as he worked steadily through the questions. He commented how interesting it was that I knew nothing about politics or cricket, but could answer the questions about rock music and Sci-Fi movies. As soon as we had eaten all we could, we made our apologies and returned to Aintree, or as my boss once described it, 'A filthy working class conurbation'.

The pay rise meant we could go abroad for our holidays again and this time we had two weeks on Evia, the biggest of the Greek islands. Greece at first sight seems to be a land cursed by deficiency. Possibly July was the wrong time to be there, but there appeared to be a chronic shortage of chlorophyll: most of the vegetation was desiccated muddy-brown. In addition there was a shortage of drinkable water. I wondered if a wrinkly epidemic had struck: all the men were wrinkled, toothless and pig-ugly, lying about doing nothing; the older women equally wrinkled were working away. The few children we saw were students of the School of Begging. Did they eat all the young girls? We never saw any in the two weeks we were there. There was also a shortage of edible food. I don't holiday abroad and demand English food but I dislike fish intensely. The Eritrea Beach hotel did offer a choice of meals but the choice was take it or leave it. The first meal we had at the hotel was fish soup; chunks of almost fresh fish with gills, bones and cartilage thrown in, presumably to make it more exciting, all floating in a turbid, watery stock: delicious! The next meal was equally gross; called calamari, it tasted like an old rubber hot-water bottle sliced up in fish water; I found out later it was squid.

We were in a group of sixty people from different backgrounds, representing a wide spectrum of personality, sense of humour and crap content. I didn't envy the guy organising the activities, there was no way to keep everyone happy all of the time. One outing to the centre of Athens was most interesting. The first thing I noticed was the police wearing funny hats, pleated skirts and pom-poms on their winkle-pickers: I considered whistling at one of them until I saw the automatic weapons they all carried. In every direction we could see the remains of massive temples. We went up the Acropolis and entered the Parthenon; this is not allowed nowadays because the visitors' feet were beginning to wreck the floor. Every statue had the nose and the willy missing, assuming it had the latter in the first place before vandals helped themselves to the weird souvenirs. We stood on Mars Hill where the apostle Paul gave his famous speech. As we looked round we could see all the temples to the various gods and as Paul pointed out in the sermon, they even had an inscription to 'the unknown god' in case they had left one out! Looking across Athens from Mars Hill it was difficult to picture the scene in Bible times, for beyond the temples were dozens of souvenir shops, coaches from all over and hundreds of tourists with cameras and camcorders. It was here that I learned to haggle over price for the first time. I fancied a brass replica Spartan helmet but the shopkeeper wanted the equivalent of £9 for it. John, the organiser of the holiday, told me to walk out the shop with him; as we did the salesman followed us and eventually took £2 for it.

Later John arranged a treat for us. Instead of returning to the hotel for another fishy delight, he had booked us into a 'genuine' Greek nightclub and restaurant. Near to the centre of Athens is a real seedy area called the Plaka, named I suspect, after the 'crud' that forms on your teeth if you don't brush them regularly. We had to jostle our way through narrow streets full of winos, perverts and other holidaymakers, past the strip joints, massage parlours and brothels to the club where we were expected. Some of our party were already freaked out before we arrived at our destination. The tables were laid out wedding style with one very long table down one wall and the banqueting tables coming off at right angles; like two big letter 'E's. We were informed that the evening consisted of a genuine Greek meal and live Greek 'entertainment'.

To my relief the main course was not fish but moussaka which was superb, washed down with retsina, a national beverage that tastes like a combination of cat urine and bleach and clears out the digestive system and sinuses as effectively as Domestos does for toilets. I don't recall what the dessert was. Some of the party were teetotal, no problem with that, but they tried to enforce their philosophy on the rest of us. They pushed their complimentary bottles of wine to the end of the table and sat glaring with curled upper lips as we kindly took the offending items off their hands and on to our table. Just as we were getting into conversation mode after the meal, three geriatric Greek dudes broke the silence with triangular guitars called bouzoukis. These guys had been informed by their mother that they could sing: she lied! I shoved an olive up each nostril because I could and forced down another glass of retsina. Each song had some 25 verses and I could feel the holiday spirit being universally exorcised despite the wine. Some of the party were enjoying it; the table with no-wine-by-choice were clapping away and really getting into the ethnic muzak. One of them was wearing a straw sombrero, a strange choice of headgear for a Greek evening out. Suddenly there was a scuffle by the kitchen door and out ran the fattest belly dancer known to man: the dismay on the faces of our swinging teetotallers was monumental. The heavy goods dancer, who by law should have had 'Keep Left' tattooed on her back, gyrated round the tables then, with amazing agility for her size, jumped onto a table. Have you ever noticed how cats are attracted to people who are allergic to them? It's a ramification of "Sod's Law'. Our belly dancer couldn't have selected a better table to strut her stuff than that of our upper crust travellers whose upper lips again curled like over-cooked bacon. The girl, I give the benefit of the doubt, totally oblivious to the sociological and psychological damage she was inflicting, continued to strut her superfluous stuff. The musicians must have felt pity for the table that was creaking and groaning, like those sitting round it, and ended the song, when the now extremely sweaty 'flobster' bounced onto the floor and out of our lives. We screamed for more just to upset the upper-crusties, but she was obviously too knackered or depressed to repeat the performance. We visited Corinth, Delphi and many other interesting historical sights. Too soon it was time to return to the UK and no more fish. Once again we were all frisked at the airport because of a terrorist attack some weeks earlier.

In 1974 the Academy award for Best Motion Picture went to 'The Sting', it was also the year when streaking became a craze. I must admit I've never had any inclination to even moon anyone, let alone streak. Ray Stevens recorded 'The Streaker' with the classic line, 'Don't look, Ethel!' 1974 was also the year our first child was born. What a load of bollocks is written about pregnancy and childbirth. Articles about how good women feel when pregnant; I don't think so. Viv was sick as a parrot for weeks and our doctor, an older man, didn't believe in new-fangled drugs and refused to prescribe a new wonder drug called thalidomide to relieve Viv's nausea and sickness when others were dishing it out like jellybeans. The wonder drug did control morning sickness OK but it also caused birth defects and we were glad our doctor was old fashioned. The television adverts showed the soft focus mother and child, a serene blonde with chubby happy baby; like giving birth was no big deal. The reality was pure agony; painful indignity; and I was only sat there holding her hand. Newborns are ugly little red-faced wizened prunes, covered with blood and slime, totally incontinent, totally self-centred: many people never progress beyond the latter.

I used to wonder what part in childbirth did the boiling of water in the Western movies represent, now I know; therapy to keep the men out of the way. A patronising obese nurse gave me the job of counting the contractions. We were left in a draughty corridor in Fazakerley Hospital's Maternity Unit, Viv on a trolley, me on a hard chair counting like a gibbering idiot. I was never in the Army, I was at university when conscription ended so I never had the joy of whitewashing coal with a toothbrush, but I now knew what it felt like. After some hours it was obvious that the pattern was changing; a lot more contractions per minute. There was a significant absence of staff but eventually I found a nurse who told me to calm down and carry on counting. I insisted she come and examine Viv and, clucking like an old hen, she grudgingly accompanied me back to the trolley. White faced she summoned help and they rushed Viv into the delivery room, telling me to wait outside. I of course did what I was told and pushed my way in! I got a stool at the head end and fought with Viv over who had the Entonox as Maddy made her entrance. In 1974 the fashion was chemical induction of birth, I suspect so the staff could plan holidays, barbecues and days off. By the time our second daughter was born, the fashion had changed again; no induction of birth - you waited until the child felt like leaving its cosy hibernaculum and joined you on Planet Earth. Contrary to the women's magazines, my eldest daughter's birth was not a quasi-spiritual occasion but a totally traumatic experience: I don't think the wife enjoyed it too much either. Visitors reckoned the baby looked just like me, virtually bald with wrinkled red skin, big eyes and a whining insomniac. It was three and a half years before Maddy slept through the night consistently; we realised later that the orange juice we gave her, supplied by the post-natal clinic, was coloured with an azo dye called tartrazine, which is known to cause allergic reactions, hyperactivity in children and trigger asthma in some people. To help the baby to sleep our family doctor prescribed a children's sedative: when I looked up its composition, as I always do, I found out it contained chloral hydrate, not something I was prepared to dose our child with. We tried brandy and whisky miniatures which only made matters worse; perhaps we should have drunk the hard stuff ourselves and left the child to party on.

I don't believe in buying sweets for children as a regular habit because the sugar causes obesity and dental problems, but Maddy had been good and we rewarded her with a small bag of Jellytots. These coloured gobbets of bone marrow squeezings were almost fluorescent, the green ones were particularly so. Being a good child she offered us one; why do children dislike green sweets? Why do the manufacturers still include green sweets? Anyway, for some reason that seemed right at the time, I took two green ones and pushed one up each nostril. Maddy was amused but too intelligent to mimic my stupidity. Viv was not amused, I almost daily confirmed her suspicions that I was an infantile yob, and today was no exception. I removed one of them and ate it to add to the grossness, but the other one was stuck firmly. The more I tried, the further up my snout it progressed. I tried pressurising the nasopharynx while closing the other nostril, and narrowly escaped pancaking my knickers. My wife suggested the Accident & Emergency clinic at Fazakerley Hospital: I tried to imagine what my answer would be when the triage nurse asked me how it got there. I decided to leave it there and just operate with one nostril. As far as I know it's still there.

At work, I commenced a new project improving the appearance of metallic auto finishes. These paints contain aluminium flakes, the orientation of which is significant to the appearance. The project involved a great deal of photo-microscopy work on samples of the paints on test panels. The research lab had a darkened microscope room and sitting in the dark, eyes pressed to the stereo eyepieces made one very sleepy, specially after dinner in the hot spell the country was

Where the Bugs wear Boots

enjoying. I was still getting little sleep as Maddy was not yet sleeping through the night, and one day I fell asleep for over twenty minutes while examining some coating panels under the microscope. I awoke when someone entered the microscope room and spoke to me. I looked up from the microscope and saw a look of terror on my colleague's face. I rushed to the washroom down the corridor and looked in the mirror. The result of twenty minutes flopped against the eyepieces had pushed my eyes back in their sockets; I looked like something from a Stephen King movie. My eyes did return to normal after a while. The last time I appeared that frightening was in my early days as a motorcyclist. I had no goggles and my crash helmet had no visor; I quite liked the sensation of my eyelids flapping at 70 mph plus, until I woke up one morning with extremely sore eyes. I looked in the mirror to find that the whites of my eyes had gone blood red. I looked like Dracula in the Christopher Lee colour version of the old movie. The sub-conjunctival haematoma subsided with time, and the bright red changed to a yukky brownish yellow. I treated myself to a pair of ex RAF pilot's goggles from a war surplus shop to prevent a repeat of the phenomenon.

But the child's insomnia continued. On another occasion I went to see the factory nurse with a splitting headache due to chronic lack of sleep. She gave me two para-Hypon tablets and a glass of water and suggested I lie on a trolley in a dark room till the tablets kicked in. Three hours later she woke me up in time to go home. My worst experience of sleepiness was some weeks later. I was so tired I just got into a cubicle in the toilet, sat down and fell asleep almost immediately. Fortunately I didn't dream I was using the facility. I woke with a start when someone in the trap next door flushed the system. I stood up, then my legs gave way as I had dead-legged myself by sitting on the bog for too long.

1975 saw the release of Jaws. I joined the millions who jumped in the air when the disembodied head rolled out of the hole in the boat. The polymer research team had an overall co-ordinator, Paul, then a number of laboratory heads responsible for various parts of the programme. One laboratory synthesised polymers, another characterised or tested the physical properties of the polymers, yet another formulated the polymers into coating systems and coated the systems onto metal test panels. I was responsible for the rheological (flow) studies on molten polymers as much of my work was on powder coatings. I was promoted to Senior Staff at the same time as a strange little man with horn-rimmed glasses and a Dracula-like widow's peak.

153

He appeared to have unlimited supplies of methane and was prepared to fart anytime, anyplace, anywhere without warning. We had a brass nameplate, 'Thunderbum', made for his laboratory but he refused to screw it to the door. He had a long suffering assistant, who worked in the small laboratory with this petomaniac. On her birthday we wrapped up a gas-mask in pretty paper, he saw her open it and still didn't get the message. One day I walked into the toilet and nearly collapsed with the stench. There he was washing his underpants totally unashamed that the vicious curry he'd had the previous night had caused him to follow through when he farted and horribly pancake his knickers. Nice man, he could never understand why he had few friends.

One day I arrived in work to find we all had polished brass nameplates on our office doors. Someone had given me a PhD, or thought I deserved one, as I had the title Dr. Russell. Later on I found out that the nameplates had been issued instead of the customary merit rise. I unscrewed mine immediately intending to ask my research manager's advice on how to pay my mortgage with a brass nameplate. His secretary had been keeping people off his back all day and she told me politely to go away. A joiner working on the roof panels outside the office saw me waving the nameplate and scuttled off to inform the Union what was going on. Within the hour the manager sent for me and I had to apologise to the union representative for removing the plate instead of summoning a joiner to do so. I then had a chance to discuss the situation for several seconds while the boss cut his nails and looked out of the window. He told me his hands were tied and there was nothing he could do about the missing merit rise, so I returned to the laboratory with an improved self-image, feeling totally motivated again. Not!

Viv's Mum and Dad had some American visitors staying for a week. One evening we invited them round for a meal and showed them some slides of Scotland, Wales, Devon and other picturesque places we had visited over the years. They invited us to visit them in North Carolina any time we were passing. How often do you just happen to pass NC? I didn't realise they had invited us to stay with them. Early in 1976 they wrote asking us if we'd like to come over for a holiday. We looked at our finances and decided to visit them in the July of that year. We flew from Manchester to New York then had our cases transferred from New York to Charlotte, North Carolina. Blanche and Euel were waiting as we walked into the terminal; they had our cases put on this huge coach that turned out to be their motor home. Since we had already had two long flights they thought we might like to sleep on the journey to Waynesville. The motor home had a shower, toilet, lounge, four bedrooms and a kitchen; Viv slept on the way to Waynesville, I dozed for a while but then sat up front to see where we were going. The road had mountains with a blue haze over them on either side, the Smokies: after about an hour we came to civilisation, Waynesville. We turned into a large drive, the entrance to their property: it took almost five minutes to wind in and out of the forested area until we arrived at their Georgian mansion. They had mentioned in a letter that a storm had uprooted eighteen of their trees and assumed they meant saplings. I knew Euel had the Ford and Buick agency for the whole of North Carolina but I didn't realise how large North Carolina was. As a teen in Greenville, South Carolina he had started rebuilding scrap cars and selling them; he progressed to hiring mechanics to do the same, then started selling new cars. With the money he made from cars he bought plots of land in strategic parts of the local network of highways, had services and building shells constructed, then leased them to large companies as shopping malls. These people not only paid rent but contracted to pay him a percentage of their profits. I guessed he must have had a few bob, in fact he was a multi-millionaire.

Our room was huge with en suite bathroom; in fact, every bedroom in the house was en suite. We were introduced to Margie, a large black lady with an ear-to-ear smile. From behind she looked like the lady whose face you never see in the Tom and Jerry cartoons; I expected any moment to hear her utter those immortal words, 'Thomas, yo is a baad cat!' She was the housekeeper and did all the washing we needed while we stayed with the Taylors. I must admit I judged my hosts wrongly when I saw they had a black 'servant'. Margie's husband had died and the Taylors gave her the job and paid her well, she was not a servant but an employee and treated as part of the family. I don't remember my head touching the pillow, but woke early next morning because Maddy did. She was almost two, a sticky fingered dynamo and we were staying in a mansion, every room full of art treasures or irreplaceable items. We had to watch her constantly, particularly when she'd been scoffing chocolate bars.

I had a traditional Southern breakfast, fried eggs, bacon, sausage and grits. The sausage was a lump of sausage meat which was dropped in the pan and flattened; it looked like a cow pat but tasted like sausage. The grits were unbelievable: hard and rice-like with no taste and dripping with water which made interference patterns with the grease from the other items. After breakfast we had a tour of the property. Euel gave us a car which always seemed to have a full tank of fuel: one night I heard a noise out back and thought I'd caught a burglar; it turned out to be a serf who had instructions to refill the petrol tank on our car each night. We had a set of house and freezer keys, but never needed the house keys as no-one locked their houses or cars except when they went on vacation. These people reminded me of upper class hillbillies particularly considering some of the things they ate: turkey and broccoli stew, corn bread, lemon jelly with tomatoes, cucumber and shredded lettuce set in it which they called salad, the ubiquitous grits and pork and turnip greens. They eat the part of the turnip that we throw away and give the turnip itself to the animals. Life operated on a real slow level and after a while we got used to it.

For several days they took us out until I had the hang of the highway system, then we explored the area in the car they had provided for us. One memorable trip was Maggie Valley where we went round a native American village called Oconoluftee. In the town of Cherokee we had our photo' taken with a genuine Indian chief. I remarked to Viv how sad that this proud man was reduced to doing this. After this bit of excitement we drove on then took a chair-lift up to Ghost Town. This is a replica western town with a dusty main street, a cemetery called Boot Hill and saloons and hotels on every corner. Every hour on the hour the streets were cleared and mean looking dudes indulged in gunfights; very noisy and very realistic. There were bodies falling from the rooftops everywhere and a tall undertaker measured them then dragged them to his premises by the heels. Later, returning through Cherokee, we noticed the old chief loading his tepee into a brand new white Cadillac, smiling past himself. Maybe things weren't so bad after all. Driving to Cherokee we had noticed a large metal cage on the side of the road with a grizzly bear lying in a heap on some straw at the back. I felt empathy for the bear, locked up just for being himself: he looked harmless and cuddly. I wanted to release him, but remembered a steel garbage container I'd seen in the Smoky Mountains which had been ripped open by hungry bears. At least I'd take a photo, maybe send him a copy. I parked the car and checked the camera, just five shots left. The bear was still lying on the straw, virtually unmoved from when we had driven past. I set up the camera and poked the lens through the bars so that they wouldn't show on the photo. I heard Viv shout, turned to look as the camera jerked out of my hands and onto the sidewalk. Turning back I found myself eyeballing the bear as he stood upright, towering over me, the dude must have been eight or nine feet high. The moment I'd approached the cage the bear had lurched forward, if Viv hadn't shouted I'd have had a slice taken out of my head, as it was the camera was destroyed. I was so glad I had only thought about letting him out. I rescued the film from my dead camera; the resultant photograph just showed a dark blur as my underwear nearly did.

We had many picnics in the Smoky mountains with the Taylors. Some of the peaks, like Mount Mitchell and Grandfather Mountain were so high we were shivering with the cold. There were many picnic places with stone shelters and slate grates built in so we could build fires with which to cook and keep warm. The views from these peaks were 'gob smacking'. One day we went out with the wife of one of Jimmy Carter's aides, a friend of the Taylor's, and we all took something to eat which we shared up in the dizzy heights of the Pisgah National Forest. Again it was very cold and to make things more interesting, the lady's contribution was a thermos of iced baked beans. We had Pringles computerised potato chips for the first time; in 1976 you couldn't get them in the UK.

At the weekend we went up to Lake Summit to meet their two sons and their families. Euel had bought the seven mile long lake with the mountain adjacent and had houses built on either side of the mountain for each of his sons. On the opposite side of the lake he'd built a large log cabin with a path leading down to a small dock and sheds which held three power boats. I was given the keys to one and we explored the lake for a few hours. Later we had a go at water skiing; Viv swallowed gallons and never managed to actually get moving on the water. I did it for three seconds then bit the water yet again. We stayed in the cabin overnight but I couldn't sleep for the shooting pains in my arm muscles. The next day we drove through a town called Canton, famous for its orchards and apple processing factory. The smell of the fermenting purulent apple waste was awful. No sooner had we passed through the town and into fresh air again than I became aware of a stench that can only be described as unbelievably evil. Our hosts were far too refined to cope with the question, 'Who's farted?' and before I could paraphrase it or beg for a window to be opened, Euel explained that the smell that had me dry retching was a skunk that had been hit or frightened on the road ahead. I made a mental note never to frighten or even approach a skunk under any circumstances.

Looking at a map I noticed that we were less than 100 miles from Kingsport, Tennessee, the head office of the Eastman-Kodak company.

Euel suggested we visit and had a Ford Gran Torino brought up to the house from his car sales premises for us to use. This is the car that Starsky and Hutch used in the series but without the white custom stripe and the dubbed in racing car sounds.

Tennessee is very similar to North Carolina and the people equally hospitable. We spent the day at the Eastman Kodak factory, some secretaries amused Maddy while we met some of the research team that I knew from 'phone calls and reports. Our first two weeks flashed by then we had a choice to make. Our hosts were going to the Southern Baptist Convention for the week, the big attraction was that Richard Nixon was speaking there, say no more! We had a choice to make; we could accompany them to the Convention, stay in Waynesville, or drive from North Carolina, through South Carolina and Georgia and tour Florida for the week. After a millisecond's consideration we opted for the Florida trip. We visited Stone Mountain and Atlanta in Georgia, Jacksonville Beach, Daytona Beach, Silver Springs and Orlando where we visited Disney World. One day was not really long enough to see everything but we wanted to visit Sea World before driving back to Waynesville. Strange the way time runs faster when you're enjoying yourself and slower when you're not. We were soon on our way back to our end-terrace after a taste of life in the fast lane.

When I returned to work after the holiday my research manager at Kodak 'went bananas' as our trip to Kingsport was an unofficial visit which he had not authorised. He had a long memory and was unhappy with me for this and another reason: I had a beard and long hair and he expressed his dislike of this fact. As I seldom ventured outside of the research department and had little or no customer contact I suggested my appearance was irrelevant and none of his business. Big Mistake!

The next year at pay assessment time I received no salary increase as punishment for failing to adjust my dress code. We went on holiday for four weeks in the USA to stay with my brother Dave and family who were now living in King of Prussia, Philadelphia: he was lecturing at Penn State and Villanova Universities. Once again I was the bad boy because the maximum holiday senior staff employees were supposed to have consecutively was three weeks only. We managed to get a flight direct from Manchester to Philadelphia and Dave picked us up in his new Chevrolet Camaro. The first week we toured fairly locally, we did the horse-drawn Philadelphia trip which is a good way to see the city. Philadelphia is very clean and has many huge fountains; Maddy managed to fall into two of them. The shopping malls were open all night and scrupulously clean. One night I couldn't sleep and drove down to the mall which had a foods-of-the-world section where you could buy Cajun, Mexican, French, Chinese and other ethnic dishes and eat them in a central dining area. On another occasion, looking for somewhere to eat, we found a Roy Rogers restaurant and decided to give it a try. All of the staff were dressed as cow persons. The cowgirls seemed to be doing most of the running about and the cowboys stood around saying 'Have a nice day!' as customers arrived or departed. Maddy, now four and a half years-old had a cowboy special with sausage, beans and varied methane generating fast food items. I had a vicious Mexican chilli that I shovelled down at high speed. Maddy seemed interested in the red kidney beans in my meal: to further the child's appreciation of the good things in life I suggested she sample the chilli and she did. In a matter of seconds she recycled the mouthful of chilli and her cowboy special, projecting her stomach contents across the table; the majority of the fallout being on my plate, which was almost empty. Before I could blink a posse of intense cow persons arrived at our table, in minutes the table and Maddy were cleaned up and I had a new plate of chilli, and an extra, 'Have a nice day'. It could only happen in America. Viv was mildly amused by the entertainment but missed out on the extra food by sitting next to the child instead of opposite.

My brother Dave and his wife were members of a private open-air swim club with four large pools; we spent a few days chilling out in the sun and cooling down in the water. We also visited George Washington's headquarters at Valley Forge, a significant site during the War of Independence. Another full day out was Dutch Wonderland, a theme park in Lancaster, operated by Amish people dressed in black with long beards and stovepipe hats. The men were interesting too! The following week we were off down the Schuykill (pronounced Skoogle) Expressway, onto the Pennsylvania Turnpike and north to the Poconos where we hired a log cabin for two weeks on the banks of Lake Naomi. The whole of the Poconos consists of mountains and freshwater lakes that have been artificially given sandy beaches by the dumping of millions of tons of white sand. One night I had a walk and saw the staff raking the beaches and spraying disinfectant to sanitise them before the next day's visitors arrived. Americans sanitise everything; in the motels they sanitise the drinking glasses and any horizontal surfaces one might touch, including the toilet seats. I suppose it's better than contracting the plague as some have done in other countries. Our cabin also had its own landing stage with a large

Indian canoe with which we could explore the other lakes which all interconnected; eventually we got the hang of paddling at speed without falling into the water.

We returned for a week around the Ocean City beach area. At a service area on the Atlantic City Expressway we found a fruit farmer selling sacks of peaches for $1.50. We ate half the sack between six of us and then a problem emerged. Maddy had sticky fingers and was bleating about it. How can you not have sticky fingers when scoffing peaches? I had to buy a bottle of cooled water to clean her hands; the rest I poured on my head in an attempt to cool off. I took my camera to the beach to get some surfing photos, and succeeded: I also had a rogue wave cover me and the camera, even though I held it at arm's length over my head when I saw the wave approaching. I put the camera under one of the fresh water showers by the boardwalk and eventually it was OK. I built the kids a tree house over the last few days, then it was time to catch a DC-10 and return to cold, rainy Liverpool again.

When I returned I found my desk missing; I had been transferred to another section, I suspect as a disciplinary measure for having four weeks off. My 'superior' was educationally well endowed, with a PhD and highly innovative, but was mortally afraid of doctors and dentists. If he had toothache, he took aspirins until the tooth crumbled, the nerve rotted and the pain subsided. This could take months and gave him breath like a hippo's litter tray. My 'inferior' was a chap with a number of inadequacies who had taken up martial arts training to improve his self image. He ate loads of garlic and spicy foods and practised judo almost every night; seldom did he get round to having a shower after his efforts. The combination of 'tandoori' and 'randori' gave him armpits like a baboon's crotch; a permanent miasma that followed him everywhere and remained when he had gone. Little imagination is required to appreciate what sharing a small office was like with these gentlemen. If I arrived first I opened the window and shivered; if one of them was present I overdosed on Polo mints to create a breathable atmosphere, or shoved cotton wool balls saturated with eucalyptus oil up each nostril. The worst scenario was to work in any breathable atmosphere then return to the office without my own air supply; the fetid atmosphere was guaranteed to produce a dry retch from anyone.

Perusing a chemical engineering journal I noticed an interesting advert: a South London ventilation engineering company was offering free quotations for fitting fume extraction units to suitable pieces of machinery. I sent off the form the same day; in the space for the item of machinery needing extraction I put the name of one of my rancid colleagues. It amused me, the idea of extraction equipment fitted to one of them, but to my surprise a week later some ventilation engineers arrived to measure up the 'equipment'. They had not telephoned to say they were coming and were not amused to find that the equipment for extraction was human. They also agreed having entered the office that something needed to be done. I had been griping for an office of my own for months, I even invited the boss to come up and sample the atmosphere, but had no success. Right out of the blue some weeks later, he ventured onto the first floor and called in at the office when I was at lunch. A small store room was cleared and I had an office of my own within the week: very speedy for the company. I still had shoulder length hair and seldom wore a suit because I seldom came into contact with the outside world.

The research manager surrounded himself with company men who carried a briefcase everywhere. The boss once told me he'd noticed that I never carried a brief case. I informed him that I didn't need one: I didn't bring sandwiches in for lunch and I didn't need to take work home, in fact, people who took work home were either overworked or incompetent; not the answer he was looking for! I have always viewed work as a necessity, I need the money, and the company need the brain power so we have a contract. I work, they pay me as an intellectual mercenary: have test-tube, will travel. Most employers don't see it this way; they want to own employees, train them to do the task required without question and be happy with the working conditions and pay.

There were two exits to the research block, one considerably nearer the car park which I used to arrive on time and leave on the dot, planning my research to fit this schedule. Many of the other laboratory heads aimed to finish 5-10 minutes later then left the building by the further exit which meant they passed the manager's window. Call it game-play or creeping, I wasn't prepared to do it; I just wanted to do my job then return to the real world. I seldom attended the parties and official outings; I have problems with people who ignore or discuss me all year round then want to lick my ear when they are worse for wear after an office booze-up. So now you know, I'm state-registered antisocial. After dinner I used to sit in my office and listen to my Heavy Metal tapes; this musical genre requires a certain volume to be fully appreciated, so the Bridge players in the adjacent office reported me to the manager, which improved my promotion chances no end. Nevertheless, I decided to try and conform a little for financial reasons. I had a short-hair wig made and bought a more sober charcoal grey business suit. I already possessed a mustard yellow suit and a red corduroy suit with white boots which were a little loud; how I had the bottle to wear them I don't know. I managed to get my hair under the wig, put on the charcoal suit and went to pick my wife up from work. I waited in the foyer and she walked right past me because I looked so different. My new image cost, not just money but comfort. The wig made my head hot and itchy and the suit was too hot as I was accustomed to T-shirt and denims. I turned up at work on Monday morning in my new gear and only a few recognised me at first. I was too smooth to work in the lab so I sat in my office and did some writing up. Throughout the day different people came to peek in the office and see the new me; the boss didn't see my effort to curry favour. By the end of the day I was melting: when I got home I shelved the suit and wig and decided the sacrifice was too great. As I got near the research block on the Tuesday morning there was no one in sight, unusual as I was one of the last to arrive. As I walked down the corridor to the office, again, no one was around. I walked into the laboratory and nearly dropped my breakfast: almost everyone in the research unit was there, all wearing wigs of some sort borrowed from wives and neighbours. Paul had engineered the joke as he did on many occasions, so it was time for payback.

He was preparing for another trip to Kingsport, Tennessee, and I heard him telling someone that he hadn't had a company medical for years. I decided it was time he had some medical treatment. I got hold of one of the works nurse's official memo pads and a blood lancet used for pricking the thumb for blood tests. I got a secretary to produce a memo to the effect that Paul's lack of medicals had not gone unnoticed and that I was authorised to do a blood test instead of the nurse. We were sitting in his office during a tea break when the memo was delivered. As he read it his face became pale. He screwed it up and threw it in the waste bin. At this point two of the assistants grabbed him and I produced the lancet from my pocket; he fainted before I even took it out of its sterile container. I know it seems like all we did was play jokes on each other, not so! We achieved success with virtually every project we undertook, but the work was classified and I remember the funny bits better anyhow.

I once accidentally set off a fire alarm, or thought I had, and this led to the longest running practical joke of them all. As a consequence of the false alarm, I received an invitation to join CAFE, the Company Accident, Fire and Emergency committee based at Harrow headquarters. This, of course, was a total figment of Paul's imagination, as was the false alarm. The equally imaginary head of this committee was a William Hampstead who sent really nasty letters sometimes, and at one stage appeared to be trying to 'come onto' me. Every letter I sent back in retaliation or refusal to meet him at home for a 'fancy dress party' was cleverly taken out of the external mail and re-routed to my persecutors who planned what the next stage in the 'relationship' would be. Occasionally I had my doubts about this character but my persecutors got official things printed to convince me otherwise. They even primed a visiting member of the Harrow staff to tell me that Hampstead had been talking about me and that I needed to be careful in dealing with him. I was all set to complain to our research manager, or to travel down to Harrow and beat the crap out of this guy, so well did they wind me up. The 'Gotcha' lasted for about four months and provided a great deal of amusement for the perpetrators.

This may surprise you, but bossy, ill-mannered people irritate me. I was working in my broom cupboard office late one afternoon when one of the managers put his head round the door and informed me that he had important visitors arriving for a tour of the laboratories on the following morning and that I should make sure I was wearing a tie. This most excellent person was not my supervisor, he had very little to do with me, and so I decided to ignore his request for tie wearing. I later had second thoughts and decided maybe I would wear a tie. The next day I heard his voice boom out as he officiously showed his visitors into the laboratory next to my office. After an interval, I heard them depart and approach my office. As they approached my office he began to describe my function in the organisation, put his head inside the door then swept his visitors past explaining that I was not present. One of the visitors looked back over his shoulder as they were escorted onwards: a look of disbelief on his face. As ordered, I was wearing a tie - a red plastic rotating bow tie, a red plastic nose and nothing else above the waist.

You may be surprised to know that I often wondered why my requests for promotion were ignored. I began writing a sitcom I called 'Boffins' based on my experiences at Kodak. Scientists are always shown demonstrating extra-white washing or teeth and stereotyped as thin, white-coated, bespectacled nerds whose life is given over to science. You may find the odd one of these around, but most scientists I know are extremely creative and highly eccentric. I sent a sample episode and series plan to ITV with no success; so I shelved the project.

Chapter 11

Big mistake!

I was setting up a rheological experiment when I received a telephone call; I had a visitor at reception. I left the equipment set up and went to see who it was; usually it was a representative trying to sell something I didn't need, in fact it was the director of a local photographic business. He had with him an acquaintance who needed advice on a photochemical project he was trying to develop. This gentleman wanted to use existing UV cure technology to customise cars and print logos at high speed on wagons or vans. Car customising never really caught on here but was very popular in the USA. Enthusiasts would get a car; jack up the rear suspension, fit spoilers, extra-wide tyres and chromium-plate anything that wasn't chromed already. The automobile bodies were painted with a variety of wild finishes and images; metal flake made the vehicle sparkle in sunlight; 'vreeble' consisted of applying two coats of contrasting colour; the top coat would crack like Mississippi mud when dry to show the colour below. The designs painted on varied from simple flames to complex artwork that took an artist several weeks to produce and cost thousands of dollars. The final step was the use of furry fabrics to cover the dashboard, seats and the rest of the interior like a rock stars' coffin. The cheap alternative was the use of decals or stickers with ready-made designs. Cars had been all-over powder coated and UV cured several years before at the Ford Motor Company in the USA and photographic images had been applied to a variety of surfaces including cars; nevertheless, the production of commercial custom UV cured images was a good idea in principle. A company was formed; as the chemist, I was to develop the polymers and photo-initiators, another guy would devise the quartz optics to cure the polymers and apply and test the systems and market the product.

Kodak were operating a voluntary redundancy scheme at this time so I got a quote and decided to take the money and work full time in developing the photopolymers. My wife had problems with the whole thing, her intuition said 'Stay at Kodak, don't get involved in the project'. I, of course, ignored her, applied for redundancy and invested a third of my redundancy payment in the company. Within weeks I realised that the company had no money. Almost every Friday morning they needed to persuade the bank manager to loan enough to pay the wages of the men in the factory. The main business that supported the research was car body repair and refinishing, which was fraught with cash-flow problems and bouncing cheques. I never got the company car that was part of the package that convinced me to leave Kodak, and I never saw the company accounts; there was always some reason why not. I don't think they appreciated the complexity of the project; apart from identifying the right UV curing paint formulation, achieving inter-coat adhesion with the existing paint and stabilising the image to light and atmospheric oxygen there was also the impossibility of projecting a flat two-dimensional image to focus sharply on the curvature of a car body. Nevertheless I obtained samples of UV cure polymers and photo-initiators and began experimentation.

I drafted a patent with the three of us as co-inventors and it was submitted to the Patent Office. The company tried to sell the idea to a millionaire. The rich dude eventually dropped us, even though we all shook hands and cracked a bottle of Dom Perignon champagne to cement some sort of deal at the time.

1979 was the year that Margaret Thatcher became Prime Minister and the year that John Wayne rode into the sunset for the last time. We decided on a new approach. As kids we used to transfer images from newsprint to paper or cloth by using turpentine or white spirit. We found that paint solvent would transfer a faint image from textile transfers onto most surfaces; suddenly the UV-cure method was on hold. Some thermally applied fabric transfers were obtained and a kit was designed. The images were faint and totally unstable, as the transfer dyes needed heat to activate them. I had become a spare part, as the company were convinced that the solvent transfer method was the way to go. I had left Kodak to work on UV polymers which were no longer flavour of the month. Some days I was polishing cars until my fingerprints disappeared, or filling little cans with solvent and packing the transfer kits they intended to sell without any proper light fastness or weatherometer testing. I was glad when it was time for my annual holiday; I had about £1500 left from my Kodak redundancy payment and decided to visit the USA again. We decided to stay at my brother's home in Philadelphia for a week then fly down to Miami and hire a car for two weeks and explore the southern half of Florida which we hadn't visited before.

We got a direct flight to Philadelphia and Dave picked us up from the airport. The house he was renting was a farmhouse with many acres of land and a big outdoor swimming pool. He was too busy to come on vacation, so we took his in-laws and children with us to stay for a week in a log cabin in the Poconos. His father in law was a state-registered moaner. I was driving an AMC Ambassador, a huge station wagon, and kept to the statutory 60 mph, but he reckoned I drove too fast: on several occasions he screeched, 'We'll all be killed!' when I was only doing 25 mph on a forest trail. He had a wooden leg of which he was immensely proud. He once explained to my niece, who was five at the time, that the doctor had taken his leg off. The next time they took the young-un to the doctors she had to be dragged into the surgery, screaming, 'Grandad's leg! Grandad's leg!'

The father-in-law sat most of the time with a handkerchief on his head, knotted at each corner, complaining that America was too hot. He was very nosy and was caught going through someone's case on two occasions, but the worst scenario was to come. One evening we had waffles and maple syrup for supper then went to bed as we had an early start the next day. One of the children knocked on our door and told us to come and see something gross. We had bought a pack of disposable paper plates to save washing up and had put the sticky maple syrupy disposables in the garbage bin. Looking round the corner we saw the father-in-law licking the syrup off the plates he'd taken from the bin and replacing them in the packet with the unused plates. This confirmed my suspicions that he was losing it!

We visited places in the northern Pennsylvania mountains we had not visited before; Winona Falls, spectacular as it had been raining overnight, and the Alpine Slide, a high speed ride on a track down a slope used for skiing in winter. The trolleys had a simple braking system to control the speed; I don't recall using the brakes at all on the breath-taking run down the mountainside. An added bonus was a chair lift to the top. They had to drag me away from the Alpine Slide, but only as far as the massive water slide which propelled the victims down a plastic tube at crazy angles for some time before dumping them in a pool. This ride had stairs to climb but I spent an hour or so leaping into it like the poor man's Superman: I was crocked the next day with painfully strained stomach muscles but it was worth it.

Wherever you went there were the golden arches of McDonalds;

they were promoting the Happy Meal for the first time so we had to call in and get one for Maddy. At the end of the week we returned to Philadelphia and flew to Miami. The flight was a little turbulent, but then so is life: the real crunch came when they served lunch; smoked salmon and caviar. They probably thought they were doing us proud and didn't know I hate fish. They had a root around in the storage area and dug out an old pie and some vegetables for my lunch. Even though I wasn't eating fish, I was surrounded by fish-eaters and the smell made me as green as a chlorophyll butty; taking a short walk outside is not an option on an aeroplane.

Arriving in Miami we picked up our air-conditioned Plymouth saloon for the Florida tour. It was early afternoon so we visited the Miami Seaquarium for a few hours then decided to find somewhere to stay for the night. We drove through Miami Beach, where hotels were offering cheap rates at $200 a room and ended up a few miles away in Hollywood Beach where we found a quaint Spanish-style motel called the 'Adobe Hacienda'. It was $20 per room and typical of almost every American hotel or motel I have stayed in, it was spotlessly clean with en-suite bathroom and colour TV. Outside was a large heated swimming pool; early next day I crept out and watched dozens of lizards sunning themselves in the rockeries that partially surrounded the pool. As soon as I splashed into the water the lizards vanished as if by magic. Some were frightened that the lizards were around, although you never saw them once the pool was inhabited; I reminded them that the lizards ate the ants and other creepy-crawlies that were notably absent at the Adobe Hacienda.

We took the Interstate A1 south to Key Largo and the John Pennekamp Coral Reef State Park. We had a swim in the bathing area which was protected by substantial shark nets. The water was hot like bath water but as I came out of the water the salt crystallised on my skin in exotic patterns. The freshwater showers were cold by comparison with the seawater but refreshing. I went to get tickets for the glass bottomed boat while Viv and Maddy were finishing their lunch. The glass-bottomed ship cruised out over the reef and had viewing panels below deck where we sat and watched the turtles, sharks and other fishes strutting their stuff. Our original intention was to drive along the Florida Keys to Key West. The Keys are a chain of islands jutting out into the ocean and connected by a highway; I realised we didn't have the time to visit the Keys and get to other places we'd planned to visit. So from Key Largo we took the Everglades Parkway, a 70 mile highway north straight up the Gulf coast. The parkway is also known locally as Alligator Alley because it cuts through parts of the Everglades Swamp and you sometimes have to give way to alligators crossing the road. About 25 miles from St Petersburg we were hit by a storm. It was not possible to drive as the windscreen wipers couldn't cope with the torrential downpour. We sat and watched the lightning flashing from cloud to cloud, cloud to sea and occasionally incinerating trees. My passengers were a bit worried so I explained the Faraday Cage effect and why we were safe inside the car; I'm not sure they believed me. Soon the storm was over, the sun ruled OK again and we continued.

After the air-conditioning of the Plymouth we felt a bit cold, but stepping out of the car in St Petersburg we were roasted alive. From the freaky inverted pyramidal building at the head of the pier we could see a beach area, so we parked the car and went for a swim. As we walked onto the beach from the street a colourfully dressed black dude, drunk as the proverbial newt, welcomed us to St Petersburg on behalf of the residents. There were a lot of black people on the beach; as I entered the water with Maddy I looked back to locate our speck on the beach and realised there were only black people on the beach. As Maddy splashed around in her armbands a large black guy, also supervising a child of Maddy's age, introduced himself with, 'You folks must be visitors!'. I generally blend in when visiting the States; I don't wear a knotted handkerchief on my head, not in public anyway, so I was surprised. He explained that no local white people ever used the beach and had a theory to back up his observation: 'Perhaps they think they'll turn black in the water!' An hour or so later, walking back to the car I saw a pelican fly past. I was about to comment on this when I realised that in St Petersburg they are as common as seagulls in the UK. Incidentally, armadillos are almost as common as hedgehogs and the ants, bigger than ours, have a nasty bite.

The next morning we drove to Sanibel Island over a causeway; not a single other person was around so we had the whole white sandy beach to ourselves. The water was warm, which was to be expected in the Gulf of Mexico, and I was splashing about and swimming underwater when I heard Viv and Maddy shouting but I was too far out to hear what they were shouting. They were also waving so I waved back, then they began to point out to sea and when I turned to look behind me, I too could see the large fin some distance out to sea but definitely cruising in my direction. Whether shark or dolphin, I wasn't going to hang about to find out; a thought flashed through my mind;

perhaps the beach was empty because there was no-one left to eat. I left the water at record speed, trying not to splash too much and we decided to go for something to eat before our finny companion ate us. Later the same day we visited the Bounty, the replica sailing ship that was built for the film 'Mutiny on the Bounty'. I wasn't prepared to pay the excessive price to board the ship so I just photographed it, then we left St Petersburg and drove across the Sunshine Parkway to Tampa and Busch Gardens.

Busch Gardens is a theme park with a difference; the Budweiser beer factory is situated in the middle of it. The theme is Africa and this is reflected in the rides and zoological features. We had a boat ride simulating some of the scenarios of the movie 'The African Queen'. As the boat progressed past the waterfall towards the African village, a monkey jumped onto the boat, removed a man's toupee then climbed back into the trees cuddling the wig as if it was a baby: the man was not happy to be the source of our amusement. His accompanying bimbo was not too impressed either; maybe she didn't know her beau was bald as a coot. We went on most of the rides with one exception, the Python, a high speed roller coaster which looked dangerous. I photographed the screaming people as they hung upside down as it flashed round two huge vertical loops, then we visited the Budweiser factory; as I expected, it was clinically clean, stainless steel and impressive. As the tour finished we entered an open veranda where we were invited to sample the products; we did! Maddy wanted to taste the amber nectar and some years on is still partial to a cold Budweiser. The veranda overlooked a pool full of alligators, not like they are in the zoo, comatose with coins on their heads, but moving and snapping in the Florida heat. For some reason that escapes me I decided to complete my photographic record of the visit with some shots from the Python. Waiting in the queue I couldn't see the people coming off it; had I done so I would probably have chickened out. As they fastened the harness to stop me falling out I set up the camera and prepared to shoot. As the thing rocketed into the first loop, the G-forces whacked the camera onto my nose which began to bleed: on the second loop the blood was squirting out in a parabola, the equation for which escapes me. The good thing about the speed of the ride was that it ended quickly and I was able to get a tissue from my back pocket and clean myself up before the family saw me.

Driving towards Orlando we noticed the signs for Cypress Gardens, the self styled 'water-ski capital of the world'. Still sensitive about my own pathetic attempts at the sport the year before, we thought, 'Why not?' as long as someone else is doing it. Cypress Gardens is a huge lake surrounded by exotic landscaped areas representing extremely large gardens from different parts of the world. The demonstrations of formation skiing, jumping, twisting and even water-skiing with no skis at all, were amazing but insufficient to ever get me on the things again. In one of the gardens a parrot show was in progress. These birds were huge red and green Amazonian types with big black beaks that could crack nuts or finger bones with ease. After the show I had my photograph taken kissing one of the parrots, viewing it when developed I realised that, large as the parrot's beak was, mine was bigger.

Our final visit was Disney World at Orlando: we stayed overnight in Kissimmee a few miles away for a fraction of the cost of accommodation in Orlando. The kids in the USA were on holiday so every ride or show had long queues, but at least they gave some indication of how long you have to wait. We waited for an hour to take Maddy on the Dumbo flying elephant ride to have her change her mind at the last moment. Later we got her a Mickey Mouse balloon which she let go and watched float into the skies. Each time she went to hug Mickey, or the sweaty student in the Micky suit, there was a crowd of parents shoving their brats into him in camcorder frenzy; I had to get pushy myself to get a good photo of Maddy with her hero. We visited the Haunted Mansion, went on the Riverboat, suffered the trauma of Space Mountain, were attacked by the Pirates of the Caribbean and, when totally 'knackered', had to wait for the illuminated procession and fireworks. Like the previous visit, it was impossible to see everything in a day. We drove back to the motel and crawled into bed.

Our last day had arrived. We drove across to the Space Centre for another highly condensed morning before returning the car to the rental agency at Miami Airport. To my horror we were presented with an invoice for refuelling the car, something I had forgotten in the rush. I had about $2 and £10 in English money: my cash card was unacceptable in the USA. I offered to send a money order when we got home and would have done so. I could think of worse things than being detained in Miami for an extra day or two but the manager sorted it out. They let us off with the cost of the petrol and bade us, 'Have a nice day!' As we boarded the aeroplane I could see a row of six DC-10s with the Miami Airlines logo. Since our last transatlantic flight there had been two DC-10 crashes with extensive loss of life. At O'Hare airport in Chicago 273 were killed when an engine fell off and, later in the year, a further 257 lost their lives when a DC-10 crashed into a mountain in Antarctica. As the stewardesses went through the safety drill I realised that we too were sitting in a DC-10 about to take off. The others didn't notice and I wasn't going to tell them: I did pray a bit more than I usually do. There were no problems with the flight other than that which I caused for myself. The fresh orange juice was free and I must have put two pints or more down my neck. I paid for my folly later when the juice worked through my system and I had to remain in the vicinity of the smallest room for the best part of the next day.

On my return to work I heard that our product had been featured on Tomorrow's World. When I mentioned this the reaction was of acute embarrassment which I found surprising. A few days later I noticed an envelope from the Patent Office which was not addressed to me. I opened it and found the latest copy of our patent, but with my name missing. The patent was obviously written by someone with a chemistry degree, namely me: with respect, the other dudes on the patent couldn't even pronounce the names of the photo-initiators, never mind formulate them into photochemical compositions. Like a good Monopoly player I went directly to the toilet, did not pass 'Go' or anything else for that matter, and certainly did not collect my £200. I stood there punching the door; could feel rage building up, the red mist that I had not experienced for 15 years or so after I became a Christian.

I sat down on the bog seat. I had a flashback to 17 years earlier. I was playing football on Walton Hall Park, the whistle had just gone for half-time. My brother Dave and a friend of his were running back from the horrible brick 'Gents' toilets which you could smell for miles in any direction. Excitedly, he asked me, 'What does 'Toss us off' mean?' Before I could start thinking of a suitable answer, with great enthusiasm he explained that this bloke in the bog had offered them a 'silver shilling' if one of them would 'Toss him off'. The second half was about to start as I reached the bog, kicked the pervert in the groin then kneed him in the face. As he fell on the floor I kicked him again, then ended his aversion therapy by jumping up and down on him, totally out of control; the red mist ruled. By this time some of our team had arrived and dragged me out of the toilet still twitching and kicking and carried me down to the pitch. The game restarted but I was so adrenalised that I was sent off within a few minutes. The pervert had gone; I doubt if he ever cruised round that particular public toilet on a Saturday afternoon again.

Then back to the reality of the altered patent. I was a Christian now and those I worked with knew it. Violence was no longer an option. We faced up and agreed that the time had come to part. He gave me a redundancy note, no money, of course, and I signed on the dole. I had left Kodak for the best reasons, the good of the family but failed to listen to my wife. I learned a valuable lesson but we payed dearly for it. I have since come to realise that my wife's intuition has a spiritual basis and is a real gift. At this time Viv was looking after Maddy who was five years old, I was the sole wage-earner, now once again a job seeker.

Almost a year later the company went bust. I lost my investment as did the other partner but, as the business was a limited company; at least we didn't lose our homes. Some years later, at the time I fractured my ankle, the boss turned up at our house wanting advice on stabilising the transfer image. He'd persuaded someone to let him adorn his old Rolls-Royce with images of warplanes which had faded after a short time. We gave him a cup of tea, not doctored with any toxic chemicals, but also informed him that there wasn't enough cash in the galaxy to get me to work for him on any project.

A friend was looking after Carla Lane's mother in West Derby while the family were away and invited us to call in for a cuppa as we were in the neighbourhood. The house was large, full of character and in the dusk looked rather eerie. As I knocked on the door, something big appeared; its eyes level with mine. My daughter observed, 'It's just a dog'. The huge beast didn't bark - it didn't need to. No one in their right mind would push their luck with a dog that big! It was an Irish wolfhound; that much I gathered from its accent, a veritable Hound of the Baskervilles, in my mind anyway. My youngest daughter climbed onto its back and it trotted off into the depths of the house. In the main lounge I sat in the chair Michael Parkinson sat in when he interviewed Carla at home. The room was a veritable Aladdin's Cave, full of interesting curios. Against one wall was a strange looking kennel. It was quite large, but far too short to accommodate the huge stuffed dog placed therein. Being nosy I investigated to find that it was only half a kennel because there was only half a dog in it! I have seen some scary sights in my time and I don't know why the idea of a half dog disturbed me, but it did! We didn't stay long but it was interesting to see how the other half lives, Carla's family that is, not the stuffed dog. Carla Lane is still one of Britain's best-loved television writers with a succession of successful TV series including 'The Liver Birds', 'Bless this House', 'Butterflies' and my all-time favourite, 'Bread' plus many episodes of the

US based 'Soap'. The series 'Bread' truly reflected my own experiences in unemployment, written with her keen sense of humour and razor sharp intuition. There are few sitcoms on TV that are remotely funny at the present - come back, Carla, all is forgiven!

Chapter 12

Re-inventing the wheel?

So I was unemployed, on the Dole, also known as 'up the creek without a paddle'. I've always been an ideas person thanks to the university training and God-given creativity. I decided while looking for work to try to sell some of my better inventions, so I set up an office above a friend's bookshop near the Bootle New Strand shopping precinct. From my office I began to blitz potential employers with my résumé and a letter requesting an interview; there were few jobs actually advertised for polymer chemists. When I did get an interview I used to take proof of my successes; printouts of my research reports and copies of the patents I had worked to produce. No one was interested in my past triumphs, just what I was doing now, which was job seeking. As soon as they realised I was unemployed it was like I'd just failed their HIV test, or had the pustule disfiguration of the Black Death on my face. The longer I was on the Dole the worse it got and the interview opportunities decreased.

I guess I was programmed from an early age to have an enquiring, scientific approach to life. I suspect I have a nosy gene anyway but a major influence was my Auntie Clara who encouraged my search for knowledge by buying me the Wonder Book series: titles like 'How it's done', 'How it works' and 'Tell me why'. I had a whole set of them and read them over and over. Knowing how a rainbow appears in terms of refraction and total internal refection within raindrops never spoiled the phenomenon for me: if anything it added to the wonder; if the refractive index of water was different, rainbows could be different or not exist at all. As a child I had to know how everything worked; I dismantled things with my Dad's tools then tried to reassemble them once I knew how they worked; sometimes I'd complete the assembly but have bits left over. I never carried this lunacy over to living things; I observed my snakes, lizards and frogs, read books about them but never felt the need to dissect them, or kill them and call it sport. I think there are serious psychological problems with anyone who gets pleasure from killing living things.

Where the Bugs wear Boots

One Christmas I got a Bayko set, a large expensive one. Bayko was one of the world's first plastic construction kits and was produced in Liverpool between 1934 and 1964. It kept me busy for days but I soon tired of making the buildings described in the booklet and designed my own bizarre castles with booby traps and secret passages. I never had a Meccano set, where construction involved nuts, bolts and metal plates and I always felt I had missed out on something significant. I hassled my parents to get me a Chemistry set which was a major disappointment: a few bubbles of gas, pathetic colour changes and weird smells. I found an older kid at school who got me chemicals from a laboratory supplier in London. I saved my pocket money and obtained some more exotic and dangerous chemicals. I had to order some over the space of a few weeks so the supplier could not tell I was making explosives. I searched the city with my Mum until we found a gas fitting shop where I got a tap to fit to our stove; I could now use my own Bunsen burner and perform some dangerous experiments.

I made my first and last explosive pressure device when I was 12 or 13. I obtained a quantity of iron sulphide, which can be used to generate hydrogen sulphide, the bad-egg gas. Using a small Brylcreem jar I constructed a pressure bomb which I threw down the garden for observation. This does not say a lot for my IQ at the time as we had a cat which was my blood-brother and my real brother and I played football there. After ten minutes with fingers in ears nothing happened; it was back to the drawing board. I decided to unscrew the lid slowly to release the pressure and recycle the container. As I leaned forward to grasp the impotent device, it exploded. Fortunately, my outstretched hand eclipsed most of my face but I still had a few dozen glass splinters to pick out of my hand. It was like a red porcupine with the acid from the reaction adding to the excitement. Over half an hour later, when I had picked out the last of the glass splinters I could see and the wounds had stopped bleeding, I was able to come to an important experimental conclusion: no more pressure bomb making.

My next project was to make some beetroot wine. This took some time, as fermentation does, and I was too impatient to wait for long. I used loads of sugar and yeast but the wine tasted like aardvark urine or my nearest guess to what it tasted like. I decided to set up a simple distillation experiment and turn the 'wine' into beetroot brandy. While this was going on Mum was trying to cook the dinner on the stove. Somehow the water supply to the condenser got switched off, the alcoholic vapours ignited and the flask exploded. Fortunately no-one

176

was near at the time, except me, but the wallpaper behind the stove was stained bright red. I was banned from the kitchen for a while and diverted my efforts onto some mechanical projects. I converted a cheap water pistol into a flame thrower using methylated spirit as the fuel. An earlier version using petrol failed; the petrol dissolved the plastic that the water pistol was made of. Just as well really; the meths version produced a jet of flame with which I fried some plastic spacemen, but the fuel leaked out of the trigger mechanism and the whole thing went on fire; had I been using petrol it could have been nasty. Like a true scientist I documented all my successes and failures; as I got older and slightly wiser I became a bit more safety conscious.

Explosives fascinated me as a child because of the power and the noise. I experimented with combinations of oxidising agents with different combustible materials, then I experimented with more dangerous compounds which I will not name in case some nut job has a go and I get blamed. I made a dangerously large quantity of compound X in the kitchen and kept it moist. I went down to Seaforth and found an old wall in a derelict area. Using a six inch nail and a brick I dug a deep hole in the wall which I filled with my detonator. I left it to dry for a few days then brought some scrofulous friends to view the explosion. I fitted the nail carefully into position and hit it with the brick again and again: nothing! My friends evaporated; I was in disgrace. I guessed that the chemical had not dried out and so I returned a week later with no witnesses to laugh at my failure. As I thwacked the brick there was a loud bang and the nail shot out of the hole, just missing me. I looked but was unable to find it. The wall at the back of the hole now had a number of cracks; while I made notes, people started appearing, gibbering about guns and irresponsibility. I realised that although the experiment was a success, the nail could have gone through me. I read a book in the library that explained how to make a simple atomic bomb by using two pieces of uranium of sub-critical mass. Fortunately they had no spare uranium in the local school suppliers. I did try nitrating glycerine; fortunately I ran out of sulphuric acid and the yield of nitro-glycerine was zilch. I then turned my attention to fireworks for a while, but my Mum realised what I was trying to make and had my Bunsen burner tap removed and replaced with an end cap which ended the research.

We were invited to the wedding of one of my many cousins. I was forced to wear a suit and wash my long hair, finishing the job by applying half an ounce of Brylcreem. These were my days as the Joker; the wedding was to be my pièce de resistance. Before we sat down for the meal I filled a small plastic wash bottle with warm water. A length of rubber tubing connected the bottle in my trouser pocket to the nozzle which I had wired to my shoelaces. By pressing the bottle in my pocket I could squirt a jet of warm water from the top of my shoe. As we sat down to eat I claimed a dog had just brushed past my feet. The hotel where the reception took place had no dogs, the room was on the first floor and most of the guests shook their heads, treating me as the black sheep should be treated. Once more I claimed a dog had touched me, some looked under the table in a patronising way and I was told to shut up and behave. Now, of course, they were programmed. All I had to do now was wait a few minutes then point my shoes and direct a stream of warm water towards the ladies' legs at suitable intervals. There was panic, disgust and mystery: they believed an incontinent dog was urinating at will. My brother Dave and I were hyperventilating with glee, my Mum knew it was me but didn't know how I was doing it. Several of the older family members were convinced it was the ghost of a family pet, a wire-haired terrier called Terry which had choked on a cinder, but which had an incontinence problem before its sad demise.

Being long-term unemployed meant that many maintenance tasks on the house were neglected because we had no money. Several of our window frames, particularly at the front of the house, were so bad you could push a screwdriver through them. I had been unemployed for four years or so and was not aware of the many grants and help available, basically because the Department of Social Security kept quiet about them. A neighbour informed me that he had obtained money to buy carpets and have rotten windows replaced so I decided to try my luck. I got several quotations for the work only to be told that there was a limit on how much I could claim. I then split the necessary jobs into smaller, less expensive portions and reclaimed. Again my claim was rejected, this time they accused me of trying to obtain money by false pretenses. I appealed against the decision and heard nothing for months. They must have known there was going to be a change in the rules; after just about a year I got a letter telling me that they were prepared to loan me the money to get the essential repairs done. The windows were held together with injections of fibreglass, plaster, cement, in fact anything that set solid. I never did understand the logic of offering loans to people who could not afford to repay them. Being long-term unemployed could have been fun if they tripled the unemployment benefit but this was not to be.

Where the Bugs wear Boots

Many people prayed for us, felt sorry for us, some despised me and very few helped practically. A kind old lady in Maghull was left some furniture when her friend died; she asked if we could use any of it so we borrowed a van and arrived at the house. As we pulled up outside, a big mangy dog attempted to mount my left shoe. I chased the dog, opened up the van and started stacking the items we wanted. My mate Ken was helping me to move the stuff but being a control freak, I supervised the stacking of the items. We had almost finished when I realised my waistcoat with the van ignition keys was under some of the furniture. As I pushed my way in the chairs shifted and I found myself trapped with just my feet sticking out the back of the van. I felt something grip my foot. I shouted to Ken to get the chairs off me and to stop trying to pull me out that way. No answer, so I twisted around so I could see behind me, Ken was lying against the wall laughing uncontrollably. The mangy dog was straddled across my foot and was 'humping' it enthusiastically. I gave the dog a kick with my other foot, and the 'lurve' it had for my foot turned to hate. It snapped at my feet, so I had to keep still and think of England until Ken got some control back and freed me from the randy dog and the heap of chairs.

Half of my working life has been in research and development of polymer systems for various applications; transformer winding wires, cars, domestic appliances etc. Inventing things for big companies is interesting, well paid, but not that well paid. When I was in Research and Development, the inventor got no share of the profits made from the invention, just his or her name on the patent. This looks good but doesn't pay the bills. This was one of the factors that convinced me to leave Kodak and make the disastrous move to Spraymagic. Also, while I was a director of Spraymagic I joined the Full Gospel Business Men's Fellowship International, a Christian outreach to business people. I was asked to speak at one of their dinner meetings at the Holiday Inn in Liverpool and agreed to do so although at this time I was unemployed and no longer a businessman. I invited a friend to attend the dinner at which I was speaking. He had never been to anything like it and decided to go to the toilet before the dinner was served. As we entered the men's rest room he stopped dead in his tracks and my nose hit the back of his head. Like a crazed turkey he pushed past me trying to get out. Looking over his shoulder, I saw two men hugging and realised they were only greeting each other. What my friend thought he saw was two gays in a clinch in the toilets of the Holiday Inn. Later I suggested to the chairman that, as the Bible teaches, we should 'avoid every appearance of evil' - perhaps we should put a ban on hugs in the toilet in case it was mistaken for snogging in the bog: my betters thought I was over-reacting; perhaps they were right.

Anyway, back to the meeting. The main speaker had prayed for a guest house in Majorca and he claimed God had provided one. My story was rather lame by comparison. After a successful research career I was now on the dole but God had promised to look after us and had provided holidays, several cars and money to pay bills as we'd trusted Him. See the next chapter for further details. In the audience unknown to me was the owner of several night-clubs in the city. Later, I was introduced to him and he asked me to visit him the next week to talk about my faith. He was a real character, a James Bond look-alike with several cars to match. He had been in advertising and had once sold a piece of paper with a drawing on it to a toy and games manufacturer for £6000. This meeting triggered the dormant urge to start inventing again; I had limited finances but plenty of spare time. At first I invented toys and a new range of board games, then anything that came into my head, including electronic novelties, educational aids and gadgets to help the disabled. In total I designed over 300 inventions but couldn't afford to patent even one of them. Like Topsy, most of the time I sat and thought; sometimes I just sat. I had all these ideas, but which one should I try to work up to commercial possibility? I felt like a fart in a colander, unable to decide which perforation through which to escape.

It was 1980. Someone found what was left of the Titanic some 12000 feet deep beneath the Atlantic Ocean. Big names were dropping like flies; I recall particularly the deaths of Peter Sellers, Alfred Hitchcock, Steve McQueen and Mae West. The same year some loony shot and killed John Lennon in New York. Back in the real world, I started to hawk my ideas, drawings and prototypes around a number of toy and game manufacturers until all our spare cash was gone. The whole procedure of disclosing ideas to big companies is dodgy. I've shown ideas to marketing executives who have promised to 'think about it' or 'get back to you' and heard no more. Then I've seen my idea on display at the Earls Court or Harrogate toy fair. When you complain you are told 'we were already thinking along those lines' or 'great minds think alike'. What they really mean is 'We have money, so go and boil your head!' I took a selection of my ideas and prototypes to a toy manufacturer in Birkenhead and they suggested I contacted a subsidiary in Peterborough. Viv and I loaded up the old car with various toys, games and gadgets and set off for Nottingham where we spent a few days with friends. From this base we arranged to see the Managing Director of the company. We were well received and complimented on our wide range of ideas, but have you ever tried to repay your mortgage with compliments? A useful spin-off was the suggestion that we needed an agent; they recommended a toy and game agency in London.

On my first visit to the agent I almost bumped into a man leaving the premises as I was entering. It was Erno Rubik, the inventor of the Rubik Cube. The managing director of the agency had been in the business for years, had many contacts and I felt I could trust him. In case you didn't know, inventing is a dodgy way to make a living because ideas are easy to steal. Be it a talented footballer, a new kitchen gadget or a novel toy, there are people whose job is to spot good ideas or players and steal or buy them. If you patent an idea, very expensive anyway, it is possible to have the idea pinched by careful improvement and re-patenting. To really succeed requires good ideas, cash to invest and marketing skills; I've never had the latter two requirements. Tom, the MD, was one of those people who said what he meant, no waffling and no respecter of feelings. It's no fun getting a true opinion but it's better than living in Cuckoo Land, deceiving yourself that an idea will make your fortune when it's not feasible or has been done before. Some of my ideas nearly made it.

A meeting was arranged for selected creative thinkers with representatives of a German ink and coatings company. They were looking for new ideas, new products and new uses for their existing product range. An artist friend, Vic, helped to create an impressive presentation of my ideas and they were interested in 12 of them. After the Germans went to Heathrow, we opened a bottle of champagne to celebrate our success. Fortunately, I didn't start spending the royalties I thought I was going to get: unknown to us and the German representatives, the company were having financial problems and the whole diversification program was dropped; a near miss and back to the drawing board.

You may remember our Irish next door neighbour who tried to saw off the branch that supported the ladder he was standing on. Phil passed in a cutting from the 20th of June issue of the Irish Post. It described a Small Industry Clinic to be held at the Tickled Trout, a motel on the outskirts of Preston. It was run by an Irish Government agency that were looking for good business ideas and offering cash grants to help set up suitable businesses. Viv and I presented 70 ideas and prototypes covering craft kits, electronic gadgets, aids for the disabled and toys and games. They were interested in eight of the ideas but seemed put off by the fact that none of them were patented. At this time I couldn't even afford to produce decent prototypes never mind having patent cover. We exchanged a few letters with the Innovation Centre in Limerick then the interest petered out; business as usual! To make things worse, Channel 4 began and the Falklands conflict was under way. I looked at an atlas to see where the Falklands were: not too far from Argentina but thousands of miles from Britain. I was not convinced that killing each other was a good way to settle a dispute over a piece of land but most of my friends revelled in it. Maybe it was not so much fun to be there in the middle of it all.

In December the toy agency contacted me with a new project for me to consider. New laws and penalties for dog-owners who allowed their pets to foul the pavements had provoked an idea to develop a spray to coat and deodorise dog droppings to make disposal by the guilty owner less objectionable. I was asked to work out a research proposal and cost the project. Past work for the agency had involved the use of our kitchen as a laboratory: Viv was not too happy about the storage of dog turds in the same room that food was prepared and I tended to agree. Also, I didn't fancy having to walk around the Aintree area harvesting selected heaps of the stuff either. There was no shortage of raw material locally as many people walk their dogs near the Racecourse. When Lisa was younger, we used to count the heaps of doggy doo on the way to school as a welcome change from Christmas trees or people wearing glasses. One day we counted 45 separate heaps in the 8 minute walk.

Not wishing to research the project I overpriced the job. If they had still wanted to go ahead we could have replaced the kitchen with the £2000 I'd estimated; in due course the project was duly shelved. In January 1985 I visited the Innovation Centre in Liverpool, a large building next to the Irish centre. When I was a student at Liverpool University this building housed the Synchro-Cyclotron particle accelerator. They suggested I contact another London-based agency. I took my ideas show down to Richmond, Surrey, once again eliciting a good response but no concrete success.

1988 saw the Michael Jackson concert at Aintree Racecourse. Not a major fan, I was not prepared to pay £17 to get in or £2 plus for a can of Coca Cola even though Jennifer Batten was his guitarist at the time. My youngest daughter wanted to see what was going on and I agreed to wander down the road with her to have a look. As I opened the front door I could see a geek parked in our drive selling overpriced drinks and tired-looking sandwiches. He informed me that I would get a slice of his profits if I let him stay. I doubted his integrity on the grounds of the prices he was charging and my suspicions were confirmed when he drove off later without giving me anything.

A month or so later I received a further call from the toy agency to travel down to discuss my involvement in some other 'interesting' projects. They needed input from a chemist to solve three problems that had arisen with some potential products. The first was a super-hero figure which they wanted to be packaged in an 'iceberg' which, when dropped in water, released the character with spectacular sounds and colour changes etc. The next was even more bizarre; a plastic skeleton which grew 'flesh' when immersed in water. Finally they wanted an injection moulded plastic character whose face melted away in water to reveal a 'Terminator' below. How I achieved these is my secret; I produced the relevant results after a week's research and they paid me around £400 for the work. This seemed a good deal until I saw the Terminator Kit in our local cash-and-carry, selling world-wide at £18 a set. Later in the year I saw a competition on TV called 'Does he take sugar' inviting submission of designs for an idea to make life easier for a disabled person. I sent in three; an electronic vision simulator for the blind, a modification to a Zimmer frame to enable the user to convey meals safely, and a conversion device to enable arthritis sufferers to open Yale-type locks more easily. I received a very nice letter informing me that the ideas were good but that I had been unsuccessful again. Once again the Halifax Building society would not accept these eulogies towards the repayment of my mortgage. Incidentally, the competition was won by a pair of extra wheels, which, when fitted to a wheelchair, could enable it to cover rough terrain more easily. I began to realise that ideas alone were not easily sold; having no money and limited marketing skills I put the whole inventing program on hold.

In my experience good listeners are hard to find; very few people possess the gift. I have always found difficulty listening to others, firstly because most people are terminally boring and, of course, because I like the sound of my own voice. So you can imagine that attending lessons in school, listening to lectures at University or hearing sermons in church has been hard going for me. Not too many speakers can instruct and entertain at the same time. One day I heard a sermon on the Emmaus Road event. Let me explain for those who don't know what

I'm on about. In the Bible, in the Gospel of Luke and chapter 24 there is a record of what Jesus said to two of the disciples returning home after he had been crucified and resurrected. Obviously depressed and demoralized, they did not recognize Jesus as he talked to them as they had seen him die and didn't know he'd risen from the dead. Jesus explained that everything that had happened was foretold in the scriptures of the time and they eventually realized he was alive and well. Being unemployed at the time and looking for things to do while, of course, trying to get another job, I decided to study the Old and New Testaments to see just how they predicted the coming of the Messiah etc. and what the real Jesus is about: not the fat baby with the golden banana on his head held by his mother also wearing the statutory golden banana on her head. The research was exciting, absorbing and scary. The Church and Society have totally misrepresented Jesus Christ: he was a carpenter, chopping down trees without a chain saw, so where they get the skinny martyr with the hang-dog look I don't know. Most of the church only recognise the human Jesus; year 2000 was not Jesus' 2000th birthday. He has always existed and before he came in human form He was hanging out with God, His father. After dying and rising from the dead to save those who accept him as their saviour, God made him the ultimate authority in the universe he created and which he upholds by his will power. One day he will judge every human being that has ever lived: for this reason I am always amazed at the stupidity of those who use 'Jesus Christ' as an expletive; even in my crazy days as a biker thug I was never that stupid! A tiny bit like swearing at the motorist in front of you and finding he's your interviewer for the job you were after or the bank manager you hoped to get a loan from! I studied for several years and decided to write up my findings. I didn't have a computer, the typewriter we had came out of the Ark, my wife was working and had limited time to type up a draft copy. I lost interest although I felt I should complete the work. A few days later I tripped over my motorcycle boots, snapping some tendons and fracturing the fibula near the ankle. This was crazy because I had eight motorcycle crashes earlier that year with little injury other than abrasions and no fractures. Thanks to my boots, for the next eleven weeks I sat around with my feet level with my head and completed the main structure of the book. The typed manuscript was rejected by one publisher and I shelved the project as I don't do rejections. This is no way to proceed as a budding author as some of the world's most successful authors had significant work rejected at first by publishers, for example: The Wind in the

Where the Bugs wear Boots

Willows, Lord of the Flies, Catch-22, Lady Chatterley's Lover, Moby Dick, Animal Farm, Barchester Towers, The War of the Worlds to name a few.

A friend, feeling sorry for my unemployed status, recommended me to his next-door neighbour who was looking for someone to tutor his daughter. She was hoping to study Medicine at university and needed a good pass in physics at GCE O and A-level. The school she attended in North Liverpool had a physics teacher who could not control his classes: anyone hoping to get a pass in the subject was getting private tuition. I taught a total of seven different students who had this teacher; eventually he had a nervous breakdown. Some classes were totally ruthless, regularly throwing his briefcase out of a first floor window, once manhandling him into a cupboard and locking him in, to be released by the cleaners several hours later. Probably the worst thing that happened was triggered by the Del Monte advert running on TV at the time. Each pupil brought in an item of fruit and when the teacher was writing on the blackboard they all shouted, 'The man from Del Monte says 'Yes'!', then pelted him with the fruit. Funny? Not if it happened to you or you needed a good pass in the physics O Level.

I tutored the good, the bad and the extremely ugly. I tutored pupils from good schools and bad schools. I tutored the rich and poor; I taught two sessions in a huge house on a hill in Aughton, then I was told on the second occasion by the man of the house to use the rear entrance in future. I informed him that I don't do tradesman's entrances and suggested they found a more servile alternative tutor. I taught a boy called David, a likeable scally who never did the work I set him. His mother excused him by claiming he spent all his spare time on the computer. I explained to her that he was probably chasing Lara Croft around the tombs, impersonating James Bond on the chat rooms or 'researching' the porn sites on the Internet. I couldn't make her see that having a computer doesn't necessarily increase the IQ or improve exam scores. Another girl I tutored had a sister who was a nurse: a nut case was stalking the poor girl and her health was beginning to suffer. I was asked to help which is not exactly part of the home tuition service. I had an interesting talk to the chap and persuaded him that for the good of his health he should leave her alone, which he did. I tutored a boy whose older brother felt he should be his tutor; for two sessions he hung about, adding his advice when 'relevant'. I explained the situation to their mother and suggested that she locked the older boy away somewhere or got a tutor who would tolerate the situation; she chose

185

the latter. The scariest situation I experienced was with a boy whose father had a terminal illness and lay on the sofa simulating a corpse in the room where I was tutoring. I'm not sure what was worse, the older 'pain in the bum' brother with delusions of grandeur hanging about or tutoring with the Grim Reaper looking over my shoulder: just like Elvis, I left the building.

What amazed me with almost all the pupils I tutored was that they had a reasonable understanding of the subject, but had never been taught basic study skills; they couldn't plan work, study efficiently or recall information they had tried to learn. I had to start from scratch covering basic study theory and practice then showing them how to arrange the necessary information in a way they could assimilate into their long-term memories. I produced a 30 page typed manual and gave a copy to the students I was tutoring: they all got As or Bs in the subject. I visited libraries and bookshops to see what help was available on applied study skills and came to the conclusion that the few books available were out of date, or were subject based study guides which summarised what you needed to know but offered no effective way of dealing with the amount of information involved. With the introduction of the GCSE to replace the old GCE came a change in philosophy; no longer was the teacher the source of all knowledge and the pupil's task to passively write down and remember the facts pumped out at him or her. The teacher was now the facilitator of learning, helping the pupils to actively learn for themselves. What this meant was less emphasis on recall of facts and more emphasis on the ability to find information and use it to solve problems or present a considered opinion on a subject. Most of the so called memory improvement systems relied on the mental hook method where a standard list of words is committed to memory then any subject information can be mentally associated with this list. Recalling the basic list means you recall the facts associated with them. This method works best with factual recall questions where the question itself triggers a response; it doesn't help too much with essay type questions in an exam.

I developed a more efficient method of memorising information permanently which I called the Structured Learning System. The material students are taught each lesson is structured; the teacher does not take a list of topics then stick in a pin to decide what to teach next! There is a detailed Scheme of Work based on the Syllabus for the subject, probably drawn up by the Department Head; this is used by the teacher to plan the content of each lesson. The learning method I devised is highly structured. It requires a working knowledge of the subject syllabus and a special way of processing students' notes. The Structured Learning method encourages students to understand the basic principles of a subject and to produce study outlines that are an overview of the course based on the syllabus. Next, students produce a condensed version of class notes with headings and essential information only. From the outline and condensed notes the students draw 'knowledge skeletons' which are diagrams illustrating significant points and showing links between related facts. The final stage involves the production of revision cards covering the essential knowledge contained in the skeletons. Once the class notes are processed there are simple revision routines which help students to transfer the information on the skeletons and cards into their long-term memories.

I adapted the Structured Learning manual for physics to cover the principles of learning and remembering for any subject and found students who were prepared to use the method for a range of subjects as a trial. Four A-level students, four GCSE students, and two Project 2000 student nurses all obtained good passes in the subjects selected for trial. One student missed almost five weeks due to illness and returned to a French test. She had been working on her vocabulary using Structured Learning and was surprised to obtain 95% in the test. I also submitted copies to selected people in education for their comments; six secondary teachers and four head teachers all expressed positive comments on the course. On the grounds of this feedback Viv and I went on a business expansion course, applied for the Enterprise Allowance and borrowed five thousand pounds to get the course professionally printed. We were assigned a mentor with an MA in Marketing and we took his advice to take the course to bookshops, police stations, schools, libraries, universities, colleges, hospitals and music festivals; in fact anywhere where people remotely interested in educational success for themselves or their children could be found. We covered most of the secondary schools in Sefton and did sell quite a few courses. I suspect that many of the schools and colleges illegally photocopied the courses for the students so I wouldn't sell too many and get too big for my financial boots.

Where the Bugs wear Boots

Again prompted by our marketing 'expert', a few weeks before the mock GCSE exams, I spent £400 advertising for a week in several local newspapers with large circulations, resulting in two enquiries and no sales! We were only asking £15 for a three-book illustrated course that could substantially improve anyone's exam success potential. No takers, but parents would happily spend £40 for a computer game to help their kid's brains to atrophy to a greater degree. I still have a few cases of the course left and copies of Structured Learning can be ordered from my website or by e-mailing me and requesting a descriptive leaflet; the course is now just £10 including postage and packing. When I got round to summarising the accounts for the taxman I found we were spending more money on petrol getting about than we were making from sales. The £80 a week enterprise allowance was just keeping us alive; after 40 weeks it stopped and we had to stop trading and try to pay off the rest of the bank loan. My attempts to get out of the slow lane were once again ineffective. I also invented several large charts which illustrated the major principles of Chemistry and Physics for the GCSE market. The quotations I got for printing these started my hair loss in a big way. There was no way I could even think of selling these in the education market and after the Structured Learning fiasco I had no intention of trying.

One day my daughter came home from school with two badges she'd bought for 40p each. They were based on monochrome fuzzy photocopies, not even centred on the badge-making machine. 'I ate school dinners and survived' and 'Preserve wildlife, pickle a squirrel' were the bladder burstingly funny messages on the wonky badges. I thought to myself, 'I could do better than that without trying!' I spent two days thinking and designing and came up with 15 different joke items as an exercise. These included the Insult Computer with health warning and the infamous Wimpworker exerciser for state registered wimps. Having no spare money and still licking my wounds from my last attempt at business, they were consigned to the filing cabinet. Some of these will soon be available on the website.

Up till the age of about eleven or twelve, Maddy, our eldest, was happy and healthy. Around the second year at secondary school she began to get a succession of virus infections followed by secondary bacterial attacks like tonsillitis or middle ear infections. Obviously, she missed some schoolwork but was bright enough to catch up. Within a short time the cycle started again. We visited our doctor so often it was embarrassing. He had no idea what the problem was but suggested she might have school phobia. My problem with this was that her symptoms were real; you could measure her temperature with a thermometer, you could see the Koplik's spots on her tonsils. She had blood tests and other tests and we were told it's only a virus, but a virus that was wrecking her health, wrecking her education and stressing us all. On the occasions she did get back into school her classmates were unfriendly, jealous because she was off school and they weren't. Some of the staff also consistently made 'smartass' comments about her being 'part-time' or 'on holiday': it was no holiday for any of us. Apparently it is OK for children to attack a teacher without any repercussions, but not for parents - what a shame! One teacher at the school was sympathetic and tried to help as much as she could, but Maddy was getting worse. I fitted a downstairs toilet because on some days she was too weak to climb the stairs without help.

She also experienced a lot of muscular pain, spasms that lasted for a long time, an attack of shingles at the age of 16, and the best the doctor could do was send her to a psychiatrist. I must admit I don't have too much time for shrinks and their like, as Crocodile Dundee commented when his girlfriend went to visit her psychoanalyst, 'Haven't you got any mates?' But the NHS child shrink was a corker. The old crone had a major twitch and did more harm than good. 'Twitch', as I nicknamed her, screwed up my daughter so much I came quite close to splitting dear Twitch's lip, had this been allowable by Law. The professionals were useless because their approach was totally unscientific; they assumed she was skiving and so ignored any other evidence to the contrary. One doctor out of the six in the practice we belonged to told her it might be Myalgic Encephalitis, ME, also known as Chronic Fatigue Syndrome, but at the time there was no way to prove or disprove it and some doctors thought it did not exist. So the professionals gave up but then the amateurs stepped in. Relatives told her to get back to school, informing her that it was all in her mind and two even laid on her the guilt trip that her absence from school would result in Viv and I getting divorced. An elder of a church, who at least believed she was ill and not imagining her symptoms, kindly suggested an alternative possibility; maybe her illness was because Viv and I had a marriage problem. How do you tell such a person they've got it wrong?

When some people prayed for her and she got no better these

cretins then suggested that she wasn't healed because she had no faith. What a fiasco: you are sick but have enough faith to ask for prayer and get sent away, still sick but now feeling guilty as well because it's 'all your fault'. There was a programme on TV about ME, apparently Clare Francis the yachtswoman had it, Esther Rantzen's daughter had it and people began to believe it existed. Maddy suffered from the symptoms and the verbal abuse of those who should have known better for more than ten years. Then one day while reading her Bible she felt God telling her she was going to be healed and that she should get public prayer for healing. This she did, God healed her and she was able to walk to the shops and do many things she was unable to do before. Each day she achieved more and now works as a well respected PA/secretary in a Liverpool city centre office.

I was still job seeking and saw an advertisement for a physics teacher; I applied and to my surprise was offered the job although I had no teaching qualifications or experience. I dug out a jacket and tie and turned up early on the Monday morning. The first few classes were small; then I noticed from the registers that there was an average 40% absenteeism at the school. The first and second year classes were responsive and well behaved and my first day as a teacher was enjoyable. The highlight of the second day's classes was a group of six 16-year-olds. These pupils wouldn't work, were basically waiting to sign on the unemployment register and were, by their own choice, taking no examinations. I was instructed to 'keep them occupied'. The problem was that my jester suit no longer fitted me and the cat had clawed the bells from the hat; also I was unable to perform my famous 'banana slide' routine as I was recovering from a groin strain procured at a football game. I did own a gorilla suit which I had loaned to a mate in exchange for a portable TV as ours had expired. I felt bad about asking for its return as our cat had raced past the set, got entangled in the mains lead, had spun through 360 degrees and ultimately smashed the telly. Having no gear with which to entertain them, I just gave each of them a broken electric motor which they dismantled and attempted to reconstruct until the bell went for the end of the lesson; it was basic occupational therapy and the nearest thing to physics that any of them had had in several months, if not years.

On the Wednesday morning the head of the department called me to one side and gave me some friendly advice. He warned me about the class I'd be taking after the morning break. He described them as 'scum' and 'animals'; he suggested that I make no attempt to teach them or write on the board but to keep my eyes on them, write out some overhead projector slides and let them copy out the notes. I just couldn't wait to meet these nice people! The first class was bad enough, consisting of twelve scraggy girls with brains in their knickers who talked among themselves incessantly. I was doing an experiment using a transformer with a bright red control knob. This caught their attention and I was quizzed by the bolder of the trainee slappers while the rest sniggered inanely, 'Have you got a red knob, Sir?' 'Can anyone play with the knob, Sir?' I determined to save their lives by not killing them but let them go five minutes early and went for my tea break. I spoke to two teachers, one of whom was still in tears after a session with the class I was due to take after the break. They told me that this 3rd year class had so persecuted my predecessor that he'd had a breakdown. So it wasn't my charisma and rugged good looks that had got me the job; no one else wanted it! I couldn't wait to meet this gaggle of geeks!

The bell went to call in the rabble from the schoolyard and the geeks arrived, muttering and shuffling as they found their places. A boy with an afro 'haircut' sat on the front row and placed his foot on the desk behind which I was standing. I placed his foot gently back on the floor; he smiled benignly and replaced his foot on the desk. When I pulled him off his chair by the same foot and flopped him onto the floor he stopped smiling. I explained that I was a temporary teacher and intolerant of bad behaviour, which silenced them for a few minutes. I picked up the register and began to call out their names when one pupil got up and stood in front of the class and began to address them. Simultaneously another walked past him and stood behind me. What I did next was instinctive: let's leave it at that, just to say that the class sat quietly after the incident and the two bad boys did recover. Later the geeks were supposed to be measuring the specific gravity of an unknown liquid. Predicting that these idiots would spill it all over the place I had substituted brine for the white spirit recommended. To get a rough idea of the value they were supposed to be determining the lab steward had left a hydrometer on the desk, one student filled it with the unknown liquid and proceeded to squirt others in the face until I removed it from him. I took him down to the head of department, explaining what had happened and asked what the recommended punishment was. He informed me that I could keep him in for thirty minutes after school. We returned to the class and they all sat quietly as I completed the lesson. When the bell rang I informed the perpetrator that he didn't have to attend detention as, with no witnesses around, I couldn't guarantee that I wouldn't damage him in some way.

I decided that my third day was going to be my last. As far as I was concerned I had not been told the whole situation and owed them nothing. All the Wednesday afternoon classes were amazingly well behaved, I guess the word in the playground was that I was a bit of a nutter. I taught a first year class after the dinner break then had a free period. I collected my stuff and was just leaving the common room when I heard a lot of noise coming from the classroom opposite. All the doors in the school had windows that had been boarded up to prevent the many pupils wandering about after being thrown out of class from making obscene gestures at staff, so I couldn't see what was going on. I listened at the door: definitely a fight; I heard a desk crashing over and the shouts of encouragement for the combatants. I slammed open the door; sure enough, two lads were rolling about on the floor, some desks had been knocked over and the spectators were still shouting despite my noisy entrance. Before I could rush in and give some grief to the participants a gentle voice asked, 'Can I help you?' A grey-haired teacher was writing on the board, totally ignoring the mayhem taking place at the back of the classroom. 'No thanks', I replied as I closed the door on his room, also closing the door on any intentions I might have had of ever doing any secondary school teaching again.

My youngest daughter, Lisa, went to a comprehensive school along with most of her friends from the junior school and was very happy for some years. I became a parent governor as I have done with both my children so I could have a say in matters affecting my children's education. Towards the end of her third year some decisions were made that concerned me; the Government chopped several hundred thousand pounds off our budget. One of the deputy heads had a brainwave to raise cash: in every big city there is a pool of pupils who have been suspended for violent or antisocial behaviour. If you take some of these into a school you get extra funding for doing so; our school did this despite my warnings to the contrary. There were bullying problems anyway as there are in most schools, but these escalated with the arrival of these new arrivals. As a governor I couldn't discuss what was happening with Lisa, I just kept an eye on her and occasionally asked how she was doing. The bullying became so bad that a room was assigned as a safe house for those being bullied. In a governors meeting I suggested perhaps we should be keeping the bullies in the room. and I volunteered to apply electro-shock therapy, or arrange for pre-frontal leucotomies for special cases. My suggestions were ignored! We took our daughter out of the mess at her request and obtained a place for her in a private Christian school in Tarleton. For two long years we spent almost seventy pounds a week on petrol and paid the school fees; I taught science and computing there for a while to offset the costs. The sacrifice was well worth it; she made a load of new friends and achieved excellent GCSE grades. She went on to obtain a BA, an MA and a PGCE becoming a teacher and marrying a brain-on-legs called Brendan. Both our daughters are a credit to us; at least I got something right for a change!

In 1984, two hundred and fifty acres of derelict Liverpool waterfront were transformed into the Liverpool Garden Festival, a vast array of theme gardens and water features, a marine esplanade, a narrow gauge railway and various play and leisure areas. Right in the middle was an impressive festival hall with an ornamental moat around it. They say great minds think alike: the day we decided to visit, so did Margaret Thatcher. We noticed a considerable police presence, but like the Grand National, assumed that it was because big occasions need more policing due to extra traffic, pick-pockets and other criminals plying their trade on these occasions. We were inside the Festival Hall, Lisa perched on my shoulders, proudly wearing the new leg-warmers that Viv had made from some old socks of her own. We saw a crowd lining part of the hall and pushed through to the front but could see nothing. Suddenly Margaret Thatcher and a group of security personnel appeared and stopped in front of us. She said, 'Hello' to Lisa who informed her that she had leg-warmers which her Mum had made for her. Maggie was suitably impressed, but before I could ask her the eternal question, 'Gizza job?' she was moved on by her security personnel. The Festival site was amazing but whoever designed the security fence had no idea of the resourcefulness of the average scouse scally. Driving past you could see hordes of them climbing over the fence to avoid paying to get in. Despite the magnificent hall, demolished in 2006, and the open air arena and gardens which could have been used for something, the place is a ghost town again. All that remains outside the closed off wasteland now is the riverside walk and the Britannia Inn pub and restaurant. There was talk of a house building project but we'll see.

1984 represented the end of an eight year period of unemployment. The unemployment benefit after paying the mortgage, gas, electricity and rates left about £15 a week to feed and clothe the four of us. People asked us how we survived and I'm not sure. As Christians we had no choice but to rely on God on many occasions; the next section describes some of our survival experiences.

Chapter 13

Coincidence or what?

Over the years we have had some remarkable experiences of God answering prayer, providing our needs and even saving from injury or worse. Many have hinted that these occasions are merely coincidental and offer helpful alternative suggestions as to what really happened. In this chapter I am going to share some of these so you can make your own minds up.

My brother Dave went on holiday to Jersey with a group from his church, including a missionary lady who was home on leave. One afternoon his daughter was stung by a large jellyfish and suffered an immediate allergic reaction; her eyes swelled up until they were closed and she had red blotches all over her skin. While they discussed what to do the old missionary got some cold chip fat in the absence of olive oil and slapped it on the child's head. She got everyone to surround her then she prayed to God to restore the child in the name of Jesus. Instantly the kid was back to normal. When my brother told me what happened I remember shaking him and shouting that it was not possible. The church I attended since becoming a Christian believed that miracles only happened when Jesus was on earth and I guess I'd been brainwashed to believe the same. My brother never lied so the whole incident rattled my cage; I dealt with it by forgetting it ever happened. As a scientist this was a real cop-out; the scientific method consists of devising theories then collecting enough information to prove, disprove or modify the theory. This is why treating the theory of evolution as the law of evolution is totally unscientific; there is no proof or disproof, there is insufficient evidence, nevertheless evolution theory is taught as fact in our schools and universities.

Almost a year later our band was playing in a Pentecostal church in Upper Gornal in the Midlands. Our amplifiers were second-hand, old and never serviced; unknown to us they were also downright dangerous. Johnny, the rhythm guitarist, plugged his guitar in and went to adjust a microphone stand. In case you are wondering, yes it's the Johnny our kitchen knife was named after. There was a flash and he folded up like a penknife and hit the floor with a thud. Someone quickly pulled the plug out of the mains socket but Johnny was going progressively blue in the face and having difficulty breathing. The pastor of the church appeared, knelt by his side and asked God to heal him in the name of Jesus. Johnny immediately sat up, his usual chubby pink, wondering what had happened. I was glad he was OK but I was also disturbed. What was happening to my theory that God no longer heals? I told my church leaders what had happened and they told me I had imagined it. One thing I don't do is see things that are not there: I've never seen aliens, ghosts, little pixies or gremlins and have no wish to; I realised my theory was long overdue for modification.

Over the years Viv and I have experienced many things that are not easy to explain. Sure, maybe the odd one could be put down to coincidence, but we have had to come to the conclusion that God is real, He does answer prayer, and He does heal some people. I say some because not every prayer is answered in the way we would like and not everyone prayed for recovers. What I am saying is if it happens at all then the theory that it doesn't has to change. When I talk about prayer I mean asking God in private, not whining in public about your problems so someone feels sorry for you and helps you; that's begging. I did try this once. We shared in a home group meeting that we were in serious financial difficulties and asked the group to pray for us, seriously hoping that they might help. Several days later we were returning home when we saw a familiar figure driving away from our house; it was the home group leader who had deposited two large bags on the front step. Excitedly we ran to see what was in the bags. To our surprise the bags were full of rotting, worm-eaten pears with a note, 'For the rabbits'. The rabbits appreciated the irony of the situation, we did not.

The examples that follow are only a selection and really happened; prayer was made in private without griping to others and God supplied the needs. Viv and I once prayed for a consultant's wife suffering intense pain from kidney stones and from the moment we did she had no more pain. Another time a group of us prayed for a young lad who had been diagnosed with leukaemia; his grandfather had recently died from the same illness. When he went for further treatment there was no trace of the problem. His doctors were confused, one reckoned the blood sample was labelled incorrectly and one suggested some kind of remission coinciding with the praying. Thirty years on he is still fit and well, healed by coincidence? I don't think so!

Sometimes God directs as we learn to recognise His way of doing it. One Saturday morning we went to Gateway supermarket in Maghull for the weekend shopping. As we started to go round the shelves I suddenly had the feeling that we should double-up on everything we were buying and give the food to someone who needed it. I told Viv, she agreed and so we did it. When we got home we filled two boxes with the goodies, but who was it for? We prayed and eventually the answer arrived in my head. This didn't make sense; the friend in question, a professional musician, had just completed a two-month tour of Germany and Holland and must have made a few thousand pounds even after paying the band. As I wrestled with this and tried to think of more needy cases, the same name popped into my mind. I jumped in the car and drove right to his home, some 20 minutes drive away. I took my eldest daughter with me so they wouldn't be too hard on me if I'd got it wrong and they thought I was patronising them. Maddy knocked on the door as I was carrying the boxes of food: his wife answered the door and burst into tears. The cheque he had received for the tour had bounced and they had no money at all. They had fed their children with the food that was left and had not eaten for several days. Earlier, his wife had gone to the local outdoor market to see if there were any odd vegetables lying around after the market had closed and had collapsed. A neighbour brought her home thrown over a pram like a bounty hunter's most-wanted. In desperation they had prayed and God had put into their minds that I was coming with food. Coincidence or what?

Our financial situation got so bad at one stage that I had to sell one of my most valued possessions, a Höfner Verithin guitar with a Liverpool music scene history. I put it up for sale in a local music shop but secretly hoped no one would buy it; someone did buy it. I sadly went to the shop to pick up my money less commission. A few hours later a friend knocked at the door. He had heard I had to put my guitar up for sale and had immediately purchased it, then he gave it to me as a present. The same generous dude gave me his car at a time that mine had expired from advanced senility.

Viv and I attended a Full Gospel Businessmen's Fellowship

International dinner at the invitation of some old friends. These meetings were held in quite 'posh' venues like the Holiday Inn or Centre Hotel; the meals were good and the after-dinner speakers were always interesting. We sat at a table against the wall out of the way and waited for the speaker to arrive and, more importantly, the dinner to be served. The speaker arrived with the chairman of the FGBMFI and walked towards the top table where the important people sat then excused himself to the chairman and came across to our table. I didn't know the guy from Adam and he didn't know me. We were wearing our best gear and looked like we had a few bob but outward appearances often deceive; I'd just been made redundant and my job prospects were looking bleak. At that time we had one child; Viv had been told that the likelihood of having a second was slim because of a medical condition she had. This total stranger told us that God had a message for us. We were not to worry about our finances as He would look after us, then turning to Viv he said, 'The Lord will add to your family', then he walked back to the top table. All that God promised happened; Lisa was born on 24th of June 1981 and we had cars given to us, anonymous gifts through the letterbox and holidays provided. Different people passed on high quality clothing for Viv and the kids, even though they didn't look tatty and we didn't cry poverty. God even had non-Christians help us on several occasions. I once needed £18 to get to London for an important appointment but didn't have enough money to go. I was all set to cancel it but Viv said, 'Let's pray' and we did. Two days before the appointment a local newsagent knocked at the door. He held £18 in old pound notes and in a very embarrassed manner told me that he didn't know why but he had to give me this cash: when I told him why he looked even more confused. Year after year God helped us as the man had said.

One Christmas Eve we took a small gift to my cousin in Blundellsands. On our way home I noticed a sign for Warren Road and remembered that someone I knew from the past lived there; she had met a mutual friend whom she asked to pass on her regards to us. The house was huge but they all are in that area. She was out but just as we were about to drive off she arrived home. We shared experiences: she had educated herself and was now a fully qualified doctor and had also become a Christian. I told her what was happening to me but didn't lay it on too thick so as not to depress her. We had coffee then had to go as it was Christmas and we had many things to do before the big day.

As we were leaving she gave us a load of Christmas goodies in several plastic sacks. For a moment I thought of refusing her charity on the grounds of pride but we were short of cash so we thanked her and left. We did have some stuff for Christmas but most of the kid's presents were second-hand, bought from rich people through the ads in the local free newspaper. We arrived home and examined the swag; a fine collection of seasonal luxuries that we couldn't have afforded, including a large chicken. I was about to put it in the freezer when I realised it needed to defrost and then suddenly I knew I had to give it to the couple next door. I know what you're thinking - surely you're not suggesting God told you?

Well yes! Even so I hesitated because although they were both unemployed, they were also proudly independent. The feeling to donate the chicken was strong so I knocked at the door and told them God had told me to give them the chicken. They looked slightly shocked but invited me in for a sherry and a few minutes in front of their roaring coal fire. They had ordered a chicken from a local farm but had found they had sold out. They had not long returned from a fruitless search for a replacement in the local shops and supermarket. Our gift was just what they needed and a total surprise. Several hours later we were watching an inane pantomime on TV with the kids when there was a knock at the door. A couple we hadn't seen for two years stood there with a large parcel containing a turkey of Dolly Partonesque proportions. God apparently told them to get an extra bird and give it to us. We hadn't even prayed for a turkey but got one anyway. Coincidence or what?

Our church decided to do some open air meetings in the Maghull town square. I was part of the music team but only had an electric guitar; I needed an acoustic for this job. Viv and I prayed for a guitar so I could play with the others. I had recently read a book by Paul Yonggi Cho called, 'The 4th Dimension'. In the book he said that prayer should be specific; he gave an example in the book of a girl in his church who asked God to provide her a husband. She made a list of the qualities she would like the man to have and she and her mother prayed specifically: she eventually married a guy that fitted the specification exactly. It sounded a bit heavy but we tried it; instead of praying for a guitar I asked for an Ovation, a round backed guitar which would just rest on my paunch for ease of playing. We told no one but believed that the next anonymous gift through the letterbox would be for the purchase of my new guitar. Two days later an envelope was pushed through the letterbox containing three £20 notes, I don't know to this day who it came from. I went down to Frets, our local guitar shop, convinced that this gift might get me at least a second-hand guitar. I looked round the shop, no Ovations, in fact no guitars in the £60 price bracket. I asked the proprietor if he had any second hand stock. He went into the back of the shop and brought out two guitars. One was an Ovation Matrix! I looked at the price tag, £59; I had the guitar I wanted and four plectrums. A week later someone I knew saw my guitar and gave me an Ovation case which he had intended selling. But there's more: over a month later a friend came round for dinner, a well known performer and session guitarist, who valued the guitar at more like £150. Is God good or what?

When I was made redundant I went to the bank to explain what had happened. They cut up my cheque card in front of me like ripping the epaulettes from the uniform of a disgraced army officer. They lumped all our accounts together to form a large sum that I had to repay. We tried to repay it but with the money the dole gave us it wasn't possible to clear the debt and it rose eventually to over £500. That summer someone paid for us to attend a music festival; we borrowed a tent and off we went. I mistakenly used the fly sheet for a ground sheet, but realised my mistake and corrected it when it began to rain. The tent was a bit small for the four of us so I found a large sheet of polythene in a skip and created an awning to double the size of the living area. All the tents around us were large and almost new; our living quarters resembled a third-world refugee camp; we certainly lowered the tone of the area. One of the speakers in a seminar on prayer asked everyone at the end of the session to think of a specific prayer need and to pray. Our finances were crippling, I didn't know any of the many dole dodges used by others, nor was I prepared to use them. I didn't even know what extra cash was available for special cases and the benefit office staff were not in the habit of informing anyone. It seemed a good idea to pray specifically for our financial situation so I did. We returned home and a few days later the three elders of the church we attended at the time sent for us. I often tend to say what I'm thinking and wondered who I'd upset or what I'd said or done wrong. They wanted to know how we were and if the church could help in any way. The bank account was now £600 in the red and I had a brainwave. If they could lend me £600, interest free,

I could get the bank off our back and eventually repay them; it was the interest piling on that made life difficult. They said they would pray about it; a week later I received a cheque for £600, not a loan but a gift: they'd prayed and felt God wanted the church to clear our debt.

I eventually got a job teaching study skills and computing in a large Further Education college. I had no suit but a friend, Toad, hassled his uncle to give him the suit in which their Guy Fawkes effigy was dressed and I wore it for almost a year. It was a bit small for me; I resembled a combination of Norman Wisdom, Alexei Sayle and Lee Evans, but it was the smartest gear I owned. Some months later an American biker friend saw me in the suit and bought me a new one that fitted. Another guy I didn't know that well felt God telling him to treat me to some decent clothes. I met him in Liverpool and he bought me £200 worth of new clothes. I hadn't even prayed for these things, but God once again motivated others to supply what was needed.

My daughter Maddy was having problems climbing the stairs because of her Chronic Fatigue Syndrome, so I got planning permission to build a bathroom/toilet downstairs. I did all the construction and plumbing work myself, then it was time to connect the system to the main drain. I guessed where it should be then dug down over two metres, completely missing the drain. My head was almost below street level, I had a banging headache, felt dizzy and was lathered in sweat. In desperation I prayed, well more like shouted at God, 'Are you really going to let me die down here?' I crawled out of the pit and got a glass of water. As I sat on the front step I noticed two beefy workmen coming up the road, with shovels over their shoulders like lumberjacks carry their axes. I stopped them and asked if they had any idea where the main drain was. To my surprise, they were council labourers who specialised in drainage; they excavated the drain and fitted an access saddle to connect my plumbing to the system for the price of a few drinks. On many occasions we got cash through the letterbox, once a banker's order for £1000. Most of the time we never found out who was obeying God and helping us. If any of you are reading this, thanks! I'm sure God has or will reward you for your generosity.

On a number of occasions God has intervened and preserved my life. We were running an old Mini, rather small but very manoeuvrable. After seeing the original 'Italian Job' at a cinema in Llandudno it took on a greater significance, then the sub-frame collapsed at the same time that the 950 cc engine gave a terminal cough. We were without transport and didn't really want to borrow money for another old motor, mainly because you have to pay bank loans back. We began praying that we would be given some cash to get another one. Some friends from a church we no longer attended had several cars including an old Rover 90 in very good condition. We had a lift in it once; it smelt of real leather; no sweaty backs or static shocks. It was very old but classy, a bit like myself really. (Who am I kidding?) One night the lady of the house woke up at 3.00 in the morning, woke her husband and informed him that they had to give us the Rover and so they did. This fine machine literally weighed a ton and was heavy on petrol but it enabled us to stay motorised until we saved up for another car. The Rover was big and black; occasionally people would jump into the back seat when we were stopped at traffic lights thinking it was a taxi. About a year later the suspension was making weird noises and I decided to investigate. The car was so heavy I had to use two jacks to lift it safely. I began to remove the large bolts that secured the massive road springs when I thought I heard Viv call so I crawled out from beneath the car. Just as I cleared the car the spring shot off like a bullet, numbing my right hand with the impact as it bounced. Simultaneously, the car slid off the jacks and onto the floor with a crash. Had I been under it, I would not be writing this account. The scary thing is that Viv had not called me at all. She was reading upstairs and had suddenly felt she should pray for my safety and did so!

On another occasion we were travelling to Devon early in the morning in the pouring rain, doing about 60 mph downhill, the Mini's limit. It became obvious that there was something wrong when the car began to slide out of the lane we were in and across to the opposite lane. Cars and lorries coming up the hill towards us were flashing their headlights but the steering was not responding; the tyres were not coping with the rainwater on the road and we were aquaplaning out of control. Braking had no effect either. The passengers were asleep, there was no point waking them and I was beginning to panic. As we got nearer the oncoming cars I tried pulling the wheel again and the car came back under control and into the right lane. The cars coming uphill were flashing their lights, honking their horns and mouthing obscenities at me. Unfortunately I can't lip read, but some of the motorists were performing reasonable replicas of Sir Winston Churchill's famous 'victory' sign, so I got the general feeling of disrespect I was intended to have.

A similar incident took place many years later; we were returning from a holiday in Devon at 1.30 am on a slippery stretch of road called the Devil's Elbow, near Taunton in Somerset. I had been driving a Ford Transit twelve seater minibus full of young people and Viv had just taken over the wheel. As she negotiated the winding road, driving slowly because the road was wet and it was pitch black, the minibus began to slide from our lane towards the other side of the road. To our left was solid rock towering upward; to the right was a flimsy fence then a yawning blackness, in fact a 120 foot sheer drop. Viv managed to stop the vehicle which had slid until it was at right angles to the road. As it stopped it tipped over, probably due to the weight of the suitcases on the roof rack and the angle of the hill. As the side of the bus hit the road, the front windscreen popped out and rocked, unbroken on the road. I got everyone out in case the petrol tank ignited but it did not. In a matter of minutes there was bedlam. The minibus was blocking both sides of the road, the luggage had spilled all over the road and the motorists who had to wait were screaming and honking because they were slightly delayed. They appeared not to give a monkey's toss for the kids scattered across the road, still in shock as most of them had been asleep. We spent the night in Taunton General Hospital then came home by train the next day. The police who attended the accident told me that the Devil's Elbow was a major black spot and that many vehicles had gone over the edge with fatal results. None of us were hurt in the crash.

The final example showing the way God moves happened about five years ago. I was returning from Preston on the M6 with my youngest daughter, Lisa. I overtook a lorry then tried to drop back into the slow lane but the accelerator stuck and the car speed began to increase. I kicked the accelerator pedal to try to release it and the speed increased further; the engine was screaming and the speedometer passed 100 mph. For some reason the ignition key would not turn to switch off the engine. I was wary about forcing it as I have had an ignition key snap off in the lock before. Lisa began to pray out loud and, unknown to us, my other daughter back in her own home was reading and suddenly had the urge to pray for our safety. Suddenly the speed dropped back to normal and the car responded to the accelerator again. The next day we compared notes; the time the accelerator mechanism stuck was 11.45 pm, the same time as Maddy felt she had to pray for us. I used the car for more than a year after the event and it never stuck again. Another coincidence? What do you think?

Chapter 14

Out of the Frying Pan

I was still unemployed and job seeking with no success. On a visit to her parents, my wife was given a large rhubarb root which she brought home wrapped in an old Liverpool Echo. I found a suitable place in the garden to plant it and was about to bin the newspaper when I noticed a job advertisement: a local factory wanted a polymer chemist with experience of epoxy resins. I was their man, but there was a slight problem; it was now several weeks past the application deadline. I sent a short note with my CV not expecting any response, but to my surprise was invited for interview a few days later. The next day I passed the medical at Park House and was offered the job of Surface Coatings Technologist. Back in paid employment again! Had I known what happened when they received my application, I would have not felt so good.

The company were facing a massive product liability claim and needed a chemist conversant with epoxy resin chemistry to investigate the claim. All the candidates had been interviewed and the position filled. The 'lucky' person had handed in his notice and was waiting to start. Because I had more experience, they back-heeled him and offered me the job instead; less than eighteen months later they had picked my brains and I got similar treatment. Never mind, it was Donald Duck's fiftieth birthday and Ghostbusters drew the queues at the cinema. As I entered the factory to start the job it seemed bleak, with a strong stench of creosote. An assistant showed me around; he informed me that I would never get a cold while working there. I asked him what he thought creosote vapour was doing to his lungs: he just shrugged his shoulders and lit another cigarette! The tour of the plant was short, but long enough to reveal that the place was a time bomb; an accident waiting to happen, with heaps of inflammable crud everywhere. The highlight of the tour was the pitch refining area. Most of the operators were wearing goggles and some had dust masks which were a total waste of time in an environment consisting of solvent vapour. Virtually everyone had pendulous black gobbets of flesh hanging from their necks or faces. My guide must have seen the look on my face and explained that they were just 'pitch warts'. These 'warts' were benign tumours induced by contact with benzpyrene, the main component of pitch, and one of the carcinogenic chemicals that cause lung cancer in cigarette smokers. The next day I went with the tea lady to get the toast for the laboratory workers. The canteen was full of factory workers, most of them were from the pitch plant. There they sat, hands covered with the black stuff, eating greasy sausage on toast. The molten pig fat dissolved the pitch readily, so each piece of toast had savoury black fingerprints, which were gobbled up along with the pigs' innards and other atrocities in the sausages.

I worked on different projects as they were assigned to me. The main work at first was to enable the company to prove non-liability in a product liability claim. After some months I moved into the Technical Service section. This involved travelling to different locations where customers had complained about our roofing products, inspecting the problem and demonstrating that the cause of the problem was incorrect application of the product by the customer rather than problems with our products. This was usually the case. Many of the roof paints and coatings were in water emulsion form; these should have been stored away from frost, yet many contractors would paint a roof in cold weather and overnight frost would damage the coating. An important part of the job was taking company directors or managers to dinner at the company's expense; reminding them that our products were reliable if applied correctly. This at first sounds attractive: a day out and a good meal for free, but you also had to spend time with a load of rich, opinionated plonkers.

I was using a bicycle to get to work but once I'd saved a bit of cash I bought myself a Yamaha DT250 motorcycle. The trail bike would not do much more than 90 mph, but it could go up and down a railway embankment with ease. I devised a route to work which utilised a large part of the disused railway cutting between Aintree and Netherton. Each day I zoomed down one side of the embankment and up the other, repeating this on the other line, then splashing through the marshy bit disturbing the frogs with my tidal wave. I know this sounds a bit childish but it isn't really: it's extremely childish! Using the same route daily I got progressively adventuresome. I started accelerating over the edge so the bike and I were in the air for several seconds before we dropped down onto the slope. Some days I left home earlier so I could repeat the lunacy several times before the monotony of work. One Thursday evening some anti-social jerk decided to tip a load of building rubbish down the slope; doors, windows and a few tons of brick rubble. Unfortunately I only noticed this in mid-air as I blasted over the edge the next morning. As the bike hit the rubbish we parted company and I flew into a pile of bricks - not recommended. The forks were horribly twisted, I was bruised in some interesting patterns but the worst was to come. I straightened the forks crudely and got to work to find that my locker and house keys were not in my pocket. I returned to the scene and searched through the rubble for over an hour until I found them: this I did in my usual calm manner.

Things were going quite well, each project was completed in reasonable time but some problems were becoming apparent. One of the managers didn't like bikers overmuch and liked to feel he owned the employees in his empire. He summoned me to his office and asked me what I thought of him; I shared my thoughts which were not exactly what he wanted to hear. Around this time the men in the factory wanted more money, safer conditions etc. and called a token one week strike. The manager sent his secretary round to recruit staff to work in the factory. The research project was in a critical stage and it made sense to carry on with it, particularly as the list of volunteers filled several pages, so I told her I'd carry on with my own work. I have always had a mercenary approach to paid employment; I work, you pay me, I obey you from 9 to 5 unless you pay overtime. My decision to work on my own projects was a big mistake! Every other member of staff was on the list. For a week they scuttled around doing very little because they were not trained to do the jobs usually done by the strikers. On the Monday after the strike the same secretary came round with a pile of envelopes, an invitation to a barbecue for every member of staff except one. Guess who! Next day when I arrived for work I had a special present, a large cardboard box containing boots and overalls. I was to spend the day steam-cleaning greasy forty-gallon drums on the far side of the factory site. The steam gun had a diesel boiler and looked like something from a Terminator movie: when the trigger was pressed a six metre jet of steam was emitted with a roar. I spent one of the most enjoyable days in a long time. It wasn't me being punished for not creeping; It was Russell Schwarzenegger clearing the universe of alien predators. Within a matter of weeks I was summoned to the office and informed I was redundant. I rode the bike around all day trying to think how to tell Viv that we were back in the slow lane again!.

Chapter 15

The slow-lane revisited

History was repeating itself; I was unemployed again. The bookshop where I had an office had closed down and I wasn't too sure what to do. I signed on at the Unemployment Benefit Office and started looking for work but jobs for chemists were few. I applied for several jobs with my previous employer's competitors but didn't even get interviews; strange considering my success with the projects. At this time some people from various churches were forming an alliance through which they hoped to do something positive in the community. They were considering running Restart courses for the unemployed as the nearest ones were in Ormskirk and Bootle; I was asked to co-ordinate the project. I had not been unemployed long enough to be sent on a Restart course so I attended a course run by Reach in Belle Vale as a voluntary participant. I was impressed with the way the course was operated by a lady called Vera who was most sympathetic to the needs of the unemployed. I made copious notes, but the course content was mainly commonsense. It involved changing the attitude of the jobless from passive acceptance of the inevitable to pro-active seeking of new opportunities to get back to work. It also involved showing those who had no experience of job-seeking how to apply, fill in forms and generate a CV that would help to sell themselves to a potential employer. There were sceptics on the course, convinced it was a government plot to make the jobless numbers look better. What if it was; it motivated many to start looking and some got jobs.

The committee negotiated a contract to run a Restart course in Maghull and hired the council chamber at the Maghull Town Hall. I began leading the Restart sessions with the help of two ladies who took some of the talks and helped participants with forms and other problems. I suspect someone who had never been long-term unemployed had dreamed up the course contents but they were easily adapted to our situation. The problem was that Maghull was not a high unemployment area, so a jobless person probably had relatively rich neighbours and felt worse having no job. Where I lived my neighbours and many in the road were in the same status; in my daughter's class more than three quarters of the kids were on free dinners. The sessions went well, people were motivated and some got employment fairly quickly. I don't tend to take life too seriously, but then you haven't seen me when the car breaks down. I made the sessions as light as I could, given the subject matter. We must have been having too much fun as the management at the Town Hall moved us to a small function room, being told the laughter was 'disturbing the typists'. The Restart course had two main parts, two weeks of morning sessions teaching participants what they needed to do to sharpen their job-hunting skills, then drop-in sessions every afternoon where people could come in and apply for jobs and/or meet socially.

One day we were approached by the Restart bosses to give a talk on our facilities and approach: it appeared that our course had more people retained during the two teaching weeks and more returning for the afternoon drop-ins than most other schemes. We drove up to the Garston Jobcentre and gave our presentation. I explained that we customised the materials supplied to suit the people we contacted and made the sessions entertaining. We were all qualified teachers or counsellors and cared about the people we were dealing with, which was true but not the whole truth. I didn't tell them the real reason we got so many at the drop-ins. Once a week the brewery delivered beer to the Town Hall bar which was adjacent to the room in which we held the course. As they finished piping in the lager from the tanker they flushed out the lager in the pipes with bitter, and then pumped the bitter into the vats and so on. We arranged to have the ale that usually went down the grid to be put into pint glasses so those who had their lunch with us got two free pints with their food.

The Committee eventually bought a shop on Liverpool Road and converted it into a centre for the unemployed with an excellent café, book shop and lounge area. It was given the name 'Cornerstone'. There were interview rooms upstairs and the large garage was converted to a resource centre for Restart and Jobclub clients. The ladies who started the Restart courses with me now operated the Jobclub and I just helped with relief tutoring as required. The café was staffed by volunteers from the various churches represented by Maghull Christian Centres and did excellent meals at very reasonable prices. Being unemployed myself gave some credibility, I did know what it was like to try and feed the family and pay your way with minimal help from the dole. I got to know many of the Restart and Jobclub clients personally, we invited many home for meals and some even stayed with us when family situations got temporarily unpleasant.

One evening there was an advert in the local paper about the closure of the miniature model village in Southport, located where Morrison's supermarket is now. It was being demolished and the plants and trees were free to anyone who came and collected them. A number of garden centres were first on the scene and got many of the trees and shrubs, no doubt selling them later. A friend told me about it and I decided to see what was available as I couldn't afford the over-priced plants from the nurseries and garden centres. I took a lad with me who belonged to the Job Club, we'll call him Leech. On the way we talked about job prospects and his plans for the future. We arrived at the site at noon, the bulldozers had levelled a large part of it but there was a small area with a few straggly shrubs left that I dug up and potted. We called at McDonald's on the way home, then I dropped my passenger off and returned home to plant the shrubs. The next day I received a weird 'phone call; someone from the committee who said, 'I wouldn't have expected it of you', then replaced the receiver. Almost an hour later I had a similar 'phone call from another committee member. Before they could hang up I asked,' What are you talking about?'

'Did you or did you not take Leech to Southport and take plants home?' 'Yes'. I replied and they hung up. I didn't bother ringing back; I didn't see what the problem was. Half an hour later a friend rang and asked me what it was all about: A committee member had telephoned him and reported that Leech had been bragging to Cornerstone staff that he'd travelled with me to Southport at midnight and we had stolen plants from somebody's garden. He was a state registered liar, but this was a whopper even for him. We knew he'd been dipping into the till at the café and that he'd been stealing books then dumping them. I told my friend I would tell him what really happened if he promised not to tell any of the committee, as they should have known better than to think that I would do such a thing and that I would be so stupid as to take a plonker like Leech with me to witness my 'crime'... He kept his word and

I parted company with Cornerstone, under a cloud that someone else had constructed. As far as I know they still think I did it. Let them eat cake! The funding for Cornerstone eventually ceased and there was no way to continue without it.

A friend who had a driving ban asked me to chauffeur him around a number of establishments in the course of his business. As I was unemployed at the time, I agreed. I generally took a bottle or two of ice cold water around with me and did on this occasion. After some hours a message was received by my brain from bladder-central; 'Empty me now!' I had parked in a side road near the Old Swan; there were no toilets, no back entries and the situation was getting desperate. My friend had been gone for ten minutes and I was beginning to lose hope, but not control. Then I noticed an old polythene bag on the car's parcel shelf and had a brilliant idea. Looking about carefully I surreptitiously relieved myself into the bag, tied a knot in it, the bag that is, and placed it under the drivers seat. Rather pleased with myself I had a further great idea: I would open the car door enough to slide the bag under the car and drive off when my friend eventually returned. I once again looked around - no one in sight - I opened the door slightly and picked up the bag, which exploded as I lifted it, all over my trousers. What a lesson to learn; never trust an old bag, no matter how sturdy she may appear.

I was running an old Vauxhall Viva which only cost me £140. This phantasmagorical machine passed its MOT without any work being necessary. By the next MOT there were a few jobs to be done, the most expensive being a rear suspension strut. The Vauxhall agents wanted £20.50 plus VAT for the part, £20.50 was more than I was prepared to pay for a bit of metal. I went down to one of local scrap yards to see if they had any Vivas: they did. The first two were in worse condition than mine; eventually I found one in a waterlogged part of the yard with a mini van perched precariously on top of it like a rampant hedgehog trying to hump a scrubbing brush. The good news was that would only cost £3 if I removed it myself; the bad news was it would cost me £8 if the crane man lifted the van off for me. I jacked up both cars and lay in the rusty water to remove my trophy, while both cars swayed with my efforts to release the strut. It's amazing the things you do when you're strapped for cash. I managed to stay on four wheels throughout both periods of employment, thanks to the scrap yards of Liverpool and second hand car manuals.

A very good friend telephoned me; he'd had a dream about a new kind of security system. He awoke with the details clearly in his mind and wrote down what he could remember. He knew a businessman who was interested in the project and together they consulted a patent agent in Manchester for some advice. The hour's consultation cost them £250; have you ever wondered whether you were in the right business? Knowing that I had years of experience of inventing, he phoned and explained the idea. I offered to help in any way and was sent copies of the eight patents that were identified as similar to his idea. This is the usual procedure for checking that a good idea has not already been thought of and patented by someone else, called a Prior Art search. Three of the patents were not in English; I translated the French one and a friend translated the two German ones for me. I then examined the basic claims of each patent and drew up a report comparing the claims and technical details in each patent with my friend's idea. In my opinion, the idea was workable, even though several patents were similar. My friend's rich contact felt that the idea was not feasible but as he was the one with the finances it was his decision to make. At this point I had not even thought about asking for any payment for the hours of work involved: I was working part-time, the brainwork was good therapy and I was doing it for a mate. My friend 'phoned and explained that his contact wanted to offer some payment for the work I'd done, so I added up the hours and based the cost on my usual hourly rate at the time, around £20 per hour. This seemed reasonable compared to the £250 he had paid for an hour's consultation. To my surprise I was sent a fraction of the amount I had calculated. It was better than a kick in the plums, but it made me question the integrity of the dude. I had to let it go because the relationship with my friend was at stake. I still feel that the said businessman thought I was trying to milk more out of him than I ought; as I indicated earlier, I'd have done the work for nothing to help my friend.

Another friend, Simon, bought a fish and chip shop in Bootle and wanted some help with cleaning it up. I turned up with my mate Ken and helped to rip out the old frontage. The tiles in the kitchen were coated in almost a centimetre thick layer of condensed grease. I ran my fingers through it to produce a ploughed field effect. We had to scrape it off the walls then wash the walls with detergent and hot water. We filled in a few hundred holes in the front of the shop; then it was time to paint. I turned up with brushes etc and parked the car. Simon had left the front door unlocked but left the metal security grille half way down. Instead of lifting it or bending to get under I decided to limbo under when I felt a stab of pain and ended up in the X-ray department where a cracked vertebra and slipped disc was identified.

Opening day loomed near and so we agreed to help in the kitchen for a few weeks until they got into a routine. I was the chip monitor; each night I came home at about 1.30 am, had two showers in succession and still smelled like an old chip butty. Simon did all the wok cookery and his wife served in the front of the shop. When a portion of chips was requested, she used to bang with a spoon on a metal bell positioned on the serving hatch between the front part of the shop and the kitchen. If the chips weren't on the hatch shelf within a fraction of a second the bell was struck again. Bells make me go mad, I always empathised with Quasimodo; two weeks of bell conditioning has made me what I am today. Simon introduced me to real Chinese food. The crap they slop out in most takeaways bears no resemblance to the food that most Chinese eat. One day he made a concoction in a huge earthenware pot; he called it 'chicken-soy-sauce'. We had some; it was mainly vegetables and thick black soy sauce. As he brought out the ladle he produced what looked like a tarantula, but it was only a chicken claw turned black by the sauce. There's not a lot of meat on a chicken claw so I asked him what it tasted like, not wishing to find out for myself. 'It's not for the taste, but the excitement' replied Simon inscrutably. I must admit I've never found the prospect of gnawing on a chicken's foot, alive or dead, exciting in any way!

When the construction work was complete, Simon and his wife invited us round for a meal. There were vegetarian options and other delicacies, but slap in the middle was a large steamed fish with translucent poached eyes. Before we started eating he explained that the eye was traditionally for the guest of honour and I could feel the brash rising in my gullet. To my relief he winkled out the eye with a fork and gave it to his good wife, and I sure was glad.

Working in the fish 'n' chip shop really opened my eyes, particularly the tricks of the trade. For example, I'll tell you about the preparation and cooking of the fries. The potatoes are peeled in a machine many hours before they are needed. To prevent them from discolouring a special oxygen bleach is sprayed on them and then, when required, they go through the chipper and into the fat. How old the fat is and where it came from is at the discretion of the chip fryer. The almost fresh fragments of potato are left in the vat of overheated fat until all the vitamins are destroyed and the plant structure has disintegrated. At this stage the slimy remnants resemble frogs' willies, steaming in the greasy atmosphere. Let's be honest, chips do for your cardiovascular system what haemorrhoids do for a professional jockey - not a lot! Chips are the bane of the technological age, virtually no nutritional value, dripping with fat, going right for the heart. There will never be redundancies for heart surgeons while people continue to stuff chips down their necks. Unless you register an objection, your amphibian's privates are made even more appetising by the addition of chemicals. First salt, solid sodium chloride, designed to add some taste to what is otherwise a bland, insipid mess; it also makes you thirsty so you have to buy drinks in the shop, with a further advantage of making your blood pressure rocket skywards. Secondly a further assault on the taste buds in the form of vinegar, dilute acetic acid, a pungent mix that helps you forget what the salt is doing to you.

Then there's the fish. Painfully thin slices of cod, dusted with flour and baking powder to make the fillet appear bigger than it is, in a gargantuan batter coat. The thick coat of batter makes the fish cosmetically more attractive; it also absorbs more scrumptious fat to clog up your arteries at no extra cost. My parents tried to tell me that fish would give me brains. Just look at the average fish close-up; gaping mouth and staring eyes like it's been to the edge and looked over; negative IQ if ever you saw it.

The final ingredient of the terrible trio is mushy peas; tasteless, overcooked, over-ripe peas with nutritional value almost zero, their only dietary advantage is to enable the eater to fart like a parrot. Few shops sell the turgid squashed vegetable in its natural graveyard-yellow colour, so green dye is added, almost always containing tartrazine, to make the peas glow in the dark. Mushy pea addicts never sleep, the tartrazine sees to that, but they do generate enough methane to cook a roast dinner for a family of five.

I was still looking for full time employment while helping out people who needed a hand. I managed to get two interviews out of a letter-writing spell; most of the companies I contacted were too ignorant to even send a 'We regret...' letter. One positive response was from a company where I did vacation work while at university. They were looking for an analytical chemist to fill a vacancy. It was a bit like visiting a time warp, I don't think the place had been cleaned or painted since I was there many years earlier. The guy who interviewed me was a bit of an old woman, I'm unsure which bit, but he wouldn't have got a job as a tea boy in Kodak and I wondered, if I got the job, how long it would be before I would feel led to chin the dude. The problem was hypothetical. As we entered the main laboratory at the start of the post-interview tour, I noticed a guy weighing out a white powder at an electronic balance. The weighing device was fairly new, so they had spent some money to try to enter the twentieth century, but my glee was curtailed as he turned to smile at his boss and myself. His moustache was white, coated with the material he was weighing. 'Ground white lead?' I asked my interviewer. He nodded, and then wished he hadn't; as I unwisely unleashed a tirade on the Health and Safety at Work Act and how he would be held responsible when that employee finally expired from cumulative lead poisoning. The assistant weighing the powder looked shocked out of his Y-fronts, my interviewer was hyperventilating and I knew right then that the interview was at an end: I didn't get the job, but maybe they started using dust masks in the laboratory.

Another interview was at one of the factories at Runcorn. They wanted an assistant to operate some instrumental analytical equipment, but they were offering a better salary than many other companies were paying their middle management. At Kodak I used to interview people for this kind of job, but I was not proud; I applied for the assistant job, my thinking being, once I'm back at work I can get promotion. Their laboratories were impressive, clean, bright and well equipped, with a computer at the end of almost every bench; a veritable chemist's Aladdin's Cave. The interview seemed to go well and a week or so later I got a letter inviting me to a second interview. I had my suit cleaned, spent an extra five minutes in the shower and went back to Runcorn thinking I had a good chance of success. What I didn't know till later was there were over 500 applications for the two jobs and they had given a first interview to 50 applicants on the grounds of their CVs. The second interviews were on the basis of the results of the first one and I was one of only 15 candidates selected. The main part of this interview was a 90 question Myers-Briggs-type psychometric test. You had to select the description that best fitted you from two options; one such choice was between, 'I am honest' and 'I am hard-working'. Obviously both statements were what you would want an employer to see, but you had to pick one. I realised the only way to do it was to tell the truth and work through the questions. At the end of the test we went for dinner in one of their canteens, which was more like a posh restaurant. After dinner I reported to the personnel department to receive the results of the questionnaire. The results were plotted on a circular graph; my results looked like Antarctica from the air. The manager explained the results which were totally accurate. They could tell for example that I could work in a team provided I was in charge of it. They also predicted that I would not be happy in a junior position and lots more. Apparently they had to pay the inventors £200 every time the test was used and they used it on director designates and before awarding promotions. So I didn't get the job. They said they would keep my CV, probably to line the cat's litter tray as I never heard from them again.

Constantly short of cash and looking for ways to economise we discovered the Netto and Aldi supermarkets. The children, particularly Lisa, would not even go into Netto in case any of their school friends saw her or found out. Lisa used to hide under a travel rug in the back of the car until we came out and drove away. I used to tease her by offering to back her school exercise books with the garish yellow and black Netto polythene bags. The items for sale were good value for money except the spaghetti, which was abysmal; twenty-something soggy pasta rings in an ocean of thin, tasteless, tomato-ish sauce. The nearest of the relatively inexpensive shops near to our home was Aldi. We started shopping there when we realised we could get a trolley full of quality food for the same price we were paying for three carrier bags-full at our local hypermarket. Granted, if you asked for something a bit different like squashes or avocados you got a withering look, like you just crawled out of a rotten apple, so we still went to the hypermarket for more exotic items. I still do our main shopping at Aldi who won the best supermarket award this year. I don't believe I'm writing this kitchen-sink banality, except to show that life goes on with limited income, but definitely in the slow lane.

There are many pleasures that the rich enjoy that are not available to the unemployed unless they are on the fiddle or have rich and generous friends. Most single, unemployed people who give their parents a few quid to shut them up have more free spending money than I've ever had, even in employment. Everyone needs a break from work or the monotony of unemployment. How often have people said to you, 'You need a holiday!'? With limited income it's easier said than done. One option is camping. My first camping trip was a week in Wales with Viv's brother Pete and Johnny, the knife boy. It was raining when we got off the bus in Bangor and it never stopped the whole of the time we were there. None of us had put up a tent before, by the time we actually finished we were soaked as was the inside and outside of the tent. We pitched it on one of the lower slopes of Snowdon and could hear and feel the rain running continuously under the groundsheet. We walked to Capel Curig for food and were informed by a policeman that there was extensive flooding in the valley and that the sheep were being moved. On the way back we saw a farm which had two railway carriages placed near the farmhouse. We knocked on the door and asked if we could live in one of them for a few days; of course we could, for a price. We moved camp and carried all the wet stuff some five miles to the carriage. It was dry inside and the floor was covered with straw. It also had other occupants, which scuttled around at night, but I slept with my mouth shut and did not drool in my younger days. Johnny and I came home early and I made up my mind never to repeat the exercise.

Within a matter of years I had forgotten how traumatic camping could be as we attended a range of music festivals, generally held on agricultural show grounds where camping was the only option if you weren't minted enough to stay off-site in a B&B or hotel. I have been involved in music festivals for many years in different capacities: as chairperson, exhibitor, customer, bin-person and these comments are a summary of all the festivals I have attended. If you are studying Psychology, why not attend a music festival - you'll get enough material for a Masters degree in behavioural anomalies in the space of a single weekend. Fortunately we humans only have five senses so we can only be assaulted on these fronts - or can we? If you arrive early you will get an unrealistic view of the situation, as most venues are green and tidy, grass cut to regulation length, rubbish skips and Tardis-style toilets clean and ready to use. In a matter of hours, a vast shanty village slum grows slowly before your eyes. The tents begin by being carefully placed, often by surly Hitler Youth Trainees with measuring poles, but as the crowds arrive the system collapses and bedlam ensues. A vast spidery network of guy ropes slowly appears; aesthetically interesting by day, but lethal after dark. The skips have a two metre fall out radius because of the sad inaccuracy of some happy campers when jettisoning their detritus; I am glad I do not have to watch these people eating or performing other bodily functions! Within a very short time, the once clinical Tardi are now utterly gross with each one boasting a crappy stalagmite and pools of human effluvia. Perhaps eye tests could be arranged for all campers contributing to the Tardis' contents: at one festival, a Sci-Fi freak with a sense of humour and sense of smell, had felt-tipped a classic statement inside an overfull Tardis, 'Beware of close encounters of the turd kind'.

A short distance from the camping area are the food vendors: like vultures who can't wait for the prey to die, desperately pressing passers-by to gobble up last night's leftovers so they can start re-heating the almost fresh morning slosh. All the facilities have washing up bowls - I've seen them, but I've never seen them used. I have seen assistants licking their burger-blown fingers and scratching their flecky heads and bottoms. Those studying biology may want to spend a few moments investigating the micro-organisms in the obscene gobbets on the top of the ketchup squirters. In this area you may also encounter some of the immigrants from the Camping Village with extreme exophthalmia: eyes that look like the owners have been to the edge and looked over. Whether it's due to lack of sleep, excessive decibel abuse, chronic constipation or the price of the food is hard to guess: but they all look the same!

In the performance areas some new phenomena greet your eyes: dozens of would-be stars, with pained expressions from the hernias induced by dragging their egos about, hordes of stewards, revelling in their moment of power, fighting to be in the main stage area rather than toilet cleaning or traffic controlling. Keep a look out for the amateur counsellors too; many of these would not be allowed to counsel the woodworm in their local church, but in the music festival they assign themselves a ministry. My advice is to keep walking, wear a necklace of garlic flowers and watch your neck.

You need carefully tuned ears to catch the whole spectrum of sound from the quiet twitter of the exhibitors' buttocks as they wait for break-even point, to the bass rattle of a tired PA system; from the squeak of thousands of bottoms reacting to beans-on-toast to the dull thud of bouncing cheques - it's all happening at the music festivals. You may wander, totally by accident, into a Dead Zone. There are certain nodal points on site where several bands and amplified seminar speakers are at precisely the same amplitude. The sound interference has been known to drive some people mad. Talking about the perils of sound, don't make the mistake of stopping near any of the dozens of guitar twanging inadequates who infest all parts of the site. These are generally no-talents who were not officially booked but who intend to play anyway; if you start listening, like Royston Vasey, you'll never leave. Moving on to the Mainstage area you can experience another strange phenomenon; the efficiency spectrum. Let me elaborate; in any music event the efficiency of sound engineering, lighting complexity and wakefulness is directly proportional to the artist's position in the programme. This is to make the top-of-the-bill sound worth the exorbitant performance fee. Almost every festival I have attended exhibits this hateful practice along with an equally despicable practice of artist discrimination: the Nosh Pit of the Elect. At all festivals there is a place where selected artistes and friends of the organisers can obtain better than average refreshments and mutually massage their egos in the absence of the general public.

In the Market Hall you can hear the distant trill of cash registers now drowning out the whimpering of the almost-stars whose egos have been bruised, possibly because they did not qualify for the NPE. As the Mainstage area is shut down, the nachtmusik begins: the distant sounds of the fringe bands, the pseudo-intellectual twaddle of week-end theologians, but mainly the gibberings of the late-night snoggers who all appear to think that the canvas walls turn to brick after midnight. Round about 4.00 am you may be dozing off when some twit will step out to visit the toilets, or baptise the side of your tent and get caught in the guy rope network. The way some people express themselves at this time of night, under these conditions, can be most interesting.

Pervading the whole site is the 24 hour miasma of old beef-burgers, unwashed humanity and, of course, the toilet block. When the children were younger we bought a special toilet tent. One night a strong wind caused it to take off; fortunately no one was left sitting on the 'throne' blinking like a toad in a sand heap. If your tent is sited near the toilet block, as it is almost impossible to judge how the wind strength and direction will vary, an ideal solution is to contract a head cold some 4-5 days before the festival so your olfactory system is desensitised. Within the tents there are the occasional propane leaks, more frequent vegetarian leaks and the all day training-shoe syndrome. Few music festivals provide showers, so life is quite interesting wherever you go, particularly on the third day (if there is one). If you lived like this at home you would be asked to leave or be subjected to personal fumigation. I have found that dusting the armpits with curry powder solves this problem: this also means you can keep pies warm under your arms and save on camping gas.

Closely allied with the olfactory system is the sense of taste. Few music festival punters have a sense of taste: most dress in a manner alien to human life as we know it. I assume all of these people, dressed the same, listening to the same type of music, eating the same fast food and contributing to the same faecal ziggurats, are expressing their individuality. I salivate as I write, recalling the gustatory glee of lukewarm stewed tea, delectable almost fresh offal-burgers, brackish stand-pipe water. It is with considerable nostalgia that I attempt to recall the cordon-bleu menus, every meal consisting of some atrocity that needs boiling water to infuse life into it. I hyperventilate at the merest thought of music festival fries drowning in a sea of insipid, congealing grease. Not even the pungent curry sauce can help them, they are beyond help, even though the 17 of them cost over £1. Most music festivals assault the senses and touch is no exception. There are few sensations to compare with the thrill of cold beetles in a warm sleeping bag, although finding a family of slugs in the wellies gets close. If you overdose on anti-histamines or a four-pack of the amber nectar, you may with a little luck sleep right through the weekend and wake up when it's time to go home. If you are unfortunate enough to wake up, your allergies will be minimal and the wasp stings a mere tingle. Most festivals have a First Aid tent, a visit to which is a good way to scab a cup of tea. There are a number of complaints which are specific to the music festival. A common problem is Pot Noodle Syndrome: nausea, breathlessness and abdominal pain from mono-sodium glutamate poisoning. Equally common are camper's throat, head banger's eardrum, groupie's gripes and the ubiquitous insomniac's eyeballs. Talk to any music festival aficionado, they will confirm the euphoric tactile sensation of the thin film of grease that coats everything and everyone.

You too can experience the deadly impact of a Tardis pyramid on the nether regions, if you dare.

Some friends owned a small caravan and most generously parked it in a caravan park in the Leicestershire area where they lived so we could have a holiday. We were driving the big black Rover 90 at the time. We arrived at Proctor's Pleasure Park in Quorn, the place where inadequates hunt dumb animals, not the vegetarian delicacy made from mushrooms. Apart from the deep lakes and bottomless pits it was an ideal holiday environment for our five-year-old to explore. It was a picturesque part of the country and we had a nice break from life in Liverpool. The caravan was nice but a bit cramped and we had to deconstruct the dining table to make a bed at night. It was a welcome change from camping; I'd rather have toast crumbs in my belly button anytime than earwigs and other creepy crawlies sharing the bed with us. One morning I awoke, my back stiff from sleeping on what was a table in day-time, and looked at my watch; it was 10.00 am but still dark. There was an awful stench inside the caravan and as I opened the door I could see the problem. The scrap tyre dump adjacent to Proctor's had been set on fire by some anonymous scallies for our entertainment and the wind was driving the thick black smoke in our direction. The fire did die out after four days but it added that bit of excitement to what might have been a too peaceful break.

A few years later some other friends had a caravan parked on a site a few miles from Lancaster and kindly offered us the use of it for a cheap holiday. They told us how to get to the site and where the caravan was located; near a big yellow sign. We arrived on site and saw the huge yellow sign in a far corner of the field with a solitary caravan under a tree nearby; the sign read 'Elsan'. The caravan was near the toilet block 'for our convenience' and would have been ideal for a chronic incontinent. As we sat at the table eating our breakfast we witnessed a continuous cavalcade of old people huffing and puffing as they brought the previous days' bowel motions to the disposal point opposite our window. We were close enough to see the strain on their faces as they emptied the plastic crap carriers with great difficulty. As they returned to their caravans miles away from us many smiled as they passed our window, so glad we were able to observe their efforts. I felt like a prize schubunkin on sale in a better class pet shop. We were also close enough to hear the obscene sounds as the savoury mixture of bowel and bladder contents slurped and splashed into the disposal point's sewage system. One night we made an aromatic vegetable curry with boiled rice but our position and the frequency with which the sluices were used made the meal a little too graphic for my taste. As the light began to fade we switched on the home-made lighting system only to find that the battery was flat: my car battery was due for replacement so when it became a bit darker we either slept or played 'I spy' in the dark, quite a challenge. As soon as it was light the birds used to come and audition for their own version of Riverdance on the roof of the caravan. Thanks to these pests we had our breakfast most mornings at 5.30. We appreciated their terpsichorean antics and happy song; I would have gladly thwacked them individually or en masse with a frying pan but we had only brought food that could be re-constituted in boiling water or just heated up. Beans, Pot Noodles and mushy peas are easy to 'cook' but the atmosphere they generate as they metabolise in humans is out of this world. The caravan was very cosy but someone had given the local earwigs a spare key, or maybe there was a secret passage we didn't know about. I had the job of evicting the poor bugs after they'd spent all night trying to employ their squatter's rights. The Lake District is always impressive in any weather and, having our annual National Trust passes, we visited every one of their properties we could to get our money's worth. It was a nice break but we were glad to get home.

One evening I got a strange 'phone call from a girl called Jackie. The basic message was, 'Could you handle a lot of money? Come round with Viv for coffee on Monday evening.' She was a teacher, her parents were like potatoes, minted, and my first thoughts were that she'd been left a lot of money and was going to invest some of it on my inventions. We turned up on time at her house in the wilds of Wigan and she let us in. She made coffee, the atmosphere was very mysterious and I was bursting to know about all this money I was going to handle. It turned out that she was trying to recruit us as Amway representatives, to be part of her team in a soap and cleaning product pyramid business. She demonstrated the Amway products and as an industrial chemist I was impressed: the big problem was the quantities you had to persuade customers to buy. For example you could get a huge bottle of concentrated detergent for £4-5 and it might last for six months or so, but people in the UK are conditioned to pay just over £1 for a small bottle when the old one is empty. Also few households in the UK have the room to store many five gallon containers. She showed how much money you could earn as you recruited others and advanced up the profit pyramid; at the top it was indeed big money. We bought some of the products to try and decided to give it a go. We worked hard but felt like we were manipulating our friends into buying from us. We did meet people who had made thousands of pounds in their spare time but we made very little. Perhaps we weren't true believers: at the meetings held in big hotels, new members were given a badge called 'the believer's pin'. These meetings were almost religious in content: smiling people told how they saw the Amway light and made their first £1000; there were arms waving and people applauding, like a typical Pentecostal congregation, there were speakers who delivered persuasive sermons on the excellence of the products and the potential earnings for the successful. I'm not sure what we did wrong but we were certainly not successful. We invited Jackie round for dinner and explained that we'd given it a try but it wasn't for us. We did continue to use Amway products as they were good value. Unfortunately, while preparing the cauliflower for dinner, I missed a caterpillar that was snoring away in a hide it had made. Sod's law applied and it was Jackie who got it, now ready cooked for her delectation. It was not deliberate, but she reacted adversely and couldn't finish her meal; our relationship seemed to sour from that point on. I am still waiting to see if I can handle a lot of money.

Another thing we tried to make a bit of money was delivering local directories. Viv and I and the children reported to the Everton Sports Centre to see what we had to do. Thirty quid was a lot of money just for delivering a few directories; it seemed an ideal way to make a little extra cash and the kids were excited about being temporary post persons. Relativity is an interesting concept; the word 'few' can mean different things. Few in this case meant almost half a ton of the directories. It took the four of us several days of hernia-inducing footslogging around industrial estates and housing developments. Towards the end of the project my car engine overheated and the radiator burst. The money we got paid for delivering the directories in no way covered the cost of the replacement radiator; it was back to the drawing board.

We had not had a proper holiday for 12 years; sure we'd had breaks from the monotony of daily life staying with friends or attending music festivals, but camping is more work than usual. Some friends were hiring a minibus to visit Holland and invited us to accompany them. I drove the minibus from Liverpool to Dover and on to the ferry. Ben drove from Calais to Holland while I attempted to sleep, not easy as the front seats of the minibus had been fitted with so called healthy seat covers comprising hundreds of large wooden beads. I don't know what therapeutic value they had but they kept me awake and produced interesting patterns on my back and rear end on long trips. This was a long trip; through Northern France and across Belgium to Bunschoten in Holland. One of Ben's brothers was on holiday and we all stayed in his home for the first week of the holiday. The house was surrounded by trees and full of cats, just the way we like it. Our second week was spent at another brother's house in Ermelo. We had the room with the water bed, a nice gesture by our hosts but what an experience: the last time I was as seasick was on the Isle of Man ferry. A short distance from Ermelo was Harderwijk (pronounced hydervike) on the edge of the Isselmeer, what is left of the old Zuider Zee after massive land reclamation. The atmosphere was bracing at Harderwijk apart from when the wind changed direction and the smell of fried eels hit me: I must have mentioned that I don't like fish. We had many days out as Ben and Sharon showed us around; we visited Utrecht, an amazing historic city with fairy-tale architecture, Delft where we saw pottery being made from scratch and Amsterdam with its intricate canal network. We visited the royal palace at Het Loo and ended the tour in a pancake house nearby. The range of choices of sweet and savoury pancakes was huge; we sampled a few.

We spent two days in Amsterdam. We visited the Reichsmuseum and the Van Goch museum, both containing vast quantities of priceless paintings. We visited a diamond processing business but there were no free samples. We did get free coffee and biscuits and free use of the toilet facilities. These were conventional UK style; whereas at the railway station was a formidable unisex bog with a huge lady, probably a mud wrestler, taking the money. On the main street was an alternative facility where men could have a burst with legs, head and shoulders sticking out, presumably so one could have a conversation with passers-by while pointing Percy at the porcelain, or rusting cast iron trough in this case. Amsterdam was over-run with people on bicycles; I was nearly run over several times until I realised that bicycles have the right of way. We had traditional Dutch coffee and free biscuits in a little shop in a back street near the Dam statue in the city centre. The coffee was strong enough to make your hair curl but the biscuits compensated and we laughed inanely for over half an hour. We found out later that the biscuits with a major feel-good factor were probably spiked with something. The Dutch people like their food, but some items had weird names: a fresh cream cake had the exotic label, 'Slagroom tart' and a sweet shop offered a two piece lolly ice they called 'Dubbel Dik'. Street vendors offered some delicious treats at reasonable prices; chips with mayonnaise, chips with peanut sauce, chicken satays and frikadellen, tasty pork burger things and baby pancakes called pofferjees. In addition, the food prepared by Ben and Sharon was excellent, particularly the Indonesian specialities, it more than made up for the pan-pipe rehearsals at three o'clock in the morning. Holland is one of the few places I have visited that I could imagine living in if I didn't live in Liverpool. The weather is similar to ours and people are friendly and hospitable. Their television, with a few exceptions, is as bad as ours with some in-your-face adverts in the early evening. I was watching a travel type programme with the children when a woman with trowelled on make up appeared on screen. I couldn't understand what she was saying but in a matter of seconds I knew what she was selling as she whipped her top off and a telephone number appeared on screen; I wondered if she was a slagroom tart. The holiday was far too short and soon we were back in Liverpool.

Chapter 16

Bytes and pieces

In 1993, pre-history came to life with the explosion of Jurassic Park onto the silver screen. Spielberg's 'Schindler's List' reminded us of the atrocities that 'civilised' human beings are capable of inflicting on each other and this was reinforced by the horrific torture, mutilation and murder of toddler Jamie Bulger by two twisted older children, incidentally now released back into society by stupid do-gooders. That same year saw the Warrington and the World Trade Centre bombs. I was still job seeking but not really expecting success. Loads of application letters sent but no replies, not even to say 'Go away!' I'd fixed most of the broken things in the house, I'd re-decorated all the rooms that just needed a bit of paint; the upstairs toilet and bathroom would have to wait as we had insufficient cash to re-tile. The garden was sorted, consisting of low maintenance plants that appeared every year and didn't need much pruning. While hawking the Structured Learning course around colleges in the area I was offered a part-time job teaching study skills and word processing at a further education college. It was a struggle leaving the dole for just six hours of work, but the money soon built up with a few extra courses and substituting for lecturing staff that were off sick. The following year I got even more hours and eventually a term-time contract. I am grateful to those who helped me break the techno-fear of computers and those at the college who gave me the opportunity to get back into paid employment. Because I learned the hard way I did have sympathy with the technophobes that came on the beginners' courses and most of them successfully gained the certificates they desired. A friend had suggested I got into computing as there were still plenty of jobs for the right people. I'd had a Sinclair Spectrum in my younger days and could program in basic, but when I tried to learn machine code I gave it up as a bad job. At Kodak I frequently had research data analysed by computer but I just put the work in a pigeon hole and took out the printouts a day or so later without ever seeing the computer.

Where the Bugs wear Boots

My friend John was into computers in a big way. He knew how they worked, how to fix them if they stopped working and loaned me an old 286 PC with screen burn to learn on. I got a book on WordPerfect for 10p from the Oxfam shop and started word processing with it. Another mate, Ken, gave me bits to update with and make the machine work a bit faster. I had many problems in the early days and pestered John with my questions. The manuals are not written for beginners, neither are the so-called 'Idiot's guides' although they help once you advance to a certain stage. John wouldn't just give me answers but made me think and try to solve the problems myself. I began writing this book with a DOS program called Word 5; Windows was just being launched and was out of my price range.

I never managed to get full-time hours at the college, so I had part-time status; equivalent to being a leper with staff and warning bell; also I was obviously a biker by appearance, although I had to sell my motorcycle to pay overdue bills. This meant that only a handful of my so-called colleagues would even say, 'Hello!', never mind helping me to produce teaching handouts and OHP slides. One 'seasoned' lecturer, well he'd been there a long time, gave me some interesting advice which I still recall but never used. He informed me there were two ways to deal with awkward questions from students. First, he suggested I tell the students I'd answer the question at the end of the class but make sure there was no time to do so. This is not a recipe for student success but was a distinct improvement on his second suggestion; his 'tried and tested' technique. He told me to turn the question back on the students: to make a fool of them because they didn't know the answer, to ask if anyone else did know and if no answer was forthcoming to call the students idiots and demand they all looked up the answer as homework. Confusion and discouragement is not the way I teach and I ignored the 'advice'. Incidentally the person in question was ultimately sacked and last I heard was spending some time in prison for theft of company property.

Like any college, the students were an interesting mixture. On my first day I returned home and described the people spectrum as 'the good the bad and the ugly' which really did not do them justice. A better description for the younger students would have been from Neanderthals to the Catwalk. The guys were mainly punky, skinhead types, glaring at everyone like they were infesting Dodge City; many were not there by choice and the body language and behaviour demonstrated the fact. Most of the girls reflected the current fashions, hot pants and boob tubes; most of them resembled would-be Big Brother contestants or part-time scrubbers. I elected to teach the over twenty-fives who wanted to learn and were relatively normal; eavesdropping on conversations in the common room convinced me that the older students were considerably less trouble.

Teaching mature students can be difficult for different reasons. Mature generally means responsible and motivated, but many of them had unbelievably bad self images. Many of them had been programmed by parents, teachers or partners to believe that they were incapable of achieving anything. This had to be overcome before laying study and computing skills on these unfortunates: I did this by adopting a no-pressure approach to teaching with a considerable injection of humour. For example, I modified many of the dry-as-dust word processing exercises with bizarre scenarios and weird characters. A formal letter inviting pensioners to visit a stately home followed by a tea dance became an afternoon at a greasy-spoon burger bar dining on 100% steak American 'Deathburgers' (so large that eating a whole one could kill you!) and two for the price of one Newcastle Brown ale. A Motörhead concert replaced the Tea Dance with a Health and Safety warning on the effect of head-banging on the over 70s. Many had major problems and I helped as much as I could; I'm not Mother Teresa but I do care about people. I have experienced many problems, some of them mentioned in the book to date, and so I could honestly say that I knew what it was like to lose loved ones to cancer or survive long-term unemployment. I have always 'told it like it is' and prefer it if people say what they mean when dealing with me.

If someone phones and asks how I'm doing I tend to reply 'What do you want?' I don't think I'm being rude, life is too short to waste time on unimportant subjects. This is probably why I hate programmes like 'Big Brother' where complete tossers vie with each other for the 'Cretin of the Year' award. Don't even get me started on the so-called 'Celebrity Big Brother'. My definition of a celebrity involves ordinary people triumphing over adversity without crying about it or achieving things that benefit mankind, not being seen on television in a crap soap opera or kicking a ball about like an overpaid performing monkey. I have met celebrities you are unlikely ever to hear about. A man crippled from birth, written off by society who achieved academic success by sheer guts; women abused by parents and partners who survived with dignity and made a new life for their families; elderly people who have gone through life's grind-mill and are still married after 50 years, not resorting to divorce at the first problem they encountered; a brave young woman with terminal cancer fading with dignity like a beautiful flower and her family rebuilding their lives after her death. These are real celebrities.

The students made my fifteen years at the college worthwhile, which is more than could be said of most of my 'colleagues' and management. On many occasions I entered the common room to use the photocopier and I might well have been the Invisible Man. Once while I was photocopying someone made a pot of tea and gave a cup to everyone in the room except one: guess who! I found people considerably friendlier outside my own department. I started walking up to the main college and having my dinner in the common room there. I soon got to know most of the people, virtually all acknowledged me and most would engage in conversation: it felt good to be visible again. One Monday around 12.30 I was sitting in my usual place resting my eyes, when I felt someone grasp my knee and a woman's voice asked me, 'What are you doing tomorrow afternoon?' I was still half-asleep and mentally grasping for a suitable answer when the woman grabbed my shaved head and turning to another lecturer from the same department said, 'Excellent!' She must have read the look on my face and quickly explained the unprovoked assault on my person. She was the manager of the hairdressing and make-up department and was on the look out for 'volunteers' for the students to practise wig making upon. Apparently they had a shortage of subjects on which to practise. I found this a little hard to believe as probably 70% of the male staff members were in some stage of baldness. Some had excessive recession at the front, what I would call the Christopher Lee, widow's peak look. Most were turning into Cadfael look-alikes, with a balding crown that was increasing day by day into a full tonsure. Some had regressed to Tefal head stage, so bald that their foreheads were disproportionately large - all the hair they could boast was a sad fringe, low down at the back of the head - like a dead ferret super-glued across the head. To this I must add the odd cheap wig wearers and the sad comb-over types, who would run into the foyer before anyone saw their minimal hair before it had been greased to slick over and camouflage their baldness. Despite the large number of baldies, they were all too mean to help the hairdressing students to construct wigs.

I decided to help out and arrived at the designated time at a large ground floor room. The students were in two distinct groups. The blokes were turning each other into ghouls and zombies with garish glee; most of the girls were glamming up, applying lipstick with paint rollers (or looked like they had) and the wig makers were sat around gibbering nervously like art students waiting for their first life drawing session. I regretted agreeing to the request as I came in and stashed my coat and briefcase. My new friend, Jean the knee grabber, arranged the group around me, showing what, if my head wasn't shaved, the baldness pattern would be. She then stretched some cling film over my head which I had to hold like an old woman with a Rain-Mate. Remember them? As I held the cling film tight, they took it in turns to stick Sellotape over the contours of my head until they had captured its shape.

Sitting there like a part-wrapped chicken joint I wondered how I ever got into this. Suddenly, a bizarre character appeared before me. A young lad covered in glam make-up, with wrists gesticulating wildly, looked me right in the eye and asked, 'Would you model for me?' As my mind said 'No', I heard myself saying, 'What have you got in mind?' It turned out he wanted to turn me into a special effects masterpiece. He asked, 'Can I age you?' My answer was, 'Nature is doing that quite well already - no chance'. He then inquired, 'Would you like to be a zombie?' Answer, not repeatable. 'Well what about a Sci-Fi character?' Then it clicked, friends who were even more Trekkie than I, had remarked on the similarity in personality between myself and Worf the Klingon. The deal was done. In a week's time he would start work on my transformation. The wig lady then snipped off samples of my beard to get the wig colour right and I was free for the moment.

A week later I was back in the special effects make-up studio. I met the course tutor, whose claim to fame was that he had done some of the zombie make up for the video of 'Thriller' by Michael Jackson. I reminded them that I wanted to be a Klingon not a zombie. They informed me that the first step was to take a moulding of my face. It sounded OK, but the experience was not habit forming. My skin was greased, including moustache and beard and then they tried to stick straws up my nose. They explained that this would keep me alive for the

30-40 minutes when my face would be covered in dentist's alginate impression mix. Although I have a big nose, my whole family were nasally challenged, I used to have frequent sinus problems. I recall as a child the doctor telling my mother that my condition was a Liverpool thing. To be free from sniffles and sinusitis would require a transfer to Florida. This doctor gave out prescriptions willy-nilly, frequently writing them before you described your symptoms. He would not, however, write us a prescription for winter in Florida.

Anyhow, back to my Klingon experience. After protests that I couldn't breathe, my make-up man let me have a small slit near my mouth through which I could. The cold set dental alginate felt weird, like snogging a dead octopus, not that I have ever done this! They kept asking if I was alright. Apparently, actors have suffocated inside the mould and so they have to check periodically if you are still OK: no wonder they have a thing about zombies! After about 15 minutes I was informed that the plaster was going on next. No one had mentioned this stage at all. The idea is that the plaster keeps the flexible mould in the shape of your head. It also gives a 100% increase in the weight of your head. For a further 20 minutes, which seemed longer, I had to try to support my heavy head on my little neck. Once the plaster was added there was no light getting through at all - and not too much air either. The plaster kept dripping across the breathing slit and the only way to keep this clear was to stick out my tongue. Just as I was about to panic and rip the whole thing off (quite common in the profession) I was told it was time to remove it. The light on my closed eyelids hurt, it took a minute before I could open my eyes. I was given a date and time for the next appointment and staggered off to give my first lecture of the day, still blinking like a toad on a sand heap.

During the weeks that went by a full plaster model of my head was made and the Klingon 'Cornish pastie forehead' was sculpted on. Yet another mould was made and painted; then a long black hair wig was built onto the face moulding. I got college passes for my kids to come and see the final fitting. They estimated three hours and that's how long it took. The latex eyebrows and forehead were glued to my skin; then my own face was blended in to match the colour of the mask. It was a spooky feeling watching the image in the mirror change from me to a mean looking Klingon. Later whilst walking to the lift to get photos taken my boss walked past and didn't recognise me. I stood to the side as the lift stopped on the way to the sixth floor. At the fourth floor a tiny student stepped into the lift and gasped with shock as she saw me. I told her she was OK as I'd already eaten but she ran out when the lift stopped at the next floor. A photographer took a number of shots for the make-up student's portfolio and I got some. I quite enjoyed being a Klingon but it was soon time to become normal again, if this is possible. The prosthesis was well stuck to my head and took some skin with it when it was removed, but sometimes you have to suffer for your art.

Some people will believe anything. I had just left the main college building and met one of my students walking in the same direction. Coming towards us was a long-legged girl in pvc trousers that looked like they'd been sprayed on, just one of my computing students who smiled enthusiastically, said, 'Hello!' then went on by. My companion's tongue was in danger of touching the floor. Another group approached, including a girl from a youth group I had been involved with some years before; she had been a baby-sitter for us on many occasions, she was now working at the college and greeted me warmly as I passed. Once again, my companion had the 'babe alert' look. As we were about to enter the college, three young girls came out skimpily dressed in hot pants and boob tubes, waving and shouting 'Hello, George!'. 'Who were they?' slobbered my companion. I turned to the lad and told him I didn't know but that women had never bothered with me until I shaved my head, now the attention I got was embarrassing. Not true, of course, but the idea amused me. The next day this sad person arrived in college with a pale, bald head covered in sticking plasters where he had cut himself. I hadn't the heart to tell him I was joking about the effect of shaving my head, but who knows, it might have worked for him.

The classes I taught were study skills like essay production, researching information, examination technique and word processing for students studying for the Access Certificate, an alternative way to get a university place without A-levels. The Access course consisted of core modules with several options and a mini research project that had to be written up as a 'Long Study' of 5000 or so words. Students also had to give a presentation based on their Long Study and one of my odd jobs was to assess these sessions. One girl gave an impressive talk on red-kneed tarantulas which she kept as pets. The OHP slides were well photographed and as she closed I went to the front of the class to see if there were any questions. The student asked if I could help with a demonstration and I agreed. She dipped into her large shoulder bag and produced what I thought was a spider cast-off skin as it wasn't moving; but, when she put it on my arm it began to crawl up my arm towards my neck. Arachnophobia is not a problem for me, if I find one in the house I take it outside and tell it to stay in the garden but this hairy dude was the same size as my hand and being this big I could see its fangs. I was ecstatically happy when she placed it back in the bag.

Most of the students were single parents, bravely finding time to study and write essays while bringing up their children alone. Many had never seen a computer before but I was well able to empathise and help as only a few years previously I had been computer illiterate myself. Eventually I moved from the Adult Division to the Computing and IT department. Around 1998, I got a new contract with the College, a term-time only contract. As usual I informed the Department of Health and Social Security of this fact when the summer term ended and my money stopped. To my horror they informed me that I was employed by the college and would get no Job Seekers Allowance. I appealed against the decision and after many months and two tribunals I won the case and got the cash they owed me. We had to borrow money to survive the summer months so the backdated payment vanished when we paid back what we had borrowed. I still don't understand which part of 'term-time only' they couldn't grasp. The following year I got a letter from the College spelling out that I would get no money from them after the end of the summer term and this kept the DHSS happy. I had found out the year before that we could have claimed both Family Credit and Job Seekers Allowance, so I approached our local Job Centre for advice on when to claim what. The information they gave me resulted in our surviving the summer on considerably less money than we should have had. Once again, I appealed, this time to the Employment Service. Almost three months later we were awarded the money we had lost through the desk clerk's misinformation. If you don't get satisfaction from the authorities, tribunals do give you a chance to object, you may even get the cash they owe you.

Each summer holiday period we survived with great difficulty until the new term started up and we had enough money to repay people we owed money to. The old car gave up the ghost and we replaced it with another old car. I bought it privately and thought we had a bargain as it was bright red and shiny, plus it was a few hundred quid cheaper than list price. Unfortunately it was a 'joey'; it had been a taxi and had two wiring looms under the bonnet, one of which had been on fire at some time. It cost more to get it right than I had saved and while it was being repaired I had to use public transport.

The train was OK if you didn't mind waiting in what could only be described as open plan toilets. The Liverpool stations are being slowly renovated but some are still highly primitive; pools of urine, obscene graffiti and unnameable smears on the walls. Many of the trains were unsanitary and dirty; I appreciate that these problems are by courtesy of a minority of throwbacks who in an advanced society would be recycled. When you could find a station which was manned, it was by half-wits or depressives who freaked out if they had to change a five or ten pound note. Are they not supplied with a cash float?

The buses all appeared to have changed the routes, numbers and even colour since the last time I used them. Again, the drivers often grizzled if they had to give change of a note. Smoking was banned on them but they all smelled smoky, sweaty and dusty. Outside many were filthy, if you could see out of the window it had probably been raining. If all else failed you could get a bank loan and call a taxi. If you believe in horoscopes, you sad person, then check if it's your lucky day as many taxi drivers are skilled at cutting in, U-turning with or without signals, giving the impression that the journey is life or death when you know they'll take as long as they can. They also suffer from change-phobia, appearing to have none so you have to give them more than the required fare. My observations are based on personal experience, if you work at a railway station, drive a bus or taxi and don't behave as I've described, I apologise.

Not having the car also puts you at the mercy of motorists. Whereas before you were just a rival for a place in the fast lane or a lone parking place, you are now pedestrian scum, to be bullied, splashed and honked at. Walking in the rain is bad enough if you forgot to take an umbrella or have leaky shoes but being splashed by a stupid motorist is the icing on the cake. Sitting in work or on the bus after getting soaked is a miserable feeling. But what do you think your house or flat thinks about being damp? Perhaps I may be allowed to tell you. We sat watching TV early one evening, rain hammering at the window, when there was a knock at the door. I had disconnected the bell to test the patience of callers; as a general rule I prefer people to telephone before calling so we can create a semblance of order and hide our alien friends in the priest hole. A woman of about 30 stood dripping like a drowned rat, wanting to know if we would like a free damp course check as they just 'happened to be in the area'. I am tired of pseudo-tradesmen trying to sell me a load of asphalt because they over-estimated a job 'down the road'. If they are so incompetent to overestimate by that much, they are too incompetent to make a good job of my drive. I felt sorry for the wet one and asked if she'd had any luck on our block. Not surprisingly she shook her head; most of my neighbours are unbelievably mean, they wouldn't give you the snot out of their noses: I once collected door to door for a children's charity and was totally amazed at their meanness. A duck's back passage has nothing on them, and that's water-tight. As she would get £10 for a contact I agreed to have one of their assessors come and see us; a big mistake.

Almost a week later a cocky moustachioed tosser turned up to assess our house. We sat down in the front room and Viv went to make coffee. After a brief spiel about the dangers of damp he produced a so-called moisture meter with a flourish and stepped up to the wall facing the street. Pushing the gadget into the plaster he gave a sharp intake of breath. The same noise tradesmen make when estimating a job, or a garage mechanic makes when you open the bonnet or hood on your car. A noise designed to temporarily paralyse your brain cells as they totally over-estimate the price they are going to charge you. He shook his head and told me that the wall was damp. I asked him what moisture standard he was using to calibrate the meter; he looked at me with the blankness of a dead goldfish. I grabbed the meter out of his hands, took a small screwdriver from a drawer and turned the screw underneath the meter dial anti-clockwise, then stuck the probe in my mouth - look, no moisture! He still appeared not to take my drift so I spelt it out. You can make these meters read moisture in the desert or dryness in a glass of water by twiddling the screw - without a moisture standard the reading and, therefore, the interpretation is meaningless. The penny dropped but he carried on regardless. I considered showing him the Vulcan death-grip, but it was the close season for salesmen and hawkers. He informed me that a damp wall was like cancer of the house and I had an instant vision of an army of pensioners handing over their savings because of his fear tactics. I grabbed his brief case, took his arm and propelled him out of the front room as Viv appeared with the coffee. 'He won't be needing that', I said as I pushed him out of the front door and thrust the brief case into his hands. He still looked like he didn't know what he had done wrong as I bade him 'Goodbye' and closed the door. The wall wasn't damp then and still isn't. He was very lucky I was in a good mood!

This episode made me very wary of sales geeks for a while. Viv and I have always enjoyed entertaining friends, visitors and occasional callers. You do have to be sensible as the caller may just be casing the joint; looking for household items worth stealing at an opportune time. I've already told you about the neighbour's son who came in out of the rain and subsequently arranged for his mates to steal my album collection, but worse things can result from undiscerning hospitality. One afternoon a kid from the youth group brought a friend of his around to meet us. We spent an hour or so, discussing life, the Universe and everything over several cups of tea and a packet of Rich Tea biscuits. As they left and I came back into the house I became aware of a weird, 'heavy' atmosphere. It was in every room; when I went outside, nothing. Coming back in was like walking through a low cloud when climbing. Even the cat was behaving strangely. I thought it was just me, but everyone felt the same. No weird noises, floating objects or spooks, but an almost suffocating, depressive 'presence'. I don't believe in ghosts, horoscopes or aliens, but this was scarily real.

Later that evening there was a Christian rock band from Bury playing locally and we decided to go, mainly to get out of the house. After the gig we sat around with tea and coffee; I sat by myself wondering whether to sell the house, book into a hotel or just torch the property. A large shadow loomed over me, the beefy bass player from the band. Observing that I was not a happy bunny, he asked if he could help in any way. I told him what had happened. 'No problem - just cleanse the house!' was his advice and he elaborated. We returned home hoping things would be normal: no such luck. Because we'd been away for a few hours the atmosphere seemed even worse. I explained to the family what the bass-man had advised and we agreed to try it. We all stood in the hall and I prayed that God would fill the place with His Presence and remove 'anything' that shouldn't be there. Nothing happened. We then repeated the procedure in each room finally arriving at the last room with no change apparent.

To my amazement I realised that the cat had followed us as we went from room to room and had stayed inside the circle as we prayed. Meep the cat was a feral farm beast and tended to keep to himself most of the time, so this behaviour was a bit scary. As we prayed in the last room the presence, atmosphere, whatever it was, vanished and the cat went back to loner mode. We found out days later that the unknown visitor that day was heavily into the Occult and specialised in astral projection. My head is shaved, not because my hair fell out during this experience, but because I hate the 'dead ferret around the ears' baldness pattern. Nevertheless my advice is simple. For Christians, ask God to give you discernment about who you let into your home. For those who are not yet Christians, there may be some reading this book, stay away from the Occult and sleep with the light on, one eye open and garlic flowers in the room.

I took some time off work to attend the Bulldog Bash with the Tribe of Judah, a Christian motorcycle club to which I belonged. The Bulldog Bash, run by the Hell's Angels was held at Long Marsden near Stratford. Long Marsden airfield was reminiscent of the opening credits of the cult Sci-Fi series, 'The Invaders'. Men too long without sleep, alien craft from another galaxy and aliens, thousands of 'em! A collection of some of the meanest dudes in the country, if not the Universe, spread across a vast cracked mud plain: thousands of motorcycles, thousands of bikers representing tribal groups from across the globe. Long hair, shaved heads, tattoos everywhere, and I mean everywhere, perforated ears, noses and eyebrows and that was just the women! Thousands of bikers and biker babes stomping about in their tribal groups like a plague of disgruntled gunfighters, glaring at rival groups but behaving themselves in the presence of the Hell's Angels and Patriots, the Law at the Bulldog Bash.

The weather was very hot and every time a bike went by a cloud of dust arose, apart from the absence of tumbleweed it felt like a weekend in Dodge City. I got my wristband and car park pass and went to park up in the required place. A little chap blocked the entrance informing me I was not allowed in, then he saw the pass and moved out of the way. He was the president of the Brotherhood of the Wheel, a club based in Kent. He showed me the tricycle he had made out of a car engine and some wrought-iron railings and bedsteads. He'd been on duty for 5 hours in the heat; I offered him a bottle of water, still cold from a night in our fridge. He knocked it back and promised to come up to the Tribe marquee for a brew later on. This he did along with others from his club. The 'Little Sisters' were an interesting group, totally puzzled by our presence at the Bash. I was puzzled by their appellation 'little' as some of them were rather large.

To my surprise the toilet facilities were excellent, reminiscent of McDonalds or ASDA: I am lying of course! The Gents facilities consisted of two steel troughs, totally blocked by cigarette-ends so that the urine overflowed onto one's boots as one relieved oneself. An alternative facility next door had urinals made of painted chipboard which were coming apart, but at least you didn't warm your feet as you took a leak. The smell of these facilities could strip the chrome from a Dynaglide and, apart from suggesting 'Gorilla's Codpiece', I will venture no further down this road. To take the punters' minds off the squalid conditions, the dust, the state of the bogs and the overpriced, greasy food, there were several fairground attractions. A Wall of Death, several gut-wrenching 'rides', but the thing that dominated the skyline was a twin towering structure which was called a reverse bungee. A hollow ball with two seats could be launched some 200 feet into the air by bungee power then it oscillated up and down, all for £15 a time, compromising the stomach contents, central nervous systems and gastric retentivity of the victims. I marvelled at the psychological profiles of the nut-jobs that queued and paid to be tortured thus: whiplash injuries for all! Such treatment would be classed as an atrocity in some countries but with ten pints down the neck it probably does seem like fun.

Few of the bikers were particularly attractive by their own choice of dress code, general cleanliness or lack of it, and permanent inebriation, Tribe members and their spouses excluded of course, so I was gob smacked to find a stall selling orthodontic equipment, called Billy-Bob Teeth to make one look even uglier. If you have ever seen the mountain men in the movie 'Deliverance' you'll know exactly what I mean. My shift at the Tribe marquee finished at midnight and some of us went for a Pakistani banquet with a Muslim businessman and his family. My main meal of the day had been two pink ladies (apples that is, I have renounced cannibalism!) and the meal with the leather clothing vendors was most enjoyable.

A small tent had been pitched for me and my companions, twenty or so baby spiders and at about 1.30 am I crashed. At 3.00 am I awoke to the dawn chorus of drunken roaring, ranting philosophers and snogging campers. I crawled out of the tent, bid 'Aloha' to my arachnid mates and staggered the quarter mile to the car to get a bit more sleep. At 5.00 am I gave up, the rising sun was turning the Toyota into a microwave. I had breakfast, a Muesli bar and a half bottle of lukewarm water with tiny shrimpy things swimming in it. Then I had a brainwave: I decided to beat the crowds in Stratford by finding a cash machine before most people were awake. The food at the Bash was expensive and greasy but I was getting fed up with Pink Lady apples for every meal. I got lost within the airfield grounds, eventually getting directions from a marshal. As I approached the gates I noticed they were closed. A large number of Hell's Angels and Patriots were standing around and a red car drew up. A Sonny Barger look-alike informed me that something had gone missing and the car would have to be searched. I inwardly chuckled at the irony of the situation, but went to unlock the boot. Before they searched I mentioned I was with the Tribe and they seemed happy with that, the gate opened and off I went to Stratford.

Being a prospect for the Tribe was, as I expected, no holiday. I became a gopher, going for ice cream, drinking water, showering water and making the odd cup of tea for visitors. The two questions I was asked repeatedly were, 'How did you become a Christian' and 'What is the Tribe of Judah all about.' I talked to many who had poor self images, like a woman who hated herself; a young Welsh girl whose husband had ditched her and was on anti-depressants; a young man, who couldn't understand what Christians were doing in a place like the Bulldog and Steve, the proprietor of Steve's Stainless Nuts and his squeaky daughter. Even as we were packing up, the Muslim businessman came over and asked me how I came to join the Tribe; I only got to how I became a Christian then he was called away. I even got to share my faith with a stripper waiting for her 'turn' in the tent where the bands played. She invited me to see her show, assuring me that she didn't 'take everything off' but I refused politely and off she went. Many of the bikers spent their time drinking, head banging to the rock music or leering at the strippers. By 3 am many had partially sobered up and this was a good time to talk, it required a major effort for me to stay awake this long, but I managed it.

As a member of the tribe you tend to forget you have 'Jesus is Lord' in glowing letters on your back but the many observers do not. Carrying out the hard work in temperatures not far off 100°F, filling a water bottle for a disabled Hell's Angel whose peg leg was sinking in the mud around a standpipe, making tea for visitors and fetching and carrying is not hard line evangelism like sharing your faith with enquirers. Each time I moaned to God I got the same answer, 'You are doing the bum jobs in the Name of Jesus' which made the effort worthwhile. I told more people how I became a Christian and what Jesus had done for me and my family in two and a half days than I had done in the last two years. The significance of what we do really hit home when I took a Council Tax form into the Walton One Stop Shop on Monday morning. I told the girl where I'd been over the weekend to find that the biker killed on the B4632 accident just north of the Bulldog Bash site was the husband of a friend of hers. The truth is out there. There are a lot of hurting people out there too. I was a prospect with the Tribe for more than three years but I realised there was no future in it for me. I could not afford a motorcycle and without one I could never become a full member of the Tribe. I could stay a prospect for ever, or take the alternative way out. I resigned from the Tribe, one of the most painful experiences of my life.

I've had motor cycles from an early age and most bikers I knew had large bellies and tattoos. I had the belly and considered possibly getting a tattoo but I'd never seen anything I'd want permanently displayed on my skin. I visited tattoo 'parlours', saw loads of pattern books but the images were generally girly, pervy or downright demonic. I had a brainwave - I'd design my own. A central theme of Christianity is the crucifixion of Jesus - to onlookers the end of an era - the end of Jesus; but God raised him from the dead and exalted him to the ultimate ruler of the Cosmos. What appeared to be a victory for satan, who throughout history had tried to eliminate Jesus and His ancestors was in fact the ultimate sting: Jesus on the cross was victorious. This was to be the theme of my DIY tattoo design; a cross pushed right through a grinning skull.

I knew that repeated stabbing with a needle was not the most pleasant treatment, probably why most people get drunk before having them (and regret doing so later in life). My idea of having: 'Death where is thy sting, Grave where is thy victory?' engraved on my skin would be more pain than I was prepared to tolerate. I decided on 'No Sting!!' I took my DIY design to a tattoo studio, having been informed that they were 'artists' and would interpret my sketch into a work of art. In fact, my rough sketch was copied exactly. From the first prick of the needle I realized that it was more painful than I thought. Secondly, because I take aspirin as a blood thinner, blood was dripping from each stab of the needle. I had to hold a swab against my elbow to absorb the gore dripping from the 'work of art'. I endured the pain until the picture was done then stopped the procedure. The 'no sting!!' would have been the straw that broke the camel's back! I decided to get Viv to write it on with a biro, totally underestimating her reaction to my piece of primitive 'art'. She freaked out when she saw the 'masterpiece' on my arm. So much so that I tried to remove the thing with a scrubbing brush and pumice stone. When it became infected I tried to solve the problem by applying neat bleach - again, not a brilliant idea. The DIY was now an eyesore and an arm-sore. I next went to Lasercare on Rodney Street to see what it would cost to have it removed. They told me, as it wasn't too big, it would only cost £60...for each of 10 'painful as a welding burn' sessions. And so it remains. My daughter reckons from a distance my tattoo looks like a diseased carrot. Nevertheless, many have asked what it is supposed to mean and I tell them, asking them first, 'Do you really want to know?

As a part-time lecturer I was always on the look-out for any extra hours and open to substitute for the pregnant, the sick or otherwise absent in most subjects. Although I have a Chemistry degree, I have taught Physics, Maths and Computing. Once I was recruited to look after a three hour English class. I was surprised to find a lady I knew from years ago sitting near the back of the room. Recounting a family anecdote to make a point, I referred to my wife, Viv as 'Sib'. The lady from the past looked puzzled and asked what had become of Viv. I explained that Viv reckoned that I was a clone of Basil Fawlty and referred to me as Baz; I in return called her Sib. If you haven't heard of Fawlty Towers you won't appreciate the full irony of the situation that followed. I should have left it at the verbal explanation but having a latent dramatic streak, I did a quick goose-step then concluded with the infamous Basil Fawlty crouch with my hands wrapped over my head. As I did so there was a loud tearing noise as the back of my trousers split from the crotch to the waistband. I felt the draught instantly and for a moment tried to remember if I was wearing the white shorts which had been turned pink in the washing machine. I completed the lesson with my back to the blackboard and refused the offer of an enthusiastic special needs lady in the class to staple my trousers temporarily. By the following day every student in the college knew about it, people I'd never met were informing me 'it's a full moon tonight!' and other less politically correct comments.

I had an hour to spare before my next class and had a choice to make. To sit in the IT department and see if anyone would speak to me or go to the Canteen, laughingly called the Refectory, and sup overpriced tea while observing the behaviour of the local unwashed: I decided to go and have a coffee with a mate in the Art department. As I entered the office there was no one there, apart from a guy who for some reason was not wearing a shirt. As I approached the table with the kettle I realised that the dude was not wearing anything at all. He was lazing back in a chair with a cup and saucer poised over his manhood. He offered to get me a drink. I quickly informed him I'd get my own to avoid his poaching of his privates. I am not easily embarrassed but this situation freaked me out a little. Realising I was slightly uncomfortable he explained that he was the 'life model' and did not wear the dressing gown provided as it caused wrinkles in his skin. I thought of suggesting that perhaps the students could omit any wrinkles in their sketches, then concluded he was a state registered exhibitionist, knocked my drink back at speed and made an exit. I mentioned my experience to a lecturer in the same department and he asked me if I'd seen the lady who also modelled 'au naturel' for them. I was glad to say I had not: apparently she was over 60, extremely wrinkly and proud of it.

For almost five years I lectured on computer applications at a school converted to a gymnasium with a small computer suite. One day the OFSTED inspectors were visiting various classes and for once I wore a suit. When I arrived that morning those that knew me were asking if I was due in court, as my usual dress code was scruffy-casual and they'd never seen me in a suit. No inspectors called in on the first session and I went for a coffee. I sat in the foyer waiting for the queue of students to get their tea, coffee or hot chocolate from the machine so I could get mine. The caretaker was dismantling two upright 'Henry' vacuum cleaners which had stopped working. No doubt this was because the cleaning ladies had the habit of dragging them around by the flex and this had loosened the wiring. One had the suction hose attached, the other did not and they just looked like Mr and Mrs R2D2. Bob fixed Mrs R2D2 and started on the man himself. Forgetting to disconnect the power supply, Bob was fiddling with the machine when he let out a screech and fell back clutching his arm. I am convinced that much humour is based on the misfortunes of others, certainly Bob's electro-shock-therapy amused everyone waiting in the drinks queue. I tried to make him feel better by sharing some good news, which to be fair was just a figment of my imagination. I told him that an American doctor had discovered that electric shocks were good for the libido; Bob was neither convinced nor amused. 'I'll have some of that!', I joked and leaned towards the vacuum cleaner when two of the plastic chair legs shattered and I fell on the floor, my coffee flying through the air until gravity caused it to rain down on me. Suddenly I was the centre of amusement. The suit went to the cleaners and my self-image recovered. The whole thing had been recorded on a security camera and was regularly replayed for a week or so to amuse the geeks.

During the summer break a friend and his wife came to stay for a few days. We took them on the 'Ferry 'cross the Mersey', a sad pageant of Liverpool in better days, with the skeletal cranes, redundant docks, Cammell Lairds' deserted shipbuilding yards and mangy beaches almost picked clean of sand by the River Mersey. The commentary by the geek trying to imitate the Scouse accent was slightly amusing. Back on dry land, the Albert Dock was our next port of call; they were both musicians and Beatle fans all their lives; they dragged us over to the Beatles exhibition; an expensive meander through a block board maze with old enlarged photos and background music. There were not even four students done up in Sergeant Pepper outfits miming to the records. It occurred to me; if the Beatles had been born in the USA how different the exhibition would have been.

My stomach was sending out distress messages and I suggested we got something to eat, but their Beatle mania was not yet satisfied. Just outside the Granada TV Studios was a bus stop marked Magical Mystery Tour: we waited there until eventually a tatty looking coach arrived. The proper tour bus had failed its MOT and the substitute had a defective tape player and no psychedelic paint job. As the coach travelled round the historical Fab Four sites, like Penny Lane or Strawberry Field only one channel of the stereo could be heard. The big woman doing the commentary was undeterred: neither were the hordes of camera-wielding American and Japanese Beatle worshippers. The tour was gruelling, no turn was left unstoned and the single channel played on. We stopped at the bus stop where John Lennon's mother was hit by a car, but there was no bronze effigy lying in the road; not even a chalk or painted silhouette. As we reached the Strawberry Field gates, with relevant half-track accompaniment, the bus emptied and almost every one surged forward to touch, embrace and even snog the stone gateposts; all recorded on camcorder of course. On to Penny Lane; the road name now painted-on so no-one with a screwdriver could 'borrow' it, and to Paul McCartney's family home at Forthlin Road bought by the National Trust a few years ago. As the coach stopped loads of the neighbours came out to get in the picture and grab a moment of reflected glory. Eventually it all ended back at the Albert Dock. The tour was interesting, but not that magical: it was a mystery to me that people would pay so much to see the humble beginnings of a load of musically creative Scouse scallies. But what do I know? I was a Rolling Stones fan in those days!

My wife used to insist that her father liked me: I have evidence to the contrary. Throughout the years he has given me things that he no longer needed and having a magpie gene, I collect what I am given. I got an old blowlamp that blew up, a clamp that didn't, several tins of paint that were totally solidified and useless, but the worst was the stepladder. I had loaned mine to a friend and never got it back; my father-in-law gave me one, the sturdy old-fashioned type that needs two people to carry it. I was painting the tiles over the front window with bright red tile paint, not tomato ketchup as my neighbours supposed. I set up the stepladder, climbed up and began painting. Suddenly I was aware of falling through the air: the rope stopping the ladder from opening too far had snapped and the ladder had collapsed. I managed to land on my feet and was thinking how agile I was for my age. Unfortunately, still obeying the law of gravity was the tin of paint, which hit me on the side of the head and coated one side of my face and most of the T-shirt I was wearing. I'd like to say I took it calmly, but I'm afraid I didn't. An old lady walking past heard my expletive, turned to look, and then started to throw a 'wobbler' as I looked as if my head had exploded. I checked the rope later, to my surprise it had not been partially cut through, it was just rotten. An accident? A quirk of Fate? An Act of God? Who knows?

I've heard it said 'Some people have all the luck!' I have never been very lucky: the events I refer to in the 'Coincidences or what?'

Where the Bugs wear Boots

chapter were beyond coincidence. I did survive many motorbike crashes, earning the nickname 'The Cat' but I believe God was looking after me, even when I didn't believe in Him. In the Spring of 2001 my youngest daughter won a short holiday in the USA in a Warner Bros competition; three days in San Francisco and four in Los Angeles. Now that was lucky, or was it? Of the optional dates they chose September. San Francisco was buzzing and they saw the sites and sampled the cuisine. Several days later they flew to LA. Touching down they travelled to their hotel which had a strangely miserable atmosphere. No enthusiastic American hospitality, no 'Have a nice day'. Flopping down in their room they switched on the TV then they knew why. It was September 11th. As their aeroplane was landing at Los Angeles, the second aeroplane was crashing into the World Trades Centre in New York. They watched the television in horror, along with many others, as the towers collapsed. These events did not make for a particularly happy rest-of-holiday. Most attractions were respectfully closed, but the worst was yet to come. Their flight home was cancelled and they were stuck in LA for another week. It doesn't sound too bad, but when you have budgeted for a week's holiday and the local hotels and taxis whack up their prices because of the tragedy, you got problems. They had to spend the money they had saved for their wedding to survive. A friendly policeman did suggest the local centre for derelicts, drunks and geeks, but they chose not to go there. September 11th saw the emergence of a new breed of heroes; the firemen and others, plus a new breed of mercenary taxi drivers quite happy to screw stranded travellers for a few dollars more. The atrocity demonstrated once again how crazy these terrorists are; the deliberate murder of innocent people to make a political or religious statement is mad-dog behaviour and you know how we deal with mad-dogs.

Talking about mad-dogs, one day whilst driving to college I saw a bloke kicking a woman lying on the pavement. I slammed on the brakes, jumped out of the car and knocked the guy down. To my amazement the woman got up and took a swing at me, screaming abuse. I got back in the car as she went to help her abuser. Perhaps she had always wanted to be a football and I had spoiled her dream. Once again I was the bad one? Maybe, but I'd do it again as I hate bullying in any form, particularly against women or children. But what do you do if the ill treatment is given and received by those you love?

My daughter had arranged to come for tea so I picked Maddy up from work and we called at her house to feed the cat. Inside the house she found items missing including all her husbands clothes. No note, no explanation - just instant heartbreak. It was weeks later that a nosy neighbour told us she had seen her husband loading up the car but had no idea he was doing a runner. Day after day my daughter cried virtually non-stop, neither eating nor sleeping. She stayed with us for a while; every time I saw her swollen tear stained face I could taste the hatred I had for him. Maddy, amazingly, still loved him. I found out that he was staying with his parents but I was not prepared to attack him in front of his parents. Several years had elapsed since I had the accident that resulted in a sub-dural (brain) haemorrhage and my former strength had returned. My daughter still loved him and there was a further problem: as a Christian, payback was no longer an option. I was trapped in a cell of grief for my daughter, hatred for her husband and my responsibility to God for my behaviour. The whole thing was painful for Viv and I, not just because of the effect on our daughter, but because we loved and treated him as a son, loaned him the car whenever he needed one, helped him to find a career and helped with their new house.

    To try and see him in a better light I tried to rationalise why he'd done it. I loved him as my own son as I said and when they told us they wanted to marry I was overjoyed. They played together in a blues band, wrote songs together and worked on Christian projects together. When Maddy was ill with ME he cared for her. Some years earlier he was attacked on his way home from the city centre. He had walked through the gates of St Nicholas Church at the Pier Head when someone leaped out of the shadows, knocked him down with a punch then punched him again and drove his glasses into his eye. We drove round to see him. He was covered in blood and when he tried to blow his nose, his eye popped forward. The hospital diagnosis was a skull fracture in the region of the orbit. The operation was a tricky one: it entailed cutting the skin at the nape of the neck and rolling back the skin over the head to the bridge of the nose; then the real operation would commence to repair the skull fracture. He was informed that the eye might be permanently damaged. We phoned around our Christian friends who promised to pray: the outcome was that God healed him physically. A friend who was a security guard informed us that   there had been a spate of attacks on long-haired people, very comforting, but the police never traced his attacker. Wounds do heal, I suspected that the attack had scarred him emotionally and psychologically. He seemed to have become less caring, more irritable and selfish; was that something to do with it'? He was a computer programmer working to some crazy deadlines; had the stress got to him'? Had he flipped?

I managed to get a grip on myself and tried to forgive him; I used to wonder what I'd do if I ever crossed his path sometime. Then it happened. Driving towards Liverpool with a friend, he mentioned he needed a better amplifier for his Karaoke show. I pulled in quickly into Frets, a local music shop, and suggested we see what amplifiers they had for sale. I raced into the shop as it was pouring with rain. There was her ex holding one of his beloved guitars. I had promised Maddy and God that I'd not harm him but at least I'd tell him what I thought of him. I spoke and what came out surprised him as much as it did me, "How are you?" I know I did the right thing, because hate is more destructive to the hater than the recipient. His doing a runner was in retrospect the best thing he ever did. Although the experience was horrific for Maddy and our family at the time, she is far better off now. The financially crippling mortgage was transferred to a repayment one, God restored her broken heart and has given her an amazing new set of friends and a full life. There's more! She has recently become engaged to a head chef who is caring and supportive; apart from his culinary skills he is also an excellent bass guitarist and an Evertonian as well!

Back at college, the novelty of teaching computing skills was wearing thin. It was good to meet new people and help them to gain skills that could improve their prospects of gaining employment or progressing in their jobs. The conditions for part-time lecturers, however, seemed to be getting worse. On many occasions I had classes taken from me and given to full timers who had lost classes, meaning substantial financial loss in terms of salary; but a worse result was that my retirement pension was based on the lower earnings. I don't think the changes in lecturing staff helped the students much either. I was due to retire in a matter of months, and apart from the obvious financial loss, I was looking forward to it!

Chapter 17

Endgame

I retired from the college at the end of the second week in July 2006. All my students presented me with cards and other goodies and wished me all the best. On the last Friday morning I completed the registers in the IT staff room and walked out. Fifteen years at the college but not one well wishing card, comment or handshake from my beloved fellow lecturers. It was like I never existed; for a moment I had a scary thought. Maybe I'm dead and I don't know it! Maybe, like everyone except the kid in 'The Sixth Sense', they couldn't see dead people. Walking to the car I felt like I'd been released from prison. Around this time my wife underwent major surgery and her father died in Arrowe Park hospital while she was recovering from the operation. She was discharged in time for her to attend the funeral. For the next three months I spent most of my time looking after her. On her return to work I was ready to begin my retirement program, the first project being the completion of this book.

Maybe you've never thought what it's like to be 65; or maybe you know exactly: this may surprise you but I feel mentally about 18 most of the time and occasionally 3! I still love motorcycles, but racing handlebars now induce back pain. I still appreciate Heavy Metal, but I can no longer headbang without going dizzy. I am still amazed that the average policeman looks as if he should be back in the 6th form. Physically of course, I certainly don't feel 20. Years of motorcycling with hard to kick-start machines, many spills taken on my knees and elbows and playing football into my forties have left me with creaky arthritic knees. I have always hated taking tablets but now have to take five a day to control my type-2 diabetes and the high blood pressure it has caused. I am still powerful for my age but ten years ago I could lift my wife over my head with ease. I'm not saying she weighs more; I am not what I was then! Strangely age has not caused me to shrink; twenty five years ago I was six foot one; now I am six foot two - wonders will never cease. I do a lot of shouting at the television on the few occasions that

Where the Bugs wear Boots

I watch it. My pet hates are game shows and so called reality programmes. How can it be reality when the would-be celebrities know that they are on camera and so perform like overpaid decerebrate monkeys? The Grumpy Old Men and Women programmes have me shouting agreement with them: I guess that says it all! I have plenty of teeth left but they're 90% porcelain and therefore not removable This, of course, disqualifies me from participating in professional gurning competitions as I can't get my lower lip over my nose. I no longer watch live football, firstly because the game has changed radically, and not for the better. I am not prepared to pay the ludicrous entrance fees to sit and watch the grossly overpaid performing monkeys leaping into the penalty area and falling over, or whining like babies at the slightest bit of rough treatment. I used to enjoy the Game standing in the ground; the problem with all seats is that you have to keep standing up to see the exciting bits as most people sitting in front of you do. Apart from the odd game, if I watch at all it's on television with the opinionated dribblings of the commentators.

Well, there you have it: I started life in the middle of the Second World War and my story thus far ends with the ongoing Iraq conflict. To summarise: I was born mid World War 2, I slept through the May Blitz, was bribed to attend Church, I lost my dinner on the Isle of Man boat, I stood on a dead horse washed up on the Cast Iron Shore, I was bashed with a cricket bat until it broke, I lynched a neighbour, I formed a skiffle group, I was blamed for everything at school and was expelled from the same school, I obtained a chemistry degree at Liverpool University, I worked as a research scientist for twenty years, I was poisoned by a ship's cook, I performed operations without qualifications, I met the Son of God, I endured two sinus washes, I was sacked from my first job, I freaked out on Catherine Street, I totally lost my memory, I watched my mother die and thought I was dying, I was attacked by a grizzly bear and buzzed by a shark, I lectured computing for 15 years, I was swindled out of thousands of pounds by a business partner, I had eight motorbike crashes in one year, I spent thirteen years on the dole, I was attacked by a mad knifewoman, I was transformed into a Klingon, I survived a brain haemorrhage despite the consultant's gloomy predictions, I was abducted by aliens, implanted and then rejected. One of these confessions is a slight figment of my imagination I'll let the reader decide.

Well now the end of my story is near and I'm wondering how do you end an autobiography?

With a terminal cough?

With 'That's all folks'?

With a soulful rendition of 'My Way'? I don't think so! If you've read this far you will realise that I did many things my way and I cocked up because I did. If all I had relied on was myself I'd be in the crap up to my neck; probably dead or in jail! Thanks to God I have much. I do have a tendency to say what I think and have paid dearly for this at times: I was sacked from two jobs for only saying what all the other workers were thinking. I have never kneeled or grovelled to anyone in my life, not even when asking Viv to marry me. If I recall correctly, after stepping out together for seven years we went into a jeweller's shop and bought an engagement ring. When we returned to where the car was parked I suggested that she wore it, seeing as I'd just paid for it. Actually I did kneel once, but only in my head. That was fifty years ago when I accepted Jesus Christ as my Saviour and Lord. I believe God has more for me to do, more people to influence that's why I wrote this book. If it has made you think, good! If it has disturbed you, good! The scary thing is that it's all true, apart from the alien abduction bit. I mentioned in the summary that I survived a sub-dural haemorrhage and I want to close this part of the book with a bit more detail.

It was Sunday December 31st 1999 at 9.45 on a bitterly cold New Years Eve morning. I set out to catch a bus at the Black Bull, Aintree. The pavement was a hazardous ice sheet so I walked on the road in the slush but the traffic made this almost as dodgy as walking on the ice. After several retards drove close and one car splashed me, I decided to get back on the pavement and took several steps on the ice when my feet shot from under me and I fell backwards onto my head. How long I was unconscious I don't know, probably a few minutes. I faded back into consciousness as an old bloke coming out of a local shop tried to help me up. I checked the ice sheet and the pavement, no obvious damage, so I walked home with a rapidly growing egg on the back of my head. At around 1.30 pm the pain in my head was still increasing and I started vomiting like a parrot. A friend drove me to Fazakerley Hospital where they gave me some painkillers and let me go home some five hours later. A junior doctor did say that I should have had an MRI scan but there was no-one around senior enough to authorise it. Two days later, still in a great deal of pain, I returned to the hospital and they gave me a neck brace which failed to reduce the pain. Early Sunday morning I woke at 2.00 am with extreme head pain; Viv drove me to hospital and again they let me go home after I swallowed some painkillers; I had to walk home as Viv expected them to keep me in longer. In total four visits to hospital, no treatment other than paracetamol, and I was getting worse. I was delirious, screeching with the pain and my daughter harassed our doctor who drove me to the Accident and Emergency department for the fifth time. My recollections are hazy as I was in and out of consciousness. One minute I was in the A and E, then out in the open air; I now know I was being rushed to the Walton Neurology Centre.

The blow on the back of the head had caused a chronic sub-dural haemorrhage. The MRI scan showed almost one third of my skull filled with fluid compressing the brain itself. I spent three weeks strapped in a chromium-plated bed, not allowed to move or sit up. I kept going unconscious then waking up again. I recognised my visitors but couldn't say much, although I tried. I lost the ability to speak for a while, just coming out with gibberish, dysphasia for the medically competent. The steroids gave me a larger than usual appetite and I frequently had two dinners as many of the patients had no appetite at all and gave me theirs. I was so hungry I ate anything edible, including the hated fishcakes and horrible liver. I wondered if I'd ever met the liver donor. Everyone in the ward seemed a little strange, in behaviour and appearance. Many had hideous metal staples holding bits of their skulls in place; it reminded me of the first sci-fi movie I ever saw, 'The Creature with the Atomic Brain'. One guy had a rectangular cuboid dent in his head, like he'd been hit with a brick. Apparently he'd fallen downstairs and needed a load of brain tissue removing. He kept leaping out of bed and falling on the floor. In the next bed to me was Frank, a nutty old guy who'd been beaten up and mugged in the city. He had a weird habit of taking all his clothes off just as they let the visitors in and walking down the ward to the toilet, his catheter and bag dragging behind him. He talked to it and whistled at it like it was a pet dog. He never quite worked out that his frequent trips to the bog were a waste of effort when connected to the bag. One night I woke up with something touching my face; it was

Frank who had again jettisoned all his clothes and was stretching across, still connected by the catheter to the bag clipped to his bed. 'Has the bus gone yet?' he asked.

That was the least of my problems. I was so convinced I was on the way out that I wrote a note to Viv and the kids expressing my appreciation of them. What I didn't know at the time is that my daughter had been advised by the consultant to say goodbye to me as it was likely that I was not going to make it. Maddy informed him that God would look after me and Viv rang round Christian friends and asked them to pray. I wrote this book as yet another proof that God does answer prayer. When you face death, there is no time for wasted words or the usual crap people come out with. If you thought you had hours to live, what would you want to write or say to your family or friends? In case you are wondering, this is what I wrote to my wife and children. The original is virtually unintelligible; this is a transcription made after I came home and recovered sufficiently.

To my daughters:
The events of last week have rattled my cage to its dodgy foundations. I realise I am as fragile as the rest of you humans, but I have deluded myself that I am not. It is in this relatively sober frame of mind that I am writing this; once I recover I may not get around to telling you, and I'm not totally convinced I will recover at this stage. I was kidding about the aliens leaving you on the racecourse for us to look after; Viv and I made you with not a little help from God. I have loved you both from your wriggling, kicking, pestering alien fetal stage, through your dramatically different entrances into our ecosystem, in the good and bad times up to now. I love you both and there is nothing you could do to change that. Viv and I are no experts on parenting, but everything we have done has been with your good in mind. You are aware of my constant fight to be normal and responsible. I am a one-off, as we all are, and a loose-cannon on occasions and you have inherited some of these characteristics. You are both highly creative, multi-talented, caring and responsible yet very different from each other in other ways. You are valued friends, mentors and wise counsellors who also happen to be my children. I am proud of your achievements to date, although I may not always appear to be, but there is so much more for you to achieve. We have never tried to

brainwash you with our faith, I am grateful to God that you have made your own decisions to follow Christ and yet are real people. Religion is a waste of good time and energy; Jesus is cool! My success rate at decision making is low, but marrying Viv, having you guys, and asking Jesus into my life were high quality decisions for which I have no regrets. Many of my decisions have cost the family dearly, particularly in terms of finance, and I apologise. My every intention has been to improve the family lot, but I'm no expert in these things. My love for Viv, yourselves and the King of Kings has kept me in a reasonable state of stability, but I am aware there is some room for improvement.

To Viv, my wife:
What can I say? As with the kids it was love at first sight. I still remember the first time I saw you, a rosy cheeked vision in a green corduroy coat and beret, with your younger sister attached permanently to your hand. No woman interested me before I saw you and none has since. You are a person of special virtue and character; your honesty, patience and discernment set you above most mere mortals I have encountered. We have seen hard times that would have crushed many but you have always been an inspiration to me, a tower of strength. I am not a bad person. I want to be a blessing to the family, I want to achieve for God, I want to be a history maker, not just history, yet I'm up and down like a frog in a bucket. I regularly say the wrong thing, I appear to offend some without even trying; many times I am my own worst enemy, but I love you with every weird cell of my being. I am a penguin.

Finally, to everyone:
So what am I saying? Has it taken a bang on the head to make me appreciate my family and friends? No, but it has stopped me in my tracks and given me a chance to express it. I don't believe I can kid anyone but myself. I do have a mean streak, especially when under pressure, but God is slowly dissolving it. I do care about people but try to create a hard veneer which no one buys anyway. I just want to express my thanks to God and yourselves for being who and what you are. I have little financially, yet substantial wealth built into my family. The codeine phosphate tablets have worn off, the head pain is back

and my muse has deserted me. I am temporarily reverting to an ungrateful oaf. 'Nurse, where's me dinner?'

It took seven months before my condition approached normality and as my wife said to the consultant, 'How can you tell when he's normal?' One morning a nurse asked how I was feeling and I told her that the little pixies kept me awake by singing too loud. I was joking, of course, but the nurse told the consultant I was still hallucinating; I'm surprised they let me out!

So you've heard my story, all of it wacky but true. Do you think it's a load of twaddle, self-delusion or reality? Many think that the world, the universe and beyond is the product of a cosmic accident. Or perhaps we are all figments of other people's imagination or that aliens did a '2001 Space Odyssey' on our Neanderthal ancestors? I believe we are not products of chance; we are special creations responsible to a Creator. So I leave you with words of Larry Norman, musician, prophet and creative genius: 'Why don't you look into Jesus? He's got the answer!"

Where the Bugs wear Boots

Glossary

A guide to some of the unfamiliar words used in this autobiography

- **A**lpha Course: a good way to investigate Christianity
- Also-ran: fairly untalented non-achiever
- Anorak: a boring person, nerd or geek
- Armadillo's knickers: decidedly unpleasant
- Atrophy: shrinkage, degradation

- **B**ack-heel: to reject
- Badger-breath: suffering from extreme halitosis
- Bananas, to go: to freak out or lose your cool
- Bangers: explosive fireworks or sausages
- Barf: vomit
- Barmy: mad, crazy, unhinged, looney
- Barp: acronym for a boring, arrogant, religious person
- Bathos: anticlimax, not one of the three musketeers
- Benzene: a toxic solvent
- Berk: an idiot, dope, buffoon or idiot
- Bikers: pleasant chaps who ride motorcycles
- Bin person: politically correct term for a refuse collector
- Bladdered: extremely drunk, pissed, legless
- Bob, having a few: rich, loaded
- Bog: a toilet, WC, khazi or rest-room
- Bog roll-in-the-freezer: a mega hot Vindaloo curry
- Boloney: lies or inaccurate assumptions
- Boneyard: a cemetery
- Brain-on-legs: a clever person, smarter than the average
- Brown bread: euphemism for dead, kicked the bucket
- Brill: brilliant, most excellent
- Bum: one who is down on his/her luck or the gluteus maximus
- Bun: a schoolmarm hairstyle, a single buttock or a bread roll
- Bunking in: entering an event without paying
- Bunking off: leaving work or school without permission
- Butties: see Sarnies

- Buttons: low wages
- Buzz: a good feeling and the sound of a bee

- **C**arcinogen: cancer causing chemical
- Cazzie: the Cast-iron shore at Otterspool
- Cheapjack: mean, tight
- Chin, to: to attack
- Chippy: a Fish and Chip shop
- Clobber: motor cycle clothing, also used by Yogi Bear to mean GBH
- Cockatrice: a mythical creature with a deadly glare
- Combo: motorcycle and sidecar
- Connie-onnie: condensed milk
- Codger: an old person, past their sell-by date
- Collywobbles: Delhi belly, suffering from diarrhoea
- Conk: a big nose, beak or proboscis
- Conky: term of abuse for a person with a big nose
- Cosh: an instrument of correction
- Counters: poker chips used to teach number theory to five year olds in the past
- Cow-person: the politically correct term for a cowboy or cowgirl
- Cozzie: swimming costume
- Crap: faeces, rubbish, unpopular opinion, rival football team
- Craw: throat or gullet
- Creeps: those who co-operate with the authorities
- Crocked: injured, broken, knackered or unserviceable
- Crone: ugly old woman
- Crud: dirt, detritus, muck or gunge
- Crumpet: opposite of Crone, qv.
- Crusty: an aged person, geriatric or coffin-dodger
- Cyclotron: particle accelerator

- **D**A: a haircut resembling the rear end of a duck
- Dicks, like a dog with two: very happy, euphoric
- Dead: adjective meaning 'very' as in 'dead clever', 'dead stupid'
- Dead leg: temporary paralysis of lower limbs caused by deliberate injury or sitting on the toilet for too long
- Diddle, to: to cheat
- Digit, thick as a donkey's: not very intelligent

- Divvy: Co-op dividend or stupid person
- Dodgy: not to be trusted
- Dosh: money, dough, filthy lucre
- Dope: an addictive substance or an idiot
- Drew Peacock: the co-inventor of Viagra
- Dunno: basic Scouse for 'I do not know'

- **E**mporium: a bespoke shop
- Enigma: a mystery, like why Donald Duck doesn't wear trousers, but has a towel hiding his bits after bathing
- En-suite: a bedroom with a toilet connected to it
- Entonox: gas/air mixture used to alleviate the pain of childbirth

- **F**ag head: a smoker
- Fanatic: someone who is more enthusiastic than you are
- Faraday cage effect: the observation that electrostatic charges reside on the outside of a hollow metal body
- Fauna: wildlife, animals
- Fibula: one of the bones in the leg
- Flash: aha! Master of the Universe or self exposure
- Flash point: the temperature below which a solvent will not ignite
- Flatulent: windy, thunderbum, vegetarian
- Flecky: flea-ridden
- Floater: a low density bowel motion, difficult to remove
- Flobster: an obese person
- Flora: vegetation or polyunsaturated spread
- Football Echo: a Liverpool Saturday newspaper
- Four-finger-split: projectile vomit between the fingers
- Foxy Lady: a babe
- Freak: to lose control
- Fuzz, the: the Police

- **G**ab, gift of: verbal diarrhoea
- Genteel: posh, snobby, richer than you
- Get stuffed: go away
- Gizmo: a gadget or device
- Gobbet: a small amount of something, particularly phlegm
- Gobbing out: expectorating, spitting

- Gob on, to have a: to look miserable or crabby
- Gobsmacked: totally surprised
- Golden boy: a creep, toady or favourite
- Golly: a lump of phlegm or the verb 'to spit'
- Goosed: ruined; also see Crocked
- Gozzy: having poor eyesight
- Greb: detritus, crud
- Green: inexperienced or a tree-hugger
- Grid: gateway to the drains, a decrepit motorcycle
- Grizzling: complaining
- Grozzling: hawking up phlegm prior to Gobbing qv.
- Guffaw: explosive laughter
- Gutted: upset or disappointed

- **H**aggling: arguing over the price of something
- Hard knocks: tough people
- Homunculus: a little man, a short-ass
- Hypothermia roulette: risking death in a cold environment

- **I**ncontinent: leaky, rubber-knickered
- Innards: offal, intestines, guts
- Invective: abusive comments directed at television 'personalities' or professional footballers who 'dive' into the penalty area

- **J**igger: a back entry, alley
- Jigger rabbit: a cat
- Job Comic: Situations Vacant in a newspaper
- Jockstrap, like a gorilla's: evil smelling
- Joey: a purchase that is not as good as you thought

- **K**ark: to die, croak, pass away, leave the building
- Kex: trousers
- Khazi: toilet, bog
- Kiddie fiddlers: paedophiles
- Knackered: broken, worn out or tired
- Knicker ripper: a loud fart
- Knickers: an expression of unbelief or a replacement expletive

- **L**ab rat: laboratory assistant
- La: term of address; pronounced 'lar' as in 'are youse alright, la?'
- Laxative: something to help you boldly go, Krap-ee-zee
- Leak, to take a: to visit the pissoir, pass water
- Legless: see Bladdered
- Lips, curled: scornful, derisive
- Long Johns: thermal underwear worn by old men and bikers
- Low-life: those you consider inferior to yourself
- Loose cannon: an unpredictable person, a nut case

- **M**arinated: soaked to absorb the flavour of the marinade
- Metal, Heavy: the music of the spheres
- Miffed: annoyed, crabby, not very happy
- Moggie: a cat
- Mooning: showing one's buttocks to those not interested
- Mr Big: God
- MSG: a food additive which causes hyperactivity
- Mugger's delight: a deserted place
- Muzak: poor quality music e.g. rap, house or country

- **N**aff: uncool or rubbish
- Navvies: labourers
- Neck-end: a low-life qv
- Nelly, wet: a sticky scouse confection
- Nits: head lice
- Nit picking: manual head louse removal, being hyper-critical
- No mark: an insignificant, unimportant person
- Nosh: scran, scoff, food
- Nutter: mentally unbalanced person

- **O**ff ones head: drunk and disorderly, high as a kite
- Omni-directional: in every direction
- One of Lewis's: motionless; like a dummy in Lewis's shop
- Oxymoron: a contradiction, like an honest politician

- **P**achyderm: thick skinned, e.g. an elephant, rhino
- Pariahs: social outcasts, scroungers or spongers
- Parky: cold weather or the park keeper

- Payback: revenge
- Pea whack: soup made from ham, peas and other vegetables
- Perv: a pervert
- Pig ignorant: very ignorant
- Pig stupid: extremely stupid
- Pig ugly: requiring a bag on the head
- Pills, happy: anti-depressants
- Pinchbeck: idea pincher, taking credit for other people's work
- Pissoir: a French public toilet, and I mean public!
- Pixilated: apparently shrunken by pixie magic
- Plaque: crud that grows on your teeth if you don't brush them.
- Plimsoles: an early thin soled precursor of training shoes
- Plums, holding your: a simple test for a hernia
- Porkies, porky pies: lies
- Porky: fat, obese, flobster
- Poser: an exhibitionist
- Posh: richer than you, used in derogatory manner
- Protuberant: sticking out
- Pseudo-cricket: cricket played to rules generated by the bat owner
- Psychometric test: a way of screening out wrong-uns
- Purgative: politically correct term for a laxative

- **Q**uack: a crap doctor
- Quaint: old fashioned
- Quorn: vegetarian meat substitute

- **R**andori: martial arts free practise
- Rat bike: a dirty, unreliable motorcycle
- Rat-assed: extremely drunk
- Reprogrammed: disciplined
- Retsina: Greek resinated wine
- Riffraff: those you consider inferior to yourself
- Rock: a musical genre; also a stick-shaped boiled sugar confectionery sold at the seaside
- Rolling pin: a device for flattening pastry and wayward spouses
- Runner, doing a: escaping to avoid responsibilities e.g not paying in a café

- **S**agging: playing truant, non-attendance at school
- Salary: posh term for wages
- Sarnies: sandwiches
- Scabbing: cadging or obtaining things without paying
- Scallies: wayward youths, yobs, scumbags
- Scare the kex off, to: to frighten
- Scouse: Liverpool accent, inhabitant, casserole with meat of dubious origin
- Scouse, blind: scouse without meat
- Scouse kiss: a head-butt
- Scrubber: a prostitute
- Shilling: old currency used to feed the gas or electricity meter
- Slash, to go for a: to urinate or empty the bladder
- Simian: monkey-like
- Snot: nasal mucus or someone who offends you
- Sod: very as in 'sod-awful', sod-ugly'
- Sod's Law: 'Anything that can go wrong will go wrong'
- Sozzled: drunk
- Squeak machine: a scooter or low powered motorcycle
- Sterrie: sterilised milk
- Stiffs: corpses
- Stiff browser: one who scans obituaries to see who is dead
- Stiff transporter: a hearse
- Stiff whinger: a professional mourner
- Streaker: an exhibitionist who runs about naked at public events
- Sycophant: a creep qv.

- **T**a: pronounced 'tar' meaning 'thank you' in basic Scouse
- Tadpole monitor: a most important responsibility
- Tandoori: Indian oven or spice
- Technophobia: fear of computers and the like
- Tickled: amused
- Tragicomic: funny and sad at the same time
- Trichloroethylene: a toxic solvent once used as a dental anaesthetic
- Tripe: stomach lining of a cow, irrelevant spoken or written rubbish

- **U**biquitous: everywhere, like traffic wardens and train spotters
- Uncle Disgusting: a pervert, particularly applied to paedophiles

- **V**ermin: MPs, DJs and traffic wardens
- Vigilantes: unauthorised revenge seekers

- **W**ellies: rubber boots
- Wobblegob: a garrulous person
- Winkle-pickers: pointy shoes
- Wonky: crooked

- **X**enomorph: a fictional endoparasitoid, the Alien
- **Y**a: a posh persons 'yes'
- Yer wot: basic Scouse for 'Could you repeat that please?'
- Yes man: a creep or toady
- Yobbo: a young thug
- Yuk: an expression of disgust

World Timeline

What was happening as I grew up

1941 (born)
Music: Deep in the heart of Texas; Chattanooga Choo Choo; Perfidia.
Film: Citizen Kane; How Green Was My Valley; Suspicion; Maltese Falcon; Road to Zanzibar; Dr Jekyll and Mr Hyde; The Wolf Man; Major Barbara.
Events: Clothes rationing; May Blitz; Ark Royal sunk; Pearl Harbour attacked; Aerosol cans, Atomic Bomb, Jet engine and penicillin invented.

1942 (1 year old)
Music: White Christmas; White Cliffs of Dover; That Old Black Magic.
Film: Bambi; Holiday Inn; Casablanca; Yankee Doodle Dandy; Cat People.
Events: Nazi gas chambers operational; Napalm invented; Battle of El Alamein; Enrico Fermi achieves nuclear chain reaction.

1943 (2 years old)
Music: Mairzy Doats; Stormy Weather; Paper Doll; Pistol Packin' Mama.
Film: The Outlaw; Jane Eyre; Son of Dracula; We Dive at Dawn; Spitfire.
Events: Round the clock bombing of Germany; Italy surrenders; Dam buster raids; Stalingrad victory; LSD found to be hallucinogenic; Biro pens, Streptomycin and the Aqualung invented.

1944 (3 years old)
Music: Don't Fence Me In; Swingin' On A Star; Accentuate The Positive
Film: Henry V; Children Of Paradise; Going My Way? To Have And Have Not; Arsenic and Old Lace; Cry of the Werewolf; Meet me in St Louis.
Events: D-day landing; 1st V-missiles (Doodlebugs); Blackout relaxed; Hitler assassination attempt fails; US invade Philippines.

Where the Bugs wear Boots

1945 (4 years old)
Music: Sentimental Journey; We'll Gather Lilacs; I'm Beginning To See The Light; Until The End Of Time; Dig You Later.
Film: Kismet; Brief Encounter; Ivan the Terrible; Dillinger; Spellbound.
Events: Last of 1050 V2s; Hitler commits suicide; Roosevelt dies; Germany surrenders; Hiroshima and Nagasaki nuked; A-bomb tested at Almagordo; UN formed; Animal Farm published; Anne Frank starved to death at Bergen-Belsen concentration camp.

1946 (5 years old)
Music: Let it Snow; Fools Rush In; Personality; Take the A train; Surrender.
Film: It's a Wonderful Life; Great Expectations; Notorious; The Big Sleep.
Events: Food shortage - Black Market; Beer production halved; H G Wells died; Bikini swimsuit named after Atomic Test island; Smoking suspected as cause of lung cancer; Biro ball point pen, Television and the zip fly invented; War Crimes trials set up at Nuremburg; National Health Service set up.

1947 (6 years old)
Music: Anything You Can Do; April Showers; Night and Day; Make Believe.
Film: Black Narcissus; The Bicycle Thieves; Brighton Rock; Walter Mitty.
Events: Al Capone and Henry Ford die; IBM Eniac calculator and the transistor invented; sound barrier broken by US pilot; school leaving age extended to 15; Pakistan and India get Independence; Big freeze then floods.

1948 (7 years old)
Music: Kiss Me Kate; Buttons And Bows; Deck Of Cards; All I Want For Christmas Is My Two Front Teeth; Red Roses For A Blue Lady; So Tired.
Film: Hamlet; Oliver Twist; Key Largo; Whisky Galore; Easter Parade.
Events: Bread rationing ends; Railways nationalised; Ghandi killed; School Certificate replaced by GCE; Big Bang theory; Morris Minor; Dead Sea Scrolls found; Israel becomes a State.

1949 (8 years old)
Music: South Pacific; Some Enchanted Evening; Baby Its Cold Outside; Rudolph The Red-Nosed Reindeer; Diamonds Are A Girl's Best Friend.
Film: The Third Man; All the King's men; Joan of Arc; Samson and Delilah.
Events: Clothes and food rationing ends; Geneva Convention agreed; De Havilland Comet commissioned; NATO formed; 1984 published; Soviet atomic test.

1950 (9 years old)
Music: Goodnight Irene; Mona Lisa; I've Got A Lovely Bunch Of Coconuts.
Film: The Gunfighter; Broken Arrow; Orpheus; Rashomon; All About Eve.
Events: Truman orders H-bomb development; Edgar Rice Burroughs dies; Matt Groening creates the Simpsons; Kon Tiki expedition; Colour TV in USA; Cyclamates used; Anti-histamines; Credit card (Diner's Club, NY); Ark Royal launched from Cammel Laird's; War in Korea; George Orwell dies at 46.

1951 (10 years old)
Music: The King and I; An American in Paris; Charmaine; Jezebel.
Film: African Queen; The Thing; The Day The Earth Stood Still; The Enforcer; David and Bathsheba; Streetcar named Desire; Quo Vadis; Showboat.
Events: The X Certificate introduced; Zebra crossings introduced; Yeti footprint found; 3D movies; Smog masks; Festival of Britain; Colour TV in USA.

1952 (11 years old)
Music: Your Cheatin' Heart; Takes Two To Tango; I Saw Mummy Kissing Santa Claus; High Noon; Unforgettable; Temptation; Winter Wonderland.
Films: High Noon; Don't Bother to Knock; Ivanhoe; The Greatest Show on Earth; Sailor Beware; Singin' in the Rain; The Crimson Pirate; Scaramouche.
Events: Fender Stratocaster and Gibson Les Paul guitars developed; Mau Mau atrocities; H-Bomb detonated; Schweitzer gets Nobel Prize; 1st sex-change operation; mechanical heart fitted; 4000 die from smog in London; Bill & Ben on TV; Death of King George VI; 26 spectators die at Farnborough Air Show.

Where the Bugs wear Boots

1953 (12 years old)
Music: How Much Is That Doggie? Diamonds Are A Girl's Best Friend; Stranger in Paradise; Secret Love; Cryin' in the Chapel.
Films: The Robe; War of the Worlds; Shane; Roman Holiday; From Here To Eternity; Gentlemen Prefer Blondes; The Cruel Sea.
Events: The Goons on radio; Queen Elizabeth Coronation; Everest climbed; Piltdown Man hoax; Korea war ends; Microwave cooker patented(USA); Smoking linked to lung cancer; Michelin-radial ply tyres; DNA structure identified; Stalin and Dylan Thomas died; Heat Wave; Quatermass Experiment on TV; Russian H-bomb test.

1954 (13 years old)
Music: Hernando's Hideaway; Three Coins in the Fountain; Secret Love.
Films: The Rear Window; The Fiends; On the Waterfront; 20,000 Leagues under the sea; Creature from the Black Lagoon; Animal Farm; Godzilla.
Events: Lord of the Rings published; 1st kidney transplant; 4 minute mile; Big Bang Theory; Boeing 707 commissioned; Matisse died; Empress Of Canada ablaze; capsizes in Gladstone Dock; Fish Fingers invented; Salk polio vaccine; 35 killed in Comet air crash.

1955 (14 years old)
Music: Davy Crockett; Sixteen tons; the Man from Laramie; Tutti Frutti.
Films: The Ladykillers; The Dam Busters; 1984; Blackboard Jungle; Rebel without a Cause; Tarantula; Henry IV; Oklahoma; Guys and Dolls.
Events: ITV starts transmission; James Dean and Einstein die; Ruth Ellis hanged; Muffin the Mule axed; Duke of Edinburgh Award introduced; Hovercraft and Deep Freeze invented; British Grand Prix at Aintree; Disneyland California opened.

1956 (15 years old)
Music: Rock Around The Clock; Hound Dog; Heartbreak Hotel; Blue Suede Shoes; Don't Be Cruel; Que Sera; Sera; My Fair Lady musical.
Film: Around the World in 80 Days; The King and I; Forbidden Planet; The Ten Commandments; Invasion of the Bodysnatchers; Seventh Seal.
Events: Suez crisis; 1st CND march at Aldermaston; Russia invades Hungary; The Liverpool Overhead Railway is demolished; Oral Polio vaccine introduced; H bomb tests at Bikini Atoll; Grace Kelly marries Rainier; Clarence Birdseye dies.

1957 (16 years old)
Music: Love Letters In The Sand; Tonight; Maria; That'll Be The Day.
Film: Bridge on the River Kwai; Sayonara; The Pride and the Passion.
Events: Little Rock Arkansas riots; Last tram removed from service; Sibelius; Bogart and Oliver Hardy die; Beatniks; Sputnik; the thermonuclear bomb; Channel tunnel recommenced; Jodrell bank telescope operational.

1958 (17 years old)
Music: Move it; Volare; Catch a Falling Star; Great Balls of Fire; Dream.
Film: Gigi; The Fly; The Blob; Quatermass and the Pit; Vertigo.
Events: Munich air crash - Manchester United; The ECU formed; Alaska becomes State no 49; Parking meters introduced; NASA established; Stereo gramophone records; M6; M1; Thalidomide birth defects; Bubble Cars; Notting Hill riots; CND founded; American Express card introduced.

1959 (18 years old)
Music: Tom Dooley; Mack the Knife; Living Doll; C'mon Everybody.
Film: Ben Hur; Rio Bravo; La Dolce Vita; Some like it Hot.
Events: Twilight Zone on TV; Sound of Music musical; Goldfinger published; Hawaii becomes State no 50; Lady Chatterley banned; Cobol invented; 1st section of M1 completed (London - Birmingham); Austin Mini Minor; Buddy Holly, Richie Valens and Big Bopper killed in air crash.

1960 (19 years old)
Music: Let's do the Twist; Are you Lonesome Tonight; Never on Sunday.
Film: Psycho; Gorgo; Spartacus; Elmer Gantry; The Magnificent Seven.
Events: Ban on Lady Chatterley's Lover lifted; JFK becomes President of USA; Smoking linked to heart disease; Laser invented; Conscription ends; Rawhide; Coronation Street and The Untouchables on TV; Clark Gable and Ernest Hemingway die; Sharpeville massacre.

1961 (20 years old)
Music: Moon River; Runaround Sue; Blue Moon; The Lion Sleeps Tonight.
Film: West Side Story; Breakfast at Tiffany's; The Guns of Navarone.
Events: Berlin Wall construction begins; Farthing withdrawn; Silicon chip; millionth Morris Minor sold; Yuri Gagarin 1st man in space; GPO tower completed; Rudolph Nureyev defects; Barbie's boyfriend 'Ken' produced.

1962 (21 years old)
Music: Blowin' In The Wind; Surfin' Safari; Green Onions; Go Away Little Girl.
Film: Lawrence of Arabia; Cleopatra; Lolita; Birdman of Alcatraz.
Events: Cuban missile crisis; Marilyn Monroe died; 2 minute warning for nuclear attack; Decca turn Beatles down; 3 day smog kills 60 in London; Amnesty International formed; Adolf Eichmann executed.

1963 (22 years old)
Music: She Loves You; Twist and Shout; Puff the Magic Dragon
Film: The Birds; Dr Strangelove; Cleopatra; Day of the Triffids; Dr No.
Events: Profumo scandal; Birmingham (Alabama) civil rights march; Kennedy assassinated; Oswald shot dead; Aug Great Train Robbery; Beatlemania in USA; Cassette recorder (Philips); Heart/Lung machine used in USA; Alcatraz closed; Vietnam war commences.

1964 (23 years old)
Music: I Want To Hold Your Hand; Can't Buy Me Love; I Only Want To Be with You; House of the Rising Sun; Walk on By; Dancin' in the Street.
Film: Hard Day's Night; Fistful of Dollars; Goldfinger; Mary Poppins; Pink Panther; My Fair Lady; Lord of the Flies; Zorba the Greek.
Events: Man from UNCLE on TV; Mods and rockers fights; Liz Taylor marries Richard Burton; Martin Luther King gets Nobel Peace Prize; Harpo Marx dies; Mandela sentenced to life imprisonment.

1965 (24 years old)
Music: Hard Day's Night; It's Not Unusual; Satisfaction; I Got You Babe; Turn; Turn; Turn; Get Off My Cloud. Mr Tambourine Man; King Of the Road.
Film: The Sound of Music; Othello; Dr Zhivago; Help! Licence to Kill.
Events: Thunderbirds are Go; Soccer 'fixing' scandal; Mary Whitehouse; Hanging abolished; Vietnam War; Cassius Clay downs Sonny Liston; Deaths of Winston Churchill, Malcolm X, Stan Laurel and Nat King Cole.

1966 (25 years old)
Music: Eleanor Rigby; Wild Thing; Strangers in the Night; Good Vibrations.
Film: 1 Million Years BC; Fantastic Voyage; Man for All Seasons; Alfie;
Events: Till Death do us Part on TV; England beat Germany in World Cup; Billy Graham London Crusade; Mini-skirts in; Hindley and Brady caught; Dog finds missing World Cup; Buster Keaton and Walt Disney die; Relaxation of fish on Friday by Pope; Aberfan landslide kills 116 children, 28 adults.

1967 (26 years old)
Music: Puppet on a String; I'm a Believer; Penny Lane; All you Need is Love; Ruby Tuesday; Strangers in the Night; Whiter Shade of Pale.
Film: Quatermass and the Pit; Cool Hand Luke; Bonnie and Clyde.
Events: Star Trek and Invaders on TV; 6 Day War; 1st heart by-pass operation (Barnard); Torrey Canyon oil spill; Donald Campbell dies at 297 mph on Coniston; Death of Jayne Mansfield, Spencer Tracy and Brian Epstein; Foot and Mouth scare; Apple Boutique opens.

1968 (27 years old)
Music: Congratulations; Hey Jude; Jumping Jack Flash; Those Were the Days; I Heard it Through the Grapevine; Dock of the Bay; Mrs Robinson.
Film: The Graduate; Thomas Crown Affair; 2001; Planet of the Apes.
Events: Mickey Mouse is 40; Martin Luther King and Robert Kennedy assassinated; Apollo 7 mission; QE2 launched;   Breath tests introduced; Decimalisation; Tony Hancock dies; Jackie Kennedy marries Aristotle Onassis; My Lai massacre.

1969 (28 years old)
Music: Honky Tonk Women; Albatross; Get Back; Come Together.
Film: Bullitt; Easy Rider; Butch Cassidy; The Wild Bunch; Midnight Cowboy
Events: Manson murders; London race riots; Maxi skirt; First Concorde flight; Intel-1st micro processor? Moon landing; Krays sentenced; Boris Karloff, Brian Jones and Judy Garland die; Woodstock Festival; Old Grey Whistle test and Monty Python on TV; Internet online.

Where the Bugs wear Boots

1970 (29 years old)
Music: Bridge over Troubled Water; Let It Be; Venus; Whole Lotta Love.
Film: Monty Python; True Grit; Catch-22; Love Story; Patton; MASH.
Events: Three atomic pacemakers fitted; Voting age reduced to 18; Jumbo Jet; 1st pacemaker fitted; No more Morris Minors; 2850 die from Hong Kong Flu; Car engines redesigned to use unleaded fuel; Beatles split; Deaths of Jimi Hendrix; Janis Joplin and Kent State students; 28 cases of Thalidomide deformities reported.

1971 (30 years old)
Music: Jesus Christ Superstar; Brown Sugar; Maggie May; Black Dog.
Film: Clockwork Orange; Dirty Harry; Silent Running; French Connection.
Events: Rolls Royce bankrupt; Decimalisation complete; Hot Pants; Disneyworld Florida opens; Queen opens Wallasey tunnel (Kingsway); Louis Armstrong dies.

1972 (31 years old)
Music: American Pie; Starman; I Can See Clearly Now; Ziggy Stardust.
Film: The Godfather; Klute; Cabaret; Deliverance; The Poseidon Adventure.
Events: Oxford University decide to admit women in 1974; Pope abolishes the tonsure (bald spot) for monks; Charles Atlas and Maurice Chevalier die; CAT scanner developed; Andes air crash cannibalism horror; Londonderry-Bloody Sunday.

1973 (32 years old)
Music: Tie A Yellow Ribbon; You're So Vain; You Are The Sunshine Of My Life; Killing Me Softly; Crocodile Rock; Superstition; Smoke On The Water.
Film: Westworld; The Sting; Magnum Force; Live and Let Die; Paper Moon.
Events: Britain joins ECU; Watergate; Push-thru beer cans; 6 million Dollar Man on TV; Deaths of Picasso, Tolkien, Noel Coward and Lon Chaney Jr; CAT scanner used; Skylab in orbit; Australia gives Aborigines the vote; Vietnam war ends; Thalidomide-£20 million compensation offered.

1974 (33 years old)
Music: The Joker; Waterloo; I Shot The Sheriff; Rock On; Radar Love.
Film: Dark Star; Blazing Saddles; Alice Doesn't Live Here Anymore.
Events: Gerald Ford President; Watergate cover-up begins; Nixon pardoned; Streaking craze; Report shows chlorinated fluorocarbons are destroying Ozone Layer; Jaws published; Miner's strike; Jack Benny dies; Paris DC-10 crash kills 346; Ohio tornado kills 324; Flixborough explosion-24 dead, 100 injured.

1975 (34 years old)
Music: Jive Talkin'; Mamma Mia; Lucy in the Sky With Diamonds.
Film: Jaws; Death Race 2K; One Flew Over The Cuckoo's Nest; Nashville.
Events: Watership Down published; Inflation increased by 25%; report: 57000 Americans killed in Vietnam; Larry Fine (3 Stooges) dies; IRA arms and ammo found in Waterloo - Liverpool; Apollo and Soyuz spacecraft link up in space.

1976 (35 years old)
Music: Don't Go Breaking My Heart; Dancing Queen; Bohemian Rhapsody.
Film: King Kong; The Omen; Rocky; Logan's Run; The Enforcer; Carrie.
Events: USA Bicentennial; Carter president; 12 die from Legionnaire's Disease; CFCs found to be destroying the Ozone Layer; Agatha Christie and Howard Hughes die; Roots published; Water shortage; Tate Gallery buy a pile of bricks for £20,000.

1977 (36 years old)
Music: Hotel California; Barracuda; Dancing Queen; You Light Up My Life.
Film: Close Encounters of the 3rd Kind; Star Wars; Saturday Night Fever.
Events: Uranus has 5 rings; Amin charged with the deaths of 1000 Ugandans; Deaths of Elvis Presley, Werner von Braun, Groucho Marx, Bing Crosby, Charlie Chaplin and PK Wrigley; Neutron Bomb tests; Space Shuttle launched; Apple II computer; Marc Bolan killed in car crash; Red Rum wins Grand National for the third time; Punk culture spreads.

1978 (37 years old)
Music: Stayin' Alive; You're The One That I Want; Wuthering Heights.
Film: Grease; Coma; Deer Hunter; Superman; Convoy; Jaws 2; 39 Steps.
Events: Bikini Island - soil and plants still radioactive; World Population 4.4 billion increasing at 400/day; CFCs banned; 1st test-tube baby; Dallas and Blake's 7 on TV; Sid Vicious kills his girlfriend; Jonestown mass suicide; Amoco Cadiz spills thousands of tons of oil.

1979 (38 years old)
Music: Another Brick In The Wall; 52nd Street; Le Freak; I Will Survive.
Film: Alien; Mad Max; Star Trek; Apocalypse Now; Kramer-v-Kramer.
Events: Margaret Thatcher becomes PM; Mother Teresa gets Nobel prize; Chicago DC-10 crash kills 273; John Wayne dies; Visicalc spreadsheet; Fire in St John's Precinct; smoking-cancer link proved; 3-mile Island atomic leak; IRA kill Earl Mountbatten; DC-10 crash over Antarctica kills 257.

1980 (39 years old)
Music: Sailing; The Rose; Another One Bites The Dust; Call Me.
Film: The Empire Strikes Back; Flash Gordon; Raging Bull.
Events: Deaths of John Lennon, Peter Sellers, Alfred Hitchcock, Steve McQueen, Jimmy Durante, Tonto and Mae West; Titanic found 12000ft deep; Liverpool Cathedral completed; Who shot JR? - Dallas gets 86 million viewers; London-Iranian embassy siege; Ronald Reagan elected US President.

1981 (40 years old)
Music: Bette Davis Eyes; Boy from New York City; Tainted Love; Don't You Want Me; 9 to 5; Physical; Imagine; Stand And Deliver; Woman.
Film: Raiders of the Lost Ark; French Lieutenant's Woman; Chariots of Fire; Day of the Triffids; Superman II; Time Bandits.
Events: Charles and Diana wedding; AIDS virus identified; Tate & Lyle closed; Meccano closed; Toxteth and Brixton riots; Bob Marley dies at 36; George Washington's dentures stolen; Bill Haley dies; Hitch-hiker's Guide to the Galaxy on TV.

1982 (41 years old)
Music: Ebony and Ivory; Come on Eileen; Our House; Eye of the Tiger.
Film: ET; Blade Runner; Tootsie; First Blood; Gandhi; Poltergeist.
Events: Mary Rose raised; Channel 4 starts; Falklands-Exocet missile changes warfare; Deaths of Ingrid Bergman, Henry Fonda and John Belushi; Pope visits Liverpool; Boys from the Blackstuff and Brookside on TV; Schindler's List wins Booker Prize.

1983 (42 years old)
Music: Flashdance; Thriller; Down Under; Every Breath You Take.
Film: Terms of Endearment; Return of the Jedi; Octopussy; WarGames.
Events: Kilauea erupts; Seat belts mandatory; Cyclosporine immuno-supressant approved by FDA; Deaths of Buster Crabbe, Muddy Waters, David Niven and Karen Carpenter.

1984 (43 years old)
Music: Thriller; What's Love Got To Do With It; When Doves Cry; Relax.
Film: Amadeus; Ghostbusters; Terminator; Dune; Gremlins; Spinal Tap.
Events: Liverpool Garden festival; Donald Duck 50; Band Aid; Report-Passive Smoking damages lungs; Deaths of Richard Burton, Diana Dors, Count Basie, Indira Ghandi and James Mason; Marvin Gaye killed by his father; Jim Fixx dies jogging; Cavern Walks and Albert Dock village open; Yorkshire Ripper caught.

1985 (44 years old)
Music: Solid; Material Girl; We Are The World; The Power of Love; Money for Nothing; Saving All My Love For You; Run To You; Axel F.
Film: Prizzi's Honour; Back to the Future; Cocoon; The Goonies.
Events: Miner's strike ends; Bradford Football Club fire kills 40; 41 die at Heysel; Live Aid makes £60 million; Crack hits NY streets; Deaths of Rock Hudson, Orson Welles and Yul Brynner.

1986 (45 years old)
Music: Graceland; West End Girls; Lady in Red; Walk Like An Egyptian; That's What Friends Are For; Walk of Life; Chain Reaction; A Kind of Magic.
Film: Crocodile Dundee; Aliens; The Fly; Short Circuit; Mona Lisa.
Events: Ozzie Osborne sued; Challenger Shuttle explodes; 25000 AIDS cases in USA; Chernobyl reactor explodes; Deaths of Cary Grant, James Cagney and Henry Moore; Clint Eastwood becomes Mayor of Carmel.

Where the Bugs wear Boots

1987 (46 years old)
Music: Bad; Joshua Tree; Livin' On A Prayer; Smooth Criminal.
Film: Lethal Weapon; Predator; Robocop; Good Morning Vietnam; The Untouchables; Abyss; Fatal Attraction; Three Men and a Baby.
Events: Zeebrugge ferry disaster; Work on Channel Tunnel commenced; Bill Gates 1st computer billionaire; Deaths of Andy Warhol, Liberace, Danny Kaye, Segovia and Fred Astaire; Hungerford massacre -14 killed; 31 die in Kings Cross underground fire.

1988 (47 years old)
Music: Teardrops; Faith; Sweet Child O' Mine; Candle In The Wind.
Film: Die Hard; Twins; Rain Man; Naked Gun; Roger Rabbit.
Events: Neighbours starts on GB TV; Salman Rushdie in trouble; Michael Jackson concert at Aintree; Piper Alpha oil platform explosion kills 150; Lockerbie air bomb kills 259 on aeroplane, 11 on ground.

1989 (48 years old)
Music: Hang Tough; Like A Prayer; The Look; If I Could Turn Back Time.
Film: The Abyss; Batman; Shirley Valentine; Driving Miss Daisy.
Events: Exxon Valdez oil spillage (11 million gallons); Hillsborough tragedy; Berlin Wall down; Largest prime number discovered (65087 digits long); Mel Blanc (voice of Bugs Bunny) dies; Ceausescu executed; Thousands killed in Tiananmen Square; Beijing.

1990 (49 years old)
Music: Nothing Compares 2U; Vogue; Blaze of Glory; Black Velvet.
Film: Arachnophobia; Total Recall; Teenage Mutant Ninja Turtles.
Events: Saddam Hussein invades Kuwait; Jim Henson dies; Mandela released after 27 years; Benzene in Perrier water scare; Greta Garbo dies at 84; Poll Tax introduced; Maggie Thatcher out; World Wide Web built onto the Internet.

1991 (50 years old)
Music: Everything I Do; Unbelievable; Joyride; Something To Talk About.
Film: Terminator 2; Silence of the Lambs; Thelma and Louise; Hook.
Events: Gulf War - Operation Desert Storm; Yugoslav civil war; Freddy Mercury dies; Terry Waite released; Lockerbie bombers indicted; Yeltsin elected; Mike Tyson arrested.

1992 (51 years old)
Music: Achy Breaky Heart; I Will Always Love You; Smells Like Teen Spirit.
Film: Alien 3; Universal Soldier; Bodyguard; Leap of Faith; Under Siege.
Events: Clinton elected; Anglicans allow women priests; EuroDisney opens in Paris; Windows 3.1 released; Windsor Castle fire; Frankie Howerd dies.

1993 (52 years old)
Music: Boom! Shake The Room; Could It Be Magic; Stay; Three Little Pigs.
Film: Jurassic Park; The Piano; Schindler's List; Demolition Man; X-files.
Events: Warrington bombing; Jamie Bulger murder; Single European Market; Nureyev dies of AIDS; World Trades Centre bomb; Babylon 5 and X-Files on TV.

1994 (53 years old)
Music: Things can only get Better; Love is All Around; All I Wanna Do.
Film: Stargate; Forrest Gump; Speed; The Mask; Pulp Fiction; True Lies.
Events: Tony Blair labour leader; Mandela president of S Africa; OJ Simpson arrested for murder; Channel tunnel open; National Lottery started; Kurt Cobain suicide; Roy Castle Lung Cancer Research Centre opened; IRA cease fire.

1995 (54 years old)
Music: Earth Song; Parklife; Common People; Back for Good; Boombastic.
Film: Judge Dredd; Johnny Mnemonic; Usual Suspects; Trainspotting.
Events: OJ Simpson trial; Oklahoma City bomb kills 167; Rosemary and Fred West murder 20; Windows 95 introduced; Diana opens £30M Women's Hospital in Toxteth.

1996 (55 years old)
Music: Firestarter; Spaceman; Wonderwall; Until it Sleeps; Macarena.
Film: English Patient; Crash; Independence Day; Madness of King George.
Events: Girl power; 'Mad Cow' panic; Ella Fitzgerald dies; Charles and Diana divorced; 16 killed and 11 injured in Dunblane massacre; The Queen opens LIPA Fame school.

Where the Bugs wear Boots

1997 (56 years old)
Music: Don't Speak; Candle in the Wind; Wannabe; Bittersweet Symphony.
Film: Titanic; LA Confidential; Fifth Element; Full Monty; As Good as it Gets.
Events: Deaths of Robert Mitchum, Jimmy Stewart, Mother Teresa and Princess Diana; 150th Grand National cancelled; Hong Kong reverts to Chinese control; Dolly the sheep clone; Versace shot dead; Louise Woodward trial.

1998 (57 years old)
Music: My Heart Will Go On; Never Ever; That Don't Impress Me Much.
Film: Godzilla; Saving Private Ryan; Thin Red Line; Mask of Zorro.
Events: Pinochet arrested; Omagh car bomb kills 200 and injures 29,10,000 die in Central American hurricane; George Michael arrested in LA public bog; Clinton-Lewinski scandal; Linda McCartney dies; Viagra introduced.

1999 (58 years old)
Music: My Vida Loca; This is My Moment; American Woman; Believe.
Film: Notting Hill; Matrix; Phantom Menace; The Mummy; Fight Club.
Events: Aug 11 Solar Eclipse; 30 die in Paddington train crash; Beckham's £500,000 wedding; Jill Dando murdered; Minimum wage introduced; Enter the Euro; Columbine High School killings; Melissa macro virus disrupts businesses.

2000 (59 years old)
Music: Babylon; Beautiful Day; Yellow; Its My Life; We Will Rock You.
Film: Gladiator; Pitch Black; Vertical Limit; Final Destination; X-Men.
Events: Shipman convicted -15 women killed; New minimum wage; RU-486 abortion pill approved; Norfolk farmer shoots burglar; Millennium Bridge fiasco; Queen Mum 100; 110 paedophile offences against UK children; Damilola Taylor murder; Sarah Payne murder; Concorde crash 113 killed; Notting Hill carnival - 2 dead, 69 injured; Air ambulance crashes into Mersey -5 killed.

Where the Bugs wear Boots

2001 (60 years old)
Music: Have a Nice day; Lady Marmalade; Teenage Dirt Bag; Rollin'.
Film: Tomb Raider; Moulin Rouge; A Knight's Tale; Monsters Inc; Hannibal.
Events: Foot and Mouth epidemic; Selby rail crash; Race riots in Oldham, Leeds, Bradford and Burnley; Lord Archer convicted; Diana's butler charged with theft; Crackdown on paedophiles; Trial of Leeds footballers; World Trade Centre destroyed - over 30,000 dead; Hunt for Bin Laden; Anthrax scare.

2002 (61 years old)
Music: Hero; Get the Party Started; Can't Get You Out Of My Head.
Film: Panic Room; Enigma; xXx; Spiderman; Die Another Day; Ice Age.
Events: End of Foot and Mouth epidemic-cost £3 billion; 7 killed in January gales; Millennium bridge re-opens 20 months late; Gulf War syndrome recognised; Potter's bar rail crash-7 killed, 70 injured; Princess Margaret and Queen Mother died; Queen's Golden Jubilee celebrations.

2003 (62 years old)
Music: Beautiful; Bring Me to Life; Where Is The Love? Changes.
Film: The Return of the King; Last Samurai; School of Rock; Terminator 3.
Events: Space Shuttle explodes; Anti Iraq war demonstrations; War declared against Iraq; Schwartzenegger elected California governor; Saddam Hussein captured; SARS identified; 9/11 mastermind captured; Bob Hope died; Last VW Beetle produced; Paris heat wave kills 3,000; Last Concorde flight.

2004 (63 years old)
Music: American Idiot; Toxic; You Had Me; White Flag; Numb; Vertigo.
Film: I Robot; Ocean's 12; Passion Of The Christ; Alien v Predator.
Events: No evidence for weapons of mass destruction in Iraq; Summer Olympics in Athens; Florida hit by hurricanes; Asian tsunami kills 225,000; Serial killer Harold Shipman hangs himself; Ireland bans smoking in enclosed workplaces; Pickled heart of Louis XVII buried; Hussein trial prelims begin; Ken Bigley killed; hypersonic jet reaches 7000 mph (Mach 9.6).

Where the Bugs wear Boots

2005 (65 years old)
Music: Crazy Frog; Push the Button; Speed of Sound; Holiday.
Film: Revenge of the Sith; Batman Begins; Crash; Aeon Flux; King Kong.
Events: London bombings-52 killed, 700 wounded; Hurricane Katrina-1000 die, millions homeless; Pope John Paul II dies; Benedict XVI new Pope; Controversial drawings of Muhammad printed.

2006 (65 years old)
Music: I Don't Feel Like Dancin'; Déjà Vu; Beep; Chasin' Cars; Photograph.
Film: Cars; Brokeback Mountain; Pirates of the Caribbean; Nacho Libre.
Events: Pluto probe launched; 1,800 die in Philippines mudslide; Mozart 250th anniversary celebrations; New species of shark discovered; Smoking ban comes into effect in Scotland; First bird flu case in UK; 171 killed in Ukraine air crash; Pluto demoted to 'dwarf planet'; Police recover 'The Scream'; Schumacher retires; North Korea claim nuclear test; Pinochet arrested.

2007 (66 years old)
Music: Rockstar; Rehab; Stronger; Smile; Umbrella; Wait a Minute; Snow; Wind it up; The Pretender; Hold On; Icky Thump; Girlfriend; Guitar.
Film: Pirates of the Caribbean 3; Spider-Man 3; Transformers; Ratatouille; I Am Legend; The Simpsons Movie; National Treasure 2.
Events: UK Floods; Sarkozy elected; Windows Vista introduced; Millennium Dome becomes O2 Arena; Live Earth concerts; Deaths of Alan Ball, Tony Wilson, Benazir Bhutto, John Inman and Evel Knievel.

2008 (67 years old)
Music: So What; I Kissed A Girl; Back to Black; Circus; Vida la Vida; Shine; Womanizer; Mercy; Gotta be Somebody; Sex on Fire; Hallelujah.
Film: The Dark Knight. Indiana Jones Crystal Skull; Hancock; Mamma Mia!; Madagascar 2; Quantum of Solace; Iron Man; WALL-E; Kung Fu Panda; The Chronicles of Narnia; Prince Caspian
Events: Northern Rock crisis; Myanmar cyclone; Beijing Olympics; Obama elected USA President; QE2 final voyage; G8 summit; Bionic eye implant in London; Large Hadron Collider inaugurated; Deaths of Heath Ledger, Bo Diddley, Charlton Heston, Michael Crichton and Arthur C Clarke.

2009 (68 years old)
Music: The Fear; Paparazzi; Use Somebody; Bad Boys; Everybody in Love; Human; New Divide; I Gotta Feeling; Sober; Ulysses; Remedy; Fire.
Film: Avatar; Harry Potter and the Half-Blood Prince; Ice Age; Dawn of the Dinosaurs; Transformers; Revenge of the Fallen; Angels & Demons; Night at the Museum: Battle of the Smithsonian.
Events: Australian bush fires; North Korea goes nuclear; Barack Obama inaugurated; G20 Summit; Taiwan typhoon; Samoan tsunami; Deaths of Michael Jackson, Farrah Fawcett, Patrick Swayze and Bobby Robson.

Where the Bugs wear Boots

The Seven Ages of Beag
(From an idea by Willy Shakespeare)

All the world's a stage,
And all the men and women merely players:
They have their exits and their entrances;
And Beag in his time plays many parts,
His acts being seven ages.

> *Beag is me! My biker name was Bald Eagle due to my shaved head and big nose: my kids shortened this to Beagle and it eventually became Beag.*

At first the Infant,
Mewling and puking in his mother's arms.
Snoring through the May Day blitzkrieg,
Unaware of everything.

Next the whining Schoolboy,
With his graffitised satchel and running morning nose,
Creeping like snail unwillingly to school,
Until they throw him out.

Then the Student, surrounded by strange oafs,
Yea, bearded like a Manfred,
Full of learning, full of crap.
Like other students, thinketh he will change the world.

And what about ye Footballer
Who fleet of foot once racèd down ye wing
Now full of pie and chips, obese?
Reduced to back-four cruncher, then spectator.

Observe ye now the Biker,
Blazing down the road at 90 miles an hour,
His rust-red steed leaketh oil from every orifice:
Eight crashes in a year.

Now analyse ye Research Chemist,
With fair round belly from fast food fancies,
Eyes severe and beard of formal cut,
Replete with wisecracks and boring anecdotes.

And finally ye grouchy Lecturer, now retired,
Too young to die; too old to rock 'n' roll.
With animosity and whining tone
Hurling invective at the TV screen.

Where the Bugs wear Boots